James F. Jaquess

JAMES F. JAQUESS

*Scholar, Soldier and Private
Agent for President Lincoln*

Patricia B. Burnette

McFarland & Company, Inc., Publishers
Jefferson, North Carolina, and London

Front cover and frontispiece: Colonel James F. Jaquess. *Latest Light on Abraham Lincoln.* Erwin S. Chapman. Fleming H. Revell Company 1917 (courtesy L. C. Page & Company, Boston).

LIBRARY OF CONGRESS CATALOGUING-IN-PUBLICATION DATA

Burnette, Patricia B., 1937–
    James F. Jaquess : scholar, soldier and private agent for President Lincoln / Patricia B. Burnette.
    p.   cm.
    Includes bibliographical references and index.

    ISBN 978-0-7864-7358-8
    softcover : acid free paper ∞

    1. Jaquess, James Frazier, 1819–1898. 2. Methodist Church — Illinois — Clergy — Biography. 3. Soldiers — Illinois — Biography. 4. United States. Army — Officers — Biography. 5. Military chaplains — United States — Biography. 6. United States — History — Civil War, 1861–1865 — Chaplains. 7. Lincoln, Abraham, 1809–1865 — Friends and associates. 8. United States — Relations — Confederate States of America. 9. Confederate States of America — Relations — United States. 10. Jaquess, James Frazier, 1819–1898 — Trials, litigation, etc. I. Title.
E415.9.J37B87 2013
973.7'78092 — dc23
[B]   2013004732

BRITISH LIBRARY CATALOGUING DATA ARE AVAILABLE

© 2013 Patricia B. Burnette. All rights reserved

No part of this book may be reproduced or transmitted in any form or by any means, electronic or mechanical, including photocopying or recording, or by any information storage and retrieval system, without permission in writing from the publisher.

Manufactured in the United States of America

McFarland & Company, Inc., Publishers
  Box 611, Jefferson, North Carolina 28640
    www.mcfarlandpub.com

To my husband, Dr. Rand Burnette

Table of Contents

Preface	1
Prologue	5
1. The Early Years, 1819–1848	7
2. Jacksonville, Illinois	21
3. Quincy, Illinois	36
4. Chaplain, 6th Illinois Cavalry	49
5. Colonel, 73rd Illinois Infantry	63
6. Private Agent for President Lincoln	79
7. Trial for Murder by Abortion	95
8. Carpetbagger in Arkansas and Mississippi	111
9. Townley Fortune in England	122
10. Trials in London and Time in Pentonville Prison	136
11. Return to America for His Last Years	153
Epilogue: A Review of James F. Jaquess' Life	165
Chapter Notes	167
Bibliography	186
Index	195

Preface

The symposium "Race and Politics in Stephen A. Douglas' America," held in the spring of 2005 at MacMurray College in Jacksonville, Illinois, introduced me to James Frazier Jaquess,* the first president of the school. After mentioning Jaquess in passing, a symposium speaker recounted the major upheaval at the school's 1854 commencement when Helen Wilmans, one of the graduating students, spoke in favor of the abolition of slavery. She had added these remarks to her graduation speech after President Jaquess approved it, and he had to convince the audience that the school did not agree with her point of view. Jaquess presented the argument that, as president of the school, he could not advocate abolitionism or anti-abolitionism or the principles held by the Whigs or the Democrats or even the principles of the Methodist Episcopal Church, the denomination that operated the school.

As a graduate of the same school as Helen Wilmans, only 104 years later, I wanted to learn more about this young woman who had caused so much trouble by advocating the abolition of slavery, a position that I had not realized was so unpopular in Illinois in the 1850s. An unusual woman for her day, Wilmans deserted her husband and children, founded a "New Thought" philosophy based on assertion of self and advocated the belief that wealth belonged to everyone. I also read the account of James Frazier Jaquess in the *Dictionary of American Biography* and decided that researching and writing about his life would be far more interesting than writing about Wilmans.

When a friend learned that I planned to write a book about James F. Jaquess, she told me that I had made an excellent choice since I would not have to search for materials outside Jacksonville — everything I needed

*Pronounced Jay-Kwess

should be available in the MacMurray and Methodist archives. Obviously, this well-wisher did not realize the broad scope of the career of James Frazier Jaquess. I discovered information about him in libraries and archives in thirteen states, Washington, D.C., and even Great Britain. Throughout the years since a symposium speaker introduced me to James F. Jaquess, I have continued to discover additional information about him and incorporate it in my book.

I owe thanks to many individuals who have shared information about Jaquess with me during my research. I am grateful to Dr. James Gillespie for providing the information that Jaquess began his academic career at Mount Carmel Academy, a fact missing from all published materials about him. I also appreciate the sincere encouragement of Dr. Robert McColley, professor emeritus of history at the University of Illinois, and Dr. David Costigan, professor emeritus of history at Quincy University, and the information about Jaquess included in his dissertation "A City in Wartime: Quincy, Illinois and the Civil War." Also helpful was Dr. Martha Steffens, professor of the Missouri School of Journalism and a descendent of the Jaquess family, who told me about a patent that Jaquess had received for an agricultural implement. The unpublished article "Preacher, Soldier, Bigamist, Thief?: The Strange Career of Colonel James F. Jaquess" by Dr. Richard B. Meixsel (James Madison University) and the information Dr. Meixsel provided about Anna Marie Peregoy, who had married his ancestor Howard Meixsel, were extremely helpful. Also very useful were copies of the Lawrence-Townley bonds and certificates provided by Sherry Jones, whose ancestors had purchased them. The staff of Pfeiffer Library at MacMurray College (Susan Eilering, library director; Jake Magnuson, public service and reference librarian; and Dee Ann Roome, circulation and interlibrary loan manager) were very helpful in finding books for me through interlibrary loan. Lauretta Scheller, archivist for MacMurray and Illinois Great Rivers Conference of the United Methodist Church, helped me greatly by locating and copying materials from both the archives located in Pfeiffer Library. I thank Steven Varble of Steven Varble Productions for photographing people and places and providing their electronic images for my book.

I also thank, for all their help and courtesies, the numerous archivists, librarians, and administrators of the institutions that I visited, wrote, e-mailed or phoned. My work could not have been accomplished without their assistance.

But the greatest assistance and support came from my husband of over 50 years, Dr. Rand Burnette, professor emeritus of history at Mac-

Murray College. He copied pages from books and articles, listened to my ideas both good and bad, proofread what I wrote, prepared the book's bibliography and even became the Burnettes' chief cook and bottle washer. Any errors are my responsibility. I cannot thank him enough for sharing with me his many talents and wide knowledge of history.

Prologue

As the sun was setting on July 18, 1864, Colonel James F. Jaquess and author James R. Gilmore crossed back from Virginia into the Union after their brief visit in Richmond, the capital of the Confederacy. The outcome of this trip was important to Abraham Lincoln, whose reelection was becoming doubtful because public opinion favored ending a war that the South appeared to be winning. President Lincoln planned all the details of this trip, arranged for Jaquess and Gilmore to cross over on July 14 and provided a pass for them in his own handwriting. Although officials in the Confederate War Department questioned the wisdom of permitting their visit, they allowed Jaquess and Gilmore to cross into the South on July 16.

Lincoln personally selected Jaquess, an excellent public speaker, and Gilmore, a popular author, as his emissaries to meet with Jefferson Davis. He chose these men because he knew that they could and would tell the people of the North what Davis stated as his conditions for ending the Civil War. Representatives from the Confederacy met Jaquess and Gilmore somewhere between Deep Bottom and Chaffin's Bluff and transported them to Richmond in an ambulance that followed a carriage displaying a flag of truce. With the Provost-Guard of Richmond keeping constant watch on them, they spent two nights at the Spotswood Hotel. After making arrangements with Judah Benjamin, Secretary of State of the Confederacy, Jaquess and Gilmore met with Jefferson Davis at 9:00 p.m. on the evening of July 17. As Lincoln had expected, Davis told them that the South was "not fighting for slavery" but "for independence" and if they failed to win, the Confederacy would accept "extermination" instead.

Shortly after Jaquess and Gilmore returned from their meeting with Jefferson Davis, accounts of their trip appeared in the *New York Times*, the

Philadelphia Enquirer and other national newspapers. Colonel Jaquess gave an oral report about this trip to the president on the evening of July 21 at the summer cottage where the Lincoln family resided from June to November. Later the Union Republicans published the colonel's account of that meeting with Jefferson Davis called "Rebel Terms of Peace" and circulated it as campaign literature to encourage Lincoln's reelection. James Gilmore also published his version of their meeting with Jefferson Davis in the September issue of the *Atlantic Monthly*. When he made this trip for President Lincoln, Jaquess was already well known in Indiana as the grandson of an early settler and as a graduate of Indiana Asbury and in Illinois as a Methodist minister and as a college president. After he returned from his meeting with Jefferson Davis, Jaquess became a national figure.

Tall, handsome and definitely charismatic, Jaquess had the ability to impress men and charm ladies, whether they knew him as a preacher, a college president or the colonel of an Illinois regiment. Whether he delivered a sermon, spoke to a group of students or addressed the men of the 73rd Illinois Infantry, he captivated his audience and held their attention. When Jaquess returned from Richmond, President Lincoln recognized his many abilities and immediately asked him to serve as one of his personal agents.

But after the Civil War ended, Jaquess' life changed for the worse. He survived an embarrassing trial in Kentucky concerning a woman dying from an abortion, then he failed to succeed as a carpetbagger in Arkansas and Mississippi. Next he convinced his family and friends in Indiana and numerous residents of New York State to invest in Lawrence-Townley bonds and share in a fortune waiting in England. This venture ended in poverty for him and a sentence in a British prison. But when he returned to America for the final years of his life, he still held the respect of the men of the 73rd Infantry and the affection of the women who had known him 50 years before as president of their college in Jacksonville. Although his misadventures had turned his black hair to white, he still possessed the charisma that had led to his national fame during his younger years.

Chapter 1

The Early Years, 1819–1848

Ironically, exactly one year before the date of James Frazier Jaquess' death, a sketch about him entitled "The Plucky Parson from Posey" appeared in the *Chicago Times-Herald*. Samuel W. Nichols, editor of the *Jacksonville Daily Journal,* wrote this tale picturing Jaquess as another Abraham Lincoln who rose from poverty to national fame. According to Nichols, Jaquess' parents "dug a sparse living from the rocks and clods of Posey county" and "could afford no luxury" for their children. This story of Jaquess as a boy who grew up in poverty is, in no way, an accurate one. The wealth of the Jaquess family began with Jonathan Jaquess, the grandfather of James Frazier Jaquess, in the 18th century and passed on to his descendents.[1]

Jonathan, who was born in Middlesex County, New Jersey, in 1753, went to sea at a young age, first serving as a cabin boy and then as a sailor. When the Revolutionary War began, colonial governors issued letters of marque to ship owners allowing them to attack British merchant vessels. Jonathan owned one of these privateers and scuttled two enemy vessels after their capture by filling their holds with stones.[2] After serving at sea for a brief time, he became a minuteman and fought in the battles of Long Island, White Plains and Kingsbridge.[3] In the battle at White Plains, Jonathan received a saber cut across his face and carried the scar for the rest of his life.[4]

At the end of the war, Jonathan returned to New Jersey, where he married his third cousin, Sally Jaquess, and settled down to farm in Middlesex County. Sally died a year later without giving birth to any children. Jonathan then married Sally's cousin Esther E. Koy (Ester Ekoy) and returned to the sea as owner of a sloop that traded up and down the East Coast. Jonathan, Esther and their children moved to Harrison County,

Kentucky, in 1789, following the same route as many other easterners through the Cumberland Gap and along Daniel Boone's Wilderness Road. A short time after they reached their destination, Esther died of consumption and Jonathan married for a third time, in November 1791. His third wife, Rebecca, was the widow of James Rankin, and their two children, James and Mary, became part of a blended family when Rebecca married Jonathan.[5]

While they lived in Kentucky, Jonathan and Rebecca became caught up in the revivals and camp meetings of the Second Great Awakening (1800–1830) and were among the almost 12,000 individuals who attended the famous Cane Ridge revival in the neighboring county of Bourbon in 1801.[6] Traveling in wagons for miles over bad roads and sleeping in tents after they arrived did not keep 19th-century Americans from attending camp meetings, because they craved fellowship with others as well as comfort for their souls.[7] Since Methodists and Baptists preached at the same camp meetings, they became rivals in winning converts. The Second Great Awakening demonstrated that the United States had come of age and could practice its own ideas of Protestantism rather than borrowing them from European denominations.[8]

Motivated by their Pentecostal experience at Cane Ridge in 1801, Jonathan and two of his brothers jointly purchased a large tract of land in the Indiana Territory in 1810 where they could live near one another and practice their shared beliefs. They purchased 2,000 acres from the land office for $4,000 in gold and silver and spent the next four years creating their personal utopia: surveying and dividing the land, building cabins for their families and planting orchards.[9] Their chief reason for moving to Indiana was a strong objection to slavery practiced by Christians in Kentucky. As William G. McLoughlin explains in *Revivals, Awakenings, and Reform*, "Southern white Christians were not averse to benevolent reform if that meant encouraging personal temperance and helping the orphan or widow, the deaf, the dumb, the blind, the insane. But if it meant rearranging the social order, tampering with slavery ... then benevolent reform was totally misguided."[10] But the Jaquess brothers were easterners who held an entirely different point of view and believed that Christians should oppose slavery, not practice it.

The Jaquess clan, consisting of forty-four Kentuckians related to one another by birth or marriage, moved together to Southern Indiana in 1815, the largest group to move as one unit from Kentucky to Indiana.[11] The three Jaquess brothers had purchased the lowest land in Indiana, Posey County on the Ohio River, as the location for their utopia. This county, which had come into existence the year before the Jaquess settlers arrived, received its name from territorial governor Thomas Posey. Their property was in Robb Township in the northern part of Posey County. Their closest neighbors were two famous utopian groups that followed one another in occupying the same land, Johann Georg Rapp and the "Harmonie on the Wabash" from 1814 to 1824 and Robert Owen and his followers between 1825 and 1827.

Indiana was still a wild and rugged land when James Frazier Jaquess was born on November 18, 1819, into this well-to-do family of farmers who owned 2,000 acres of fertile land. His middle name came from the maiden name of his grandmother, Rebecca Frazier (Rebekah Fraser), the third wife of his grandfather, Jonathan Jaquess. James was the second child of Jonathan's oldest son, Garrison (Garretson), and Mary Smith. When Mary became Garrison's wife, his father gave him, as he did to all of his children, a quarter section (160 acres) of land from Jonathan's original purchase. This concentration of Jonathan's children and stepchildren in one area of the county became known as the Jaquess Settlement.[12]

Like other pioneers who settled in Kentucky, Indiana, and Illinois, Jonathan and Rebecca became devout members of the Methodist Episcopal Church, a Protestant denomination that John Wesley had founded as the "Methodist Society" in England in 1729. Members of this society met in groups during the week for prayer and study but attended Anglican church services on Sundays and relied on this denomination for such rites as baptism and communion.[13] By 1783, the Society had become the "Methodist Church" but, as Frank Baker points out in *From Wesley to Asbury: Studies in Early American Methodism*, John Wesley claimed all his life that he remained "a loyal communicant of the Church of England."[14]

Once planted in America, Methodism grew rapidly by means of frontier camp meetings such as the one that the Jaquess family had attended at Cane Ridge and religious revivals called quarterly conferences. Methodism grew rapidly in Delaware, Maryland and Virginia and soon became a strong and expanding denomination. Most of the presiding elders who were the leaders of this new denomination came from the South and took Methodism with them to such locations as New York, New England, Pennsylvania and Ohio. Peter Cartwright, a well-known leader in the Methodist Episcopal Church for fifty years, probably set the record for spreading the gospel by taking the Methodist message from Virginia to Kentucky and also to the states of Ohio, Indiana and Illinois.[15]

The first Methodist congregation in Posey County, Indiana, met in a room in the home of Jonathan Jaquess in the fall of 1816.[16] Later the Jaquess family added an additional room to their home, called the Preacher's Room, for the use of Methodist circuit riders. Jonathan and Rebecca gave two of their sons distinctively Methodist names, John Wesley for the founder of the denomination and Asbury Cloud for Francis Asbury, one of the first two bishops of the Methodist Episcopal Church in the United States. John Schrader, who introduced Methodism to Southern Indiana, married Jonathan and Rebecca's youngest daughter, Pamela.[17] As devout Methodists, Jonathan and Rebecca were strong believers in temperance and, unlike most of their neighbors, did not serve whiskey at house raisings, corn huskings, or log rollings.[18] Jonathan was a supporter of the Whig Party and Henry Clay and, following Jonathan's lead, his sons and grandsons became Republicans and supporters of Abraham Lincoln. Thomas Jaquess, a younger brother of James, was elected twice to the Indiana state legislature. In 1867 he represented Posey County and part of neighboring Vanderburgh County and in 1869 Posey County and part of adjacent Gibson County. His election was the first time that Posey County went Republican.[19]

When James Jaquess was six years old, Jonathan's stepson, James Rankin, left the Jaquess Settlement to join Robert Owen's communal group in the neighboring village of New Harmony. Owen had recently purchased this property from a communal group called Harmonists or Rappites, who had moved back to Pennsylvania to start another communal settlement called Economy. Unlike the Rappites who had lived in New Harmony for ten years, the Owenite experiment lasted for only two years, from 1825 to 1827. When James Rankin returned from his brief experience in this communal group, he proposed the idea that the descendents of Jonathan Jaquess create their own communal experiment and name it Goshen,[20] a place mentioned in the biblical account of Joseph.

Jonathan's stepson and sons and the husbands of his daughters established Goshen near the center of the Jaquess Settlement. Four families dismantled their log homes and reconstructed them at the new location. James' father, Garrison, and his uncle Ogden did not need to move their houses because they were already close to the central location that became known as "the town." Nor did bachelor brother Fletcher have to relocate, since he lived on or near his father's (Jonathan) place. The Goshen families depended on one another for their social life, but they continued to farm their plots of land independently. They considered the harvest from all of their farms as the property of the communal organization. Several of them now had to travel to farms that were located a long way from where they lived.[21]

In 1834, the Goshen community decided to send its surplus pork, oats and corn from the fall harvest to New Orleans on the flatboat *Davy Crockett*. All members of the crew on this trip belonged to the Goshen community. Asbury Cloud, who was Jonathan's youngest son, kept a journal of their experiences on the three-month round-trip on the Ohio and Mississippi rivers to New Orleans. Because of the huge success of the first trip, the community pooled their surplus crops for a second trip to market the following year. This time the flat boat sank after traveling only a short distance on the Ohio River and nearly all of their cargo was lost. After this disaster some of the men began to grumble about the downside of communal life, such as the long distance that they had to travel between their relocated houses and their farmland. After declaring that he no longer wanted anything to do with the Goshen project, John Wesley Jaquess moved his house back to his farm. Soon the others followed his example and Goshen came to an end.[22]

Unlike many other 19th-century pioneers, Jonathan Jaquess had received a basic education and wanted his children and grandchildren to be educated. A letter written by Jonathan to George Rapp in March 1819 provides some information about both Jonathan's education and his importance in Southern Indiana. Rapp was the charismatic founder of the Harmonist Society, which was located near the Jaquess Settlement. George Wall, from nearby Cynthiana, asked Jonathan to use his influence with Rapp to persuade the Harmonists to vote for Samuel C. Hirons, a candidate for clerk of Posey County. Wall evidently considered Jonathan Jaquess a man whose opinions were highly regarded in that part of Posey County and who was a friend of the Rappites. Hirons won the election because of Jonathan's endorsement and became his son-in-law two years later when he married Jonathan's daughter Elizabeth. More significant, the letter from James Jaquess' grandfather to George Rapp reveals a great deal about Jonathan's education and intelligence. The word choice, spelling, and sentence structure in this letter show a man with an education above that of many of his contemporaries. Also, his subtle flattery of Rapp with such phrases as "lay me under obligation to you never to be forgotten" and "I remain yours with the highest degree of respect and esteem" indicates Jonathan's intelligent application of the art of persuasion.[23]

As an educated man, Jonathan wanted his children and grandchildren to have the same advantage. However, formal education was hard to come by on the frontier. The first schoolhouse in Posey County opened in 1814 in a small log building in McFadden Bluff (now Mt. Vernon), the county seat.[24] It is doubtful that Jonathan's grandchildren attended this school, because it was more than 20 miles from the Jaquess Settlement. However, in 1820, the Rev. John Schrader, one of Jonathan's sons-in-law, donated some of his land for the Poseyville Log School House. It was built one-half mile north of Poseyville on the road to Black River. This school is very likely the place where James, his brothers and sisters, and his cousins received their basic education in reading, writing and arithmetic.[25]

Relying on this minimal preparation, James Frazier Jaquess entered Indiana Asbury (now DePauw University), a Methodist college in Greencastle, Indiana, in 1841 when he was nearly 22 years old. Like Abraham Lincoln and other Indiana boys, James was expected to work on his father's farm until he reached the age of 21. James was not the only child or grandchild of Jonathan who received a college education. James' uncle, George F. Jaquess, attended medical school at Transylvania University in Lexington, Kentucky, in 1819 and 1820. Twenty-six years later, James' younger brother, George D. Jaquess, studied medicine at the same school and received an M.D. degree in 1848. His thesis was on "Bilious Remittent Fever,"[26] a relapsing fever associated with malaria.

At the time James attended Indiana Asbury, it was a college for men only. The school's catalog lists knowledge of geography, English, grammar, arithmetic and also first lessons in algebra, Latin grammar, historia sacra, Caesar's *Commentaries*, Virgil, Greek grammar, and Greek Testament as requirements for all entering students. An incoming student also had to provide a testimonial to his good character.[27] It is uncertain whether James Jaquess could meet such strict academic requirements, but he was certainly not the only student with this problem. One way for students to correct their deficiencies was by attending a preparatory academy in Greencastle. But like his fellow student James Harlan, Jaquess chose instead to suffer a year of hard study and slow academic progress.[28]

Harlan and Jaquess entered Asbury the same semester and graduated together; they formed a friendship during their time at the school that lasted for the next thirty years. Harlan, who later served as U.S. senator from Iowa, also became a friend of Abraham Lincoln. Harlan's daughter, Mary Eunice, married Lincoln's son Robert Todd in 1868. Harlan walked 18 miles from his family's farm in Rock County to Indiana Asbury in Putnam County.[29] James Jaquess probably made the trip to Greencastle in a carriage or on horseback since his home in Posey County was 150 miles away. The graduation requirements at Asbury, looked at from the modern viewpoint of 120 semester hours, were these: Latin — 20 hours, Greek — 25 hours, mathematics — 25 hours, chemistry — 10 hours, physics — 5 hours, geology — 5 hours, philosophy (partly psychology) — 13 hours, history —

5 hours, physical science — 5 hours, English (logic, rhetoric) — 5 hours and additional work in speech and forensics — 2 hours. Public speaking was an important part of the Asbury educational experience. Four students spoke each morning at chapel so that each student was able to give a declamation once a month. This arrangement provided excellent experience for students who, like Harlan, became attorneys or, like Jaquess, Methodist ministers. There were two 21-week terms each year at a cost of $12 each. Students were also responsible for the cost of room and board, usually with a local family.[30] James Harlan joined the Platonean Literary Society at Asbury. He represented the Platoneans in their annual debate with the other literary society, the Philologicals, and also served as the group's president.[31] Jaquess did not join either of the literary societies. His chief extracurricular activity was courting a local girl named Mary Sciple.

Mary Sciple (also spelled Cyple, Syple and Sipple) remains something of a mystery woman. Conrad and Catherine Sciple, who were residents of Greencastle when James Jaquess attended Indiana Asbury, were probably Mary's parents.[32] James Jaquess married Mary Sciple on April 2, 1843.[33] Their wedding took place in Putnam County, the location of Indiana Asbury; and the Rev. S.C. Cooper, the Agent for the college (today's institutional advancement officer), officiated at their wedding.[34] Sixteen days after their wedding, James and Mary's daughter, Margaret Wesley Jaquess, was born on April 18, 1843, in Sugar Grove, Harrison County, Indiana, on the Ohio River. A family genealogy, prepared by Margaret's husband many years later, conveniently moves the wedding of his wife's parents back one year, from 1843 to 1842. Why Margaret was born in Sugar Grove rather than Greencastle or Posey County remains a mystery.[35]

The Asbury rolls for 1841, 1842 and 1843 list James Jaquess as a student with the hometown of Posey County. Then he disappears from the college rolls the following year. Sometime between Margaret's birth and her mother's death, the James Jaquess family moved to Mt. Carmel, Illinois, the home of James' "half cousin" Isaac Newton Jaquess. Jonathan was grandfather to both James and Isaac, but Isaac's grandmother was Jonathan's second wife, Esther E. Koy. Isaac had moved to Mt. Carmel in 1831 after visiting his uncle William F. Jaquess and deciding that he liked the town. James needed a job to support his wife and daughter and may have moved to Mount Carmel because Isaac told him about a teaching position and encouraged him to accept it.

Although Isaac himself had little formal education, having attended school for only six months, he valued education and those members of his family who had received it. His lack of formal education did not prevent him from becoming a licensed Methodist minister, chaplain of the regiment led by James F. Jaquess and a member of the Illinois legislature after the Civil War.[36] The James Jaquess family relocated in Mt. Carmel sometime before Mary's death on March 22, 1844. She was 22 and her daughter was only 11 months old. Mary was buried in the Jaquess family plot in Rose Hill Cemetery, where two of Isaac's children and his wife Jane were already interred.[37] As was usually the case with a motherless child in the 19th century, Margaret was sent to live with a female relative, her paternal grandmother in Posey County.

Jaquess spent only one year teaching at the Mount Carmel Academy. The only surviving record of his connection with this school is an advertisement on October 2, 1844, in the *Mt. Carmel Register* about the upcoming school session. This ad announced that James F. Jaquess and Gilbert Cook Turner planned to "open a school at the Seminary on the corner of Chestnut and 4th streets" on Monday, October 14, 1844.[38] Turner was one of Mount Carmel's pioneer residents who had come to Southern Illinois from Pennsylvania in 1835. Both were young men; Turner was 31 and Jaquess was 25.[39]

The seminary building where Jaquess and Turner taught their classes was the property of the stockholders in a corporation created by special act of the Illinois legislature on January 16, 1836. Jaquess and Turner may have rented this building from the corporation and paid their own salaries and operating expenses directly from the students' tuition. Or, as was more common in schools of that day, the two teachers may have been employees of the corporation that paid their salaries based on fixed percentages of the tuition received.

Unlike most 19th-century schools, the Mount Carmel Academy had no church affiliation. In fact, the incorporation papers stated that "no particular religious faith shall ever be required of those who become President and Trustees, students, pupils, teachers, officers or servants" of the academy. A share of stock in the school corporation cost $10 at the time. Each stockholder had the right to send one student to the academy free of charge for each share of stock owned by the stockholder. This system was supposed to enable the corporation to amass a large sum of money that could then be invested in the expectation that interest from the investment would be greater than the lost tuition fees. Many 19th-century schools tried this plan or one similar to it.[40]

The academy, as advertised in 1844, had both a primary department, and a "higher" department, or what was usually referred to as a preparatory department. The advertisement mentions pupils and students rather than boys and young men, suggesting that the school, or at least the primary department, was coeducational. The primary classes included the educational basics of spelling, reading, writing and arithmetic. The preparatory department offered classes in the subjects listed as entrance requirements at such colleges as Indiana Asbury. Male students had a choice of Illinois institutions, such as McKendree College in Lebanon and Illinois College in Jacksonville, in which to complete their studies. However, a college education was not yet an option for females on the frontier. The tuition cost at Mount Carmel Academy ranged from $2.50 to $4.50 per session depending on the level of instruction.[41]

James Jaquess and James Harlan, who had entered Indiana Asbury together in 1841, graduated together in 1845 with B.A. degrees. There were eleven men in their graduating class. The cost for Harlan, and very likely it was similar for Jaquess, was $266.72 from June 1, 1841, to August 20, 1845. Both Harlan and Jaquess had been enrolled on campus less than three of the usual four years. It was possible at that time for a student to study independently and then prove that he had learned the required material by passing an examination. Harlan had spent time away from campus as a member of a group making a lengthy trip to the Iowa Territory. After graduation from Indiana Asbury, Harlan settled in Iowa, where he was admitted to the bar. He served as president of Iowa Wesleyan in Mt. Pleasant from 1853 to 1855 before beginning a long political career.[42] After receiving his undergraduate degree, Jaquess was also admitted to the bar in the informal manner typical of that day, but he did not practice law.[43] He decided instead to become a Methodist preacher. Although the Jaquess family had expected James to become an attorney, his decision to enter the ministry pleased his family even more.

When Jaquess chose the Methodist ministry instead of a career in law, he already knew the denomination's expectations of its preachers. During his time in Mount Carmel, he had served as a licensed minister on the Palestine Circuit for part of a year, probably during the months when the Mount Carmel Academy was not in session.[44] Francis Asbury had brought John Wesley's itinerant system with him when he moved from England to the United States. An itinerant Methodist pastor did not serve one church but several parishes scattered along a lengthy circuit that covered 300 to 500 miles. This system allowed the circuit riding Methodist minister to serve 25 to 30 congregations over a period of about four weeks. Asbury himself set the standard by traveling more than 250,000 miles visiting Methodist churches during his 45 years in this country.[45] A license to preach in the Methodist Episcopal Church authorized an individual not only to preach but also to perform the sacraments of baptism and holy communion. A Methodist bishop or other church official had to renew his license from year to year. The Palestine Circuit was one of nine circuits in the Mount Carmel Conference, including one served by Isaac Newton Jaquess, who was also a licensed preacher.[46] While riding the Palestine Circuit, James Jaquess met Sarah Jane Steel, the woman who would later become his wife.

At the 22nd session of the Illinois Conference of the Methodist Episcopal Church, Jaquess was officially "recommended and admitted," the first step toward full acceptance into the Methodist ministry, and sent "on trial" to the Shawneetown Circuit. The Methodists met in the hall of the house of representatives in Springfield from September 17 to 22, 1845.[47] The usual story is that Peter Cartwright, known for his objection to educated clergy, was behind the decision to send Jaquess to this circuit as his trial of fire. A powerful elder in the Illinois Conference, Cartwright supposedly insisted that Jaquess serve the toughest part of the conference to test whether this college graduate had what it took to survive the rigors of circuit riding.

But assigning Jaquess to the Shawneetown Circuit was a logical decision since it was located in the Mt. Carmel District where Jaquess was living. Also, the Illinois Conference appointed an experienced clergyman, J.M. Massey, who had traveled in southeast Illinois and Indiana for many years, to share this arduous circuit with the newcomer.[48] Jaquess certainly did not have to ride all of the rigorous Shawneetown Circuit by himself. A history of Methodism in Shawneetown describes James Jaquess as "a young man but a widower, a man of fine address and pleasant and fluent of speech."[49]

At the next meeting of the Illinois Conference, held in Paris, Illinois, in September 1846, Jaquess was examined and "continued" on his path toward becoming a deacon, the title for a Methodist minister ordained by the bishop. This time the conference assigned him to the Petersburg Circuit in Menard County.[50] It was during this year that James Jaquess and Sarah Jane Steel were married, on March 30, 1847, in Crawford County, Illinois.[51] The Steel family owned land in this county near Robinson, Illinois, a location only a few miles from Palestine, the town from which the Palestine Circuit got its name. James and Sarah Jane had become acquainted while he was riding this circuit. She was the daughter of William N. and Mary A. McMullen Steel, who had moved from Philadelphia to Terre Haute, Indiana, before settling north of the town of Robinson when Sarah Jane was 12. As described by Joy Steel Williams in *My Ancestry*, Sarah Jane's mother, Mary, who was always referred to as "Lady Steele," had "lovely manners, was well educated, and was a devout Christian."[52] Her daughter was much like her. As the wife of James Jaquess, Sarah Jane supervised and taught students at both colleges where he served as president. She was also a model of correct behavior and set the standard of proper decorum for all the female students.

According to Henry B. Rankin, Abraham Lincoln and James F. Jaquess met for the first time while Jaquess was serving the Petersburg Circuit. Robert Bray, in his biography of Peter Cartwright, calls Henry B. Rankin a "very late (and dubious) entrant into the 'I knew Lincoln — though no one knew I did' competition." Bray is referring to Rankin's *Personal Recollections of Abraham Lincoln* published in 1916 when the author was 80 years old.[53] The date that Rankin gives for the meeting between Jaquess and Lincoln is not correct, but there are good reasons for accepting some of the other details of Rankin's account. Rankin claims that Lincoln met the Reverend Jaquess at the home of Rankin's father in June 1846 when Jaquess, the Methodist preacher assigned to the Petersburg Circuit, boarded with the Rankin family.[54] Although Jaquess did ride the Petersburg Circuit, Methodist preachers received assignments at the annual conference in September that usually extended from one September to the next. Because Jaquess received his appointment in September 1846, he would not have been riding the Petersburg Circuit in June of 1846.

But it is probable that Jaquess would have stayed at the home of Amberry Rankin, Henry Rankin's father, when the preacher needed a place to spend the night in Petersburg. There was a connection between the Rankin and Jaquess families dating back to the time when they both lived in Harrison County, Kentucky. James Jaquess' grandmother Rebecca was the widow of James Rankin when she married his grandfather Jonathan Jaquess. The two children from her first marriage became Jonathan Jaquess' stepchildren and were raised in his family. Jonathan Jaquess moved his family from Harrison County, Kentucky, to Indiana in 1815. Amberry Rankin made a similar move from Harrison County, Kentucky, to Illinois thirteen years later.[55] Two probable times for a meeting between Jaquess and Lincoln are December 1846 and May 1847, when Lincoln was involved in cases at the Petersburg court for three consecutive days.[56]

According to the minutes of the Illinois Conference in the fall of 1847, Jaquess "left his work [on the Petersburg Circuit] to accept the agency for the conference Female Academy" with permission from his presiding elder.[57] The college that would select him as president in fall of 1848 hired him as their agent in May of 1847.[58] Lincoln and Jaquess had certainly met one or more times before 1863 when Lincoln mentions his "slight acquaintance" with this Methodist minister, now colonel of the 73rd Illinois Infantry Regiment.[59]

When James Jaquess attended the next meeting of the Illinois Conference in September 1847, everyone there realized that the constitutional convention scheduled the following year would address the issue of finally abolishing slavery throughout Illinois. For some Methodists, as well as other residents of Illinois, the abolition of slavery would raise the problem of what to do about the freed Negroes. The first two circuits assigned to James Jaquess had been in the section of Illinois where slavery existed. Between one and two thousand slaves, sometimes referred to as indentured servants, lived in the Shawneetown area where they toiled at the salt wells. The white operators of this industry often leased these workers from slave owners in Kentucky and Tennessee.[60] The formation of the Southern Illinois Conference of the Methodist Episcopal Church that took place in 1852 resulted chiefly from the growth of Methodism in Illinois.[61] However, the Methodists of South Illinois and Central Illinois had different attitudes toward slavery and what to do about Negroes when they were free.

Illinois was part of the territory created in 1787 by the Northwest Ordinance that contained "Article VI" prohibiting slavery. This article did not end slavery or involuntary servitude because it allowed the French in Illinois to continue "'their laws and customs now in force.'"[62] The original French settlers in the southern part of Illinois considered their slaves essential to preserving their economy and the national government chose to ignore their practice of slavery. Although there was little interest in becoming a state, Illinoisans approved a constitution in 1818 that also failed to clarify the issue of slavery within its borders.[63] As Robert P. Howard points out in *Illinois: A History of the Prairie State*, "In its first years, Illinois was hardly a Northern State. Cairo is further south than Richmond Virginia, and most of the people came from or through the South. They imported southern customs and traditions, including a prejudice against Negroes and a belief in the desirability of slavery."[64] An attempt to call a second constitutional convention with the goal of establishing slavery in Illinois failed in 1824. The constitutional convention of 1848 was definitely intended to achieve the opposite, bringing an end to slavery in Illinois.

Some residents who favored abolishing slavery believed that the best solution would be to send the freed Negroes back to Africa. Abraham Lincoln was among those who considered, but rejected, this solution.[65] After formation of the American Colonization Society in 1816, Richard Allen, founder of the African Methodist Episcopal Church, brought together a group of Negroes to oppose all efforts to force them to leave the United States.[66] Peter Cartwright, a power both in Illinois and in the national church, was lukewarm about colonization being a workable solution.[67] Congregations of the Methodist Episcopal Church in the southern states had already split from the national body three years before and formed a denomination of their own. In 1847 the future of a united America was already beginning to look dim.

The meeting in September 1847 was also a memorable one for James Jaquess but for a different reason. After the brief period of three years in the Illinois Conference, he became a deacon in the Methodist Episcopal Church. After answering satisfactorily "the questions in Section 9 Chapel of the Disciplines," he and several others were ordained by Bishop Baugh on Sunday, September 26, at the East Charge Methodist Church in Jacksonville.[68] This time Jaquess was sent to an important call within the conference, the Methodist Episcopal church in Springfield, the capital of Illinois.[69]

James and Sarah Jane spent a highly successful year at the church in Springfield while James hoped that at the next Methodist Conference he would be appointed president of Illinois Conference Female Academy for which he had raised funds in 1847. Meanwhile James received an A.M. degree from McKendree College, probably by examination, since serving Methodist congregations did not allow him time off to attend classes.[70] Master of arts was the highest earned degree offered by American colleges and universities at that time. The only doctorate awarded was the honorary doctor of divinity. Brother Peter Cartwright changed his attitude about Methodist ministers with college degrees after he received his D.D. (doctor of divinity) degree from McKendree College in 1845. Previously, Brother Cartwright had insisted that D.D. signified "double dunce," but now, according to Robert Bray, he expected to be "deferentially addressed everywhere in the Methodist Connection, as 'Dr. Cartwright.'"[71]

Peter Cartwright claims in his *Autobiography* that there were "some splendid revivals, and an increase of over five hundred members in Springfield, under the faithful labors of Brother J.F. Jaquess."[72] But as James Leaton points out in *Methodism in Illinois*, this statement about Jaquess, like many of Cartwright's claims, is "a great exaggeration." Leaton says that the conference lists an increase of only 112 people in the Springfield congregation.[73] The records of the next annual conference in Belleville in 1848 reported that the Springfield church had 215 members and 105 probationers.[74] Among the many Springfield converts of Brother Jaquess was Governor Augustus C. French's wife, who became a close friend of

Sarah Jane.[75] Whatever the exact figures were, Jaquess' ministry in Springfield was clearly a success. He was definitely an excellent public speaker, an ability that he used to his advantage not only in the pulpit but also to persuade others throughout his life.

Almost all colleges on the frontier wanted to hire educated easterners to be their presidents because the trustees considered these men better educated than men who graduated from schools like Indiana Asbury or McKendree and so were more likely to attract students and donors. Trustees of the Methodist school for females that was about to open in Jacksonville were no different. In November 1847, they elected John T. Newman from New York to be the school's first president but he turned them down. Next they elected James F. Jaquess to this position, in August 1848, but his congregation in Springfield refused to release him until the Illinois Conference assigned someone else to their church at its next annual meeting. The trustees were not willing to wait that long and asked another easterner, O.R. Howard, to become the school's first president. But he also declined their offer. Finally, the Illinois Conference appointed another minister to the Springfield church at its meeting in September 1848 and approved the trustees' choice of Jaquess as president of Illinois Conference Female Academy. McKendree College sent one of its professors to take charge of the new Methodist school for females until James and Sarah Jane Jaquess could move to Jacksonville.[76] New careers awaited both of them.

Chapter 2

Jacksonville, Illinois

When James and Sarah Jane Jaquess moved from Springfield to Jacksonville in 1848, their new hometown had existed for twenty-three years. The 1840 census reported that Jacksonville had a population of 1,900; this figure grew to 2,745 during the next ten years. Located in the center of Morgan County, Jacksonville became the county seat and the county's largest community.[1] The Illinois state capital started out in Kaskaskia then moved to Vandalia as the state's population spread northward. When discussion began about moving the capital from Vandalia to the middle of Illinois, Jacksonville was one of several towns that vied to become the new capital. A referendum took place in 1834 to poll public opinion about relocating the Illinois seat of government, but voting was light and no town received a majority. A third of the votes went to Alton with the towns of Springfield and Vandalia close behind. Only a few voters favored a location in the geographical middle of the state (now the site of Illiopolis), Peoria or Jacksonville.[2]

Having little chance of becoming the state capital, Jacksonville set out to become a town known for something else — its many private and state institutions — and became unique among communities in West Central Illinois. Although many American towns and cities called themselves the "Athens of the Midwest," Jacksonville came closest to earning this title with its colleges, academies and public institutions. These educational and charitable institutions addressed many of the concerns of the national reform movement before the Civil War.

The first of Jacksonville's many institutions was Illinois College, founded in 1829 by the Yale Band, a group of Home Missionaries traveling from New England to establish a seminary in the West. Presbyterians and Congregationalists cooperated in this educational undertaking on the frontier. Like other missionaries traveling from the East, the Yale Band believed that the real purpose for founding a college was to enable social reform.[3] This Jacksonville school promoted the formation of literary groups for men and for women as well as charitable groups of various kinds. Jonathan Baldwin Turner, who became nationally known for the Morrill Land Grant College Act, joined the Illinois College faculty in 1833. When he wrote home, he claimed that, compared to Jacksonville, there was no "'village east of the Hudson, of the same number of inhabitants, possessing so many men of literary eminence and moral worth, nor a community of greater refinement in taste and manners.'"[4]

The murder in November 1837 of Elijah Lovejoy, publisher of an abolitionist newspaper in Alton, caused a large crowd of angry residents and college students to gather on the campus of Illinois College. This gathering on the campus, along with knowledge that Illinois College's President Edward Beecher had served as chair of an antislavery convention in Alton, caused people to identify Illinois College as the home of abolitionists. Although this charge was inaccurate, it greatly upset Jacksonville resident Governor Joseph Duncan, who threatened to submit his resignation from the Illinois College Board. The chairman of the trustees, Samuel D. Lockwood, persuaded the governor that this charge was not true.[5]

Although Illinois College was not a hotbed of abolitionism, some historians argue that faculty member Jonathan Baldwin Turner was involved in the Underground Railroad in Jacksonville. Late in his life, Turner wrote to Wilbur H. Siebert, author of *The Underground Railroad from Slavery to Freedom*: "I am and have always have been a native-born abolitionist," but he also said, "I took no interest in running slaves off to Canada." When an abolitionist friend asked Turner to help three female slaves, he did not shelter them in his house because his well-known opposition to slavery would cause the slave-catchers to check there. Instead he took them to the house of a pro-slavery neighbor who took pity on the women and housed them until someone could transport them to the next station.[6]

Several members of the local Congregational Church and at least two black residents from the part of town called "Africa" took part in Jacksonville's Underground Railroad activity. In a paper read to the Morgan County Historical Society in February 1906, Julia Wolcott Carter identified her father, Elihu Wolcott, her father-in-law Ebenezer Carter, Timothy Chamberlain, Henry Miller and two African Americans, Ben Henderson and the Reverend A.W. Jackson, as participants in the local Underground Railroad operation.[7] Charles M. Eames, in *Historic Morgan and Classic Jacksonville*, interviewed W.C. Carter, the son of Ebenezer Carter, and

Benjamin Henderson about the Underground Railroad and its time span in Jacksonville. They agreed that the Underground Railroad operated from the late 1830s until 1857 or 1858.[8] Although runaway slaves did pass through Jacksonville, the town was never a major Underground Railroad station.

There was little recognition among members of the general public that they had any responsibility for the care of indigent individuals and persons with mental and physical disabilities until the state established institutions for the care of these unfortunate citizens.[9] When Illinois did recognize this obligation, Jacksonville became the site of all the state facilities to care for and educate its deaf, blind and mentally ill citizens.

The town's first public institution, originally called the Deaf and Dumb Asylum, was the brainchild of state senator Orville H. Browning, from Quincy, whose meeting with a deaf man schooled in Kentucky convinced him that deaf individuals were educable. Browning's bill passed the Illinois senate and house in 1839, chiefly because of the influence of William Thomas, a state senator from Jacksonville. The bill stipulated that Jacksonville residents must provide five acres of land where the institution could be built; the people of Jacksonville had raised $979.50 for purchasing land by 1842. A three-story building with an attic was ready for occupancy three years later. It was nicknamed the "State's Folly" because the residents of Illinois thought the building was too grand and would exceed what was needed for the next century. But the need for the school was much greater than anticipated and this building was remodeled in 1871 to become the south wing of a much larger structure. Today's Illinois School for the Deaf remains at its original location, and an upgraded version of the 1845 structure houses the administration.[10]

Jacksonville's second charitable institution, a state hospital for the insane, owes thanks to Dr. Edward Mead, a teacher in Illinois College's medical school, for helping to convince the general public of the need for medical care for mentally ill individuals.[11] This medical school lasted only 6 years (1842 to 1848) because of insufficient funds to pay its faculty and public objection to the school's method of obtaining its cadavers.[12] Jacksonville merchant J.O. King persuaded Dorothea Dix, famous nationally for her many reform activities to provide care for the insane in the eastern part of the United States, to come to Illinois. He transported her in his buggy from town to town to see the miserable care for the disabled and the insane throughout the state.[13]

Although this trip convinced Dix that Illinois needed a hospital to care for the insane, her choice for locating this institution was Peoria, not

Jacksonville. A bill to this effect passed the Illinois senate in 1847, but William Thomas used his influence in the Illinois house to persuade the representatives to amend the bill to change the location of the institution from Peoria to Jacksonville.[14] Built just south of the town, the Illinois State Hospital for the Insane received its first patients in 1851. In November 2012, Illinois governor Quinn closed the Jacksonville Developmental Center after 160 years, while the City of Jacksonville uses most of the property for a community park.

A different and highly effective approach brought a school for the blind to Jacksonville without opposition from another community or its representatives in the Illinois legislature. A blind man named Joseph Bacon came to the town in 1847 at the invitation of unidentified Jacksonville boosters. He had graduated from the Ohio School for the Blind and, with financial support from local citizens, opened his own school for a class of six blind students in June 1848. William Thomas then prepared a bill that Richard Yates introduced in the state legislature in 1849.[15] According to Don Harrison Doyle's *The Social Order of a Frontier Community: Jacksonville, Illinois, 1825–70,* this was "part of a shrewd strategy to avoid another battle over location" and also allowed Yates to request support for "an already established institution."[16] When the Illinois Institution for the Blind opened its doors on April 7, 1849, Joseph Bacon became the first superintendent, at an annual salary of $600; there were 14 students in attendance by that summer.[17] Now called the Illinois School for the Visually Impaired, this state institution remains in the same location, several blocks east of the location where the Methodist school for women would soon appear.

Jacksonville had already proved itself to be a community ahead of its time in attitudes about the education of women. As Dr. Joseph R. Harker points out in his article "A Century of Educational Progress in the Illinois Conference, 1824–1924," there was a widespread opinion in the 19th century that "'Females' could not be educated." This viewpoint maintained that "an examination of their brain showed that it was much smaller and less convoluted than that of men, and their physical constitution and their normal calling as mothers and wives in charge of the home all forbade any thought of their attempting anything but the merest rudiments of education."[18] Jacksonville did not share this point of view. Wives of members of the Illinois College faculty organized in 1832 a group called the Ladies' Association for Educating Females to make education possible for women through financial aid. This organization, now called the Ladies' Education Society, still exists and provides support to females who cannot pursue education because of insufficient funds. A school called Jacksonville Female Academy opened its doors to girls shortly after the founding of Illinois College and received its charter in 1835 along with three all-male schools: Illinois College,[19] Shurtleff College in Alton and McKendree College in Lebanon. Jacksonville Female Academy merged with Illinois College, changing the men's college to a coeducational institution in 1903.

Methodist preacher James H. Dickens takes credit for persuading the two most powerful men in the Illinois Conference of the Methodist Episcopal Church, Peter Akers and Peter Cartwright, to favor the founding of a school for females. He won the support of Akers by proposing that this school be built on property that Akers owned near Ebenezer, four miles northwest of Jacksonville. However, persuading Peter Cartwright to support the founding of a college posed a much greater problem.[20] Cartwright, like Abraham Lincoln, was a learned man who was self-taught. Dickens claims that he won Cartwright's support by convincing McKendree College to honor Cartwright with a doctor of divinity degree in 1845[21] and persuading Cartwright to accept this degree for "his many sacrifices and labors for the Church and her literary institutions." Cartwright gladly accepted the D.D. degree and from then on insisted on being called "Dr. Cartwright."[22] Dr. Akers' land at Ebenezer lost out in favor of Jacksonville as the academy's location, but the Ebenezer Manual Training School that Akers had founded in 1836 became widely known.[23] Because both Akers and Cartwright favored establishing a Methodist school for women, the Illinois Conference approved the founding of this school. Both ministers served on the school's board of trustees and continued to provide guidance and support during its early years.

When James and Sarah Jane Jaquess arrived in Jacksonville in the fall of 1848, Illinois Conference Female Academy had existed on paper since October 10, 1846, when Methodist leaders founded the school at a meeting in East Charge Church. This new Methodist school probably would have come about sooner if McKendree College had been able to survive at an earlier date without receiving support from the Illinois Conference. Governor Augustus C. French signed the new school's charter four months after its foundation and classes began in October 1848. A.W. Cummings, a professor on loan from McKendree College, was in charge until James and Sarah Jane arrived to take over. Classes began in the basement of East Charge Church (now Centenary United Methodist Church) and continued to meet there until the first college building was completed more than two years later.[24]

Virtually all 19th-century schools, both those for men and those for women, started out as academies and were later rechartered as colleges after they had prepared students who were ready for college-level courses. Illinois Conference Female Academy followed this model and began by providing both primary and secondary education for girls and young women. The Reverend James H. Dickens called this new school a "high school for young women, under Conf. patronage." Dickens was a strong advocate of educating a young woman, because "if she was educated, she would lift up man: if she was not she would ever drag man down."[25] Under the guidance of James Jaquess, the school changed from Illinois Conference Female Academy to Illinois Conference Female College within three years of his arrival.[26]

The reason why some colleges began as academies was the lack of nearby public or private schools to prepare students for higher education. But this was not the case in Jacksonville. When the Methodists founded their female academy, the Presbyterians had operated a similar institution, the Jacksonville Female Academy, for about 13 years. The Presbyterians clearly did not want Methodist competition and feared that there were not enough donors or, for that matter, enough females desiring higher education to support two such institutions in Jacksonville. Horace Spaulding, who later taught at Illinois Conference Female College, warned trustee Dr. Peter Akers that there was an anti–Methodist party dedicated to preserving the Presbyterian school at any cost.[27] Two schools for women grew to three when the Young Ladies' Athenaeum opened in 1864. Unlike the other two schools, the Athenaeum was nonsectarian. It failed to flourish and closed its doors before the end of the 19th century.[28] The Jacksonville Female Academy lost its separate identity when it merged with Illinois College. The Illinois Conference Female College still exists as MacMurray College but became a coeducational school when it added men in 1957.

Jacksonville could boast that it had a college for men and both a college and an academy for women, and then, for a few years between 1854 and 1861, a coeducational institution, a revolutionary idea for that day. Although named Berean College, this school began as an academy if it followed the same path as most educational institutions. The Disciples of Christ Church opened their school in a frame building on a five-acre campus across State Street and slightly east of Main Hall of Illinois Conference Female College. The 96 students attending the first year included 59 men and 37 women. The following year a spacious brick building replaced the original structure. Walter Scott Russell, who was also pastor of Jacksonville's Disciples of Christ Church, became president of Berean College in 1857. He became involved in a theological argument that led to the closing of the school four years later. Eliza Ayers bought the Berean College building and donated it to the Rev. W.A. Passavant's Lutheran Association for Works of Mercy in 1875; it became the east section of the first building that housed Passavant Memorial Hospital.[29]

When it became evident that the Methodists were determined to operate a school of their own in Jacksonville, a group of prominent residents argued that another school with a different religious affiliation would be "one too many to support" and would threaten the existence of Jacksonville Female Academy and Illinois College, which were struggling to keep together "soul and body."[30] Because of the danger that a new school posed to two schools already in operation, the board of the new Methodist school had the choice of constructing its own building or buying an existent building as the location for the new school. Judge Samuel D. Lockwood, acting for the Jacksonville Female Academy, made an offer to the Methodist trustees. The Methodist school could have the property of the Presbyterian academy if the board of Illinois Conference Female Academy made a reasonable offer and assumed the debts of the Jacksonville Female Academy. The Methodist board appointed a committee to look at the property of the Jacksonville Female Academy and, based on the committee's opinion, the board decided to construct their own building. Although Bishop Janes laid the cornerstone for this building on September 6, 1849, the year after James and Sarah Jane arrived, the school's first building, Main Hall, was not completed until the winter of 1851-1852 Meanwhile, classes were still taught in the basement of East Charge Church.[31]

Although there is no record of where James and Sarah Jane resided when they arrived in Jacksonville, the 1850 census[32] reported that they were living in the home of the Milburn family, which had left Jacksonville for an extended period of time. Nicholas Milburn was a trustee of Illinois Conference Female Academy and father of the Rev. William Henry Milburn, the nationally famous "blind preacher eloquent" who served as chaplain of the U.S. Senate.[33] This house was located on State Street a short distance from the Methodist church where classes met in the basement. In the cellar of the house there is evidence of the log cabin of John Henry, the cabinet maker who built the many coffins needed to bury Jacksonville victims of the cholera epidemic of 1833.[34] Sometime before the turn of the 20th century, an alteration of the Milburn home incorporated the old house within a new one and changed the structure into what became the residence of MacMurray College's president.[35]

Their first years in Jacksonville were memorable ones for both James and Sarah Jane. The Illinois Conference elevated James from deacon to elder of the Methodist Episcopal Church on September 18, 1849, at their annual meeting, this time held in Quincy.[36] Their only child, Willie (William Garrison Jaquess), was born the following month, on October 29. Margaret, James' daughter from his first marriage, joined James and Sarah Jane by 1851 when she enrolled in the primary department of the school. James' youngest sister, Rachel Jaquess, also lived with them and enrolled in Illinois Conference Female Academy as an "irregular student."[37]

When the school outgrew the classrooms in the basement of East Charge Church, the Methodist Academy began renting rooms in private homes to serve as additional classrooms. The school's first building, completed in the winter of 1851-1852, cost $100,000 and left the school with a debt of $13,930.40. Referred to as Main Hall, this structure could house 150 to 200 students and contained a dining room, classrooms and a chapel that could hold 300.[38] The Jaquess family, some of the faculty and many of the students moved into Main Hall after its completion. While James served as president of the academy, Sarah Jane was the school "governess," a 19th-century dean of women.[39] Illinois Conference Female Academy was definitely a Jaquess family operation.

Probably the most valuable asset that Jaquess gained from his seven years in Jacksonville was the friendship of Richard Yates. They were less than two years apart in age and both were college graduates, Methodists and Whigs who became Republicans. Yates, who was Illinois College's first graduate, served as Civil War governor of Illinois and became an important link between Jaquess and Abraham Lincoln. The Yates family resided on East State Street across from the college's Main Hall, the home of the Jaquess family. Yates' law partner, William Brown, was a member of the college's first board of trustees, which sometimes met at the Brown and Yates law office before the completion of Main Hall. Richard Yates himself was elected to the board in 1854 and served as a college trustee during Jaquess' last year at the school. Into the 1870s Jaquess depended on Richard Yates, along with James Harlan, his friend from college days at Indiana Asbury, for assistance and support.

Illinois Conference Female Academy became a college for women on January 29, 1851.[40] The primary department was discontinued three years later because there was adequate elementary education available in the Jacksonville schools. Illinois Conference Female College offered a curriculum in classical studies that was virtually the same as those in male colleges such as Jaquess' alma mater, Indiana Asbury. This course in Greek and Latin classics led to a "mistress of liberal arts" degree. There was also an

"Old Main" the original building of Illinois Conference Female College, Jacksonville, Illinois (courtesy MacMurray College Archives and Special Collections).

alternate course of study, the "mistress of English literature" degree. The college offered works in English, rather than in the classical languages, but included all of the other requirements for the mistress of liberal arts.[41] Apparently, the idea of awarding female students bachelor degrees offered to graduates of men's colleges was considered unfitting.

Few women, especially those from the Midwest, attended college in the 1850s. As Mary Watters explains in her history of MacMurray College's first 100 years, it was generally accepted that "the chief function of the educated woman should be as companion and counsellor to her husband and instructor to her children." Although there was interest in learning the fundamentals of reading and writing, college-educated women had no occupational choice except teaching and seldom found husbands. Also, female teachers were paid half the amount paid to their male colleagues. Although during its first year, students of Illinois Conference Female Academy came from Jacksonville and Morgan County; young women from Kentucky and Missouri appeared the next year and by 1855 there were students coming from Indiana, Ohio, Kansas and Wisconsin. Near the end of the decade a few students arrived even from the distant locations of California, Canada and Texas.[42]

Jaquess himself gave instruction in mental and moral philosophy and also in chemistry. During his seven years as president, the school attracted more students than at any other time, until the 20th century. When he was absent on college business, Sarah Jane taught his courses for him.[43] During his administration the faculty grew from 5 to 12 teachers, a large number for that time. However, most of these teachers would be called adjunct professors today.[44] Both James and Sarah Jane Jaquess were popular with the students. According to the issue of the *College Greetings* issue published for the school's 50th anniversary, women who attended in the 1850s described him as "firm, but never severe, affable but always dignified, lenient, but never over indulgent." These students also had fond memories of Mrs. Jaquess, who had "pretty glossy black wavy hair, snapping eyes, and conscious power."[45] She gave "lectures on healthful living, care of person and premises and the proprieties of life." The students remembered that they even tried to walk like Sarah Jane Jaquess.[46]

Minutes of the Board of the Illinois Conference Female College record Jaquess' decision to leave the school as a matter-of-fact event: "Bro. Jaquess tendered his resignation as President of this Institution to take effect at the close of the present collegiate year & as Trustee to take effect from this date, which on motion was accepted."[47] But the fact that Jaquess left the position of president of a Methodist college encourages speculation that he was anxious to get away from the school and Jacksonville.

One reason for his resignation was the school's financial difficulties and the money problems that they caused the faculty. When Jaquess came to the institution, the school had paid him and all faculty members set salaries established by the board. This arrangement assured that employees knew what to expect in annual remuneration.[48] But this was not the usual policy in 19th-century colleges and academies. Then, on October 11, 1852, the board voted to switch to the method of payment used in most other schools. The college ceased paying fixed salaries and began paying wages based on percentages of what the school received in tuition and in interest from the school's endowment.[49] This system, which worked at other institutions, might have also been successful at Illinois Conference Female College if the trustees had not already adopted a "Perpetual Scholarship Plan" earlier the same year. Jaquess himself introduced this idea,[50] that was similar to the arrangement at Mount Carmel Academy that allowed stockholders to send students to the school without tuition charges.

The goal of the Perpetual Scholarship Plan was to raise money for the college's endowment. The argument for this plan was that a significantly increased endowment, if wisely invested, would produce more income for the school than what was currently received from tuition. Under the Perpetual Scholarship Plan, the college guaranteed free tuition for one family member at a time, presumably forever, if the family gave $100 to the institution. This arrangement might have worked if there had not been two special clauses. First, a family did not have to pay the entire $100 before sending one daughter to the school tuition free. This benefit began as soon as the family had paid $25 in cash. The college allowed the remaining $75 to be pledged in the form of promissory notes. However, many families failed to pay these notes. In addition, Methodist ministers received the special benefit of tuition for half the regular cost although the daughters of clergymen accounted for a large part of the school's enrollment. But even if the college received the full $100, this payment was certainly far too small for the long-term benefits that it provided.[51] The college was expecting the president and the faculty to survive on fixed percentages of tuition payments while the school promoted a Perpetual Scholarship Plan that significantly reduced the amount of tuition the school received.

To make matters worse, the Perpetual Scholarship Plan attracted so many additional students to the institution that the board decided to add a wing to the college building. This decision meant that the school must raise more money to pay for adding a wing to the college's only building. The total cost of Main Hall, including this addition, was about $100,000. At the time when the Jaquess family moved on to the Paris Station of the Illinois Conference, the college owed money to him, to his wife and, in fact, to every faculty member. When Jaquess resigned, the rest of the faculty resigned with him. The college now owed more than $28,000, an "embarrassing indebtedness"[52] for any school.

It is likely that the money problems caused by the Perpetual Scholarship Plan were not the only reason for the decision of President Jaquess to leave. An incident at the 1854 graduation ceremony provided even greater motivation for his departure. At commencement ceremonies seniors read aloud essays that they had written especially for this occasion. As was customary in 19th-century schools, graduating students had to submit their compositions to the president in advance of the public reading so that he could review them for correct grammar and appropriate subject matter. One student, a girl from Fairfield, Illinois, named Helen Wilmans, submitted her essay to President Jaquess, then changed it after he had approved the composition. While attending the school, Helen roomed with the James H. Dickens family, who were her distant relatives. This was the same Reverend Dickens who maintained that he influenced Akers and Cartwright to support the founding of the school. Dickens claimed that he asked Helen to add the statements that caused the uproar at the graduation ceremony.[53]

There are several versions of what happened on graduation day, but all of them agree that whatever took place caused quite a sensation. The *Illinois Journal*, a Springfield newspaper, reported that "one of the girls" read "a composition strongly tinctured with FREEDOM—a sentence or two of which had been added after passing the proper ordeal of correction and examination."[54] These additions were statements favoring the abolition of slavery, a radical position unpopular in 1854 not only in Jacksonville but also in most of the United States. There was sentiment against the extension of slavery, but the complete abolition of slavery had few advocates.

Helen Wilmans and James Dickens agree that the sentiments added to her speech were his idea not hers. She maintained that "it was the well-meant mistake of my friend, Mr. Dickens.... It was only the methods we used that were wrong."[55] Dickens himself wrote, "A talented young lady appealed to me to aid her to graduate in this college. I did so. Her graduating address, by request, was against slavery."[56] Dickens was known to be an abolitionist who had taken part in circulating copies of the sensational novel *Uncle Tom's Cabin* in Jacksonville.[57] He claims that "proslaveryism was strong in the [college] Board, the community and the School" in the 1850s.[58]

Although eight of the original nine trustees came from Southern states, it is wrong to assume that everyone from the South was pro-slavery. Like James Jaquess' grandfather Jonathan, these trustees had moved to the North to escape the evils of slavery. But dislike of slavery was not the same as advocacy of its abolition. There was only one board member, the Rev. John Mathers, who shared Dickens' point of view. There were also two abolitionists, Horace Spaulding and Paul Selby, on the faculty of Illinois Conference Female College.[59] Selby's main occupation was serving as editor of the *Morgan Journal*, known to be an abolitionist newspaper.

Dickens may have given Helen the idea for changing her speech, but she very likely savored causing a public sensation. Years later, claiming that she had been treated with less consideration than the hired hands and the horses, Helen simply walked out on her husband of twenty years and their four children. She became a journalist who advocated reform and praised the woman's era. Eventually she founded a "New Thought" philosophy based on the "assertion of selfhood" and maintained "that wealth ... was the 'birthright' of all." She and her second husband opened a mental science university at Sea Breeze, Florida, where they became rich in the Florida real estate boom. She also increased their fortune by publishing her own books of advice on successful living and selling them directly.[60]

Helen Wilmans and an unidentified alumna who was present at the 1854 graduation tell different stories about what happened. Helen recounts that the brief essays of the twenty graduates "were as jejune and insipid as such essays usually are." She also asserts that her presentation would not have caused excitement if President Jaquess had not called attention to her comments by publicly denying that the college "was becoming tinctured with the anti-slavery feeling." Jaquess then accused faculty members of using "the pen of a gifted but misguided girl" to express their own sentiments.[61] The alumna suggested that Helen was not telling the whole story since she failed to mention that after the ceremony was over, she stood on the edge of the stage and shouted, "If there is no other soul in all the world who dares lift voice to defense of an outraged people I dare."[62]

It is clear that Jaquess made certain that the audience knew that Helen made "material alterations and additions" to her essay after he had read and approved the paper and that the Illinois Conference Female College did not advocate what Helen said in her essay. At this point in the proceedings the abolitionist trustee, John Mathers, sent a curt note to Jaquess stating, "I think your remarks after Miss Williams' [sic] speech were contemptible" and immediately left the room. Apparently, Jaquess did not realize that Mathers was no longer present and read his note aloud. Then he advanced a moving argument that he, as president, should "inculcate neither the principles of Abolitionism or anti–Abolitionism, nor the principles held by the Whig or Democratic party," nor the principles of the Methodist Episcopal Church even though the college was under its control.[63]

James H. Dickens also recalled his role in what followed. He reported that the Jacksonville papers printed both pro and con letters and that he "was in the thick of the fight" that followed. There were thirteen members, including the president, on the college board when Jaquess made his impassioned speech at the 1854 commencement. Six of these trustees published a joint letter supporting the principles on which Jaquess had based his action. They also threatened that if the conference prescribed "any other principles of action," it would be necessary to find other men to serve as trustees. Finally, they made it clear that they would not debate with trustee Mathers about such matters as "the liberty of speech, or freedom of the press." The incident at the graduation ceremony and the continuing argument in the newspapers pitted Dickens and Jaquess against one another. The Reverend W.D.R. Trotter, the school's financial agent, finally warned them that if they did not reconcile their differences, "it would imperil the very existence of the Institution." According to Dickens, he and Jaquess followed Trotter's advice and settled all of their differences.[64]

But the damage had already been done. No college, then or now, would want bad publicity in the newspapers. It was definitely time for Jaquess to move on; however, he did not leave immediately but waited until the following year. If he had chosen to leave in 1854, the college would certainly not have had enough time to find a replacement during the short time between the sensational publicity in July and the Methodist conference in September. Methodist ministers with the qualifications necessary to become college presidents were hard to find on the frontier. Illinois Conference Female Academy had tried unsuccessfully to persuade two easterners to come to Illinois before hiring Jaquess. A Methodist school could select its president, but that minister had to be a member of the Illinois Conference of the Methodist Episcopal Church and the conference had to officially appoint him at its annual meeting.

If Jaquess hoped to become the president of another Methodist college in Illinois, he had limited possibilities in 1854. McKendree College did not have an opening, since the Reverend Dr. Peter Akers was then serving his third term (1852–1857) as president. Also, the recently founded Methodist school in Quincy, Illinois, had just selected the Reverend Jesse H. Moore as its principal. And, although founded in 1850, Illinois Wesleyan had not yet selected its first president when the Illinois Conference met in the fall after the graduation incident in Jacksonville. Clinton W. Sears, an easterner from Ohio, became Wesleyan's first president the following year.

Then a vacancy opened in Paris, Illinois, in the fall of 1855. The Reverend Jesse H. Moore, principal of the Paris Male and Female Seminary, and pastor on the Paris Circuit since 1851, moved to Quincy in March of 1854. When a committee from the Illinois Conference evaluated the Paris school at the conclusion of its first year, they had praised Professor Moore as "a man of decided talents and ability."[65] Because of his fine reputation, the conference later appointed him as the first principal of the new Quincy English and German Seminary and pastor of the Vermont Street Church where classes were meeting until a building to house the new school was completed.[66] Moore, who grew up in Lebanon, had graduated from McKendree College in 1842 with honors in the Classical Department. Although Moore taught school in Nashville and served as principal of schools in Georgetown and Paris,[67] he lacked the advanced degree that Jaquess held that enabled him to become a college president. The appointment to Paris was the first of three occasions when Jaquess and Moore crossed one another's path.

There are only a few pieces of information about the one year that Jaquess and his family spent in Paris, Illinois, and no clear evidence that Jaquess handled both the school and the church as Jesse Moore had done before him. The Reverend James Leaton, a contemporary historian of 19th-century Methodism in Illinois, reports that the conference's appointment of Jaquess to Paris included an allowance of $600, and when he left for Quincy, everything in Paris was in a "healthy and prosperous condition."[68] It is also likely that an advertisement for the Paris Male and Female Seminary dated 1858 also applies to Jaquess' residence in Paris three years earlier. This ad mentions a staff of three professors and one teacher and describes the principal's residence as located next to a three-story brick school "pleasantly situated on rising ground ... in a beautiful grove of forest trees."[69] When the conference appointed Jaquess to the presidency of the Quincy English and German Seminary, Jesse Moore left Quincy and moved on to another call. Their paths would cross again when they both formed infantry regiments to fight the Confederate army.

Chapter 3

Quincy, Illinois

When James and Sarah Jane moved from Paris to Quincy, they quickly discovered that their new home was different from any of the other towns where they had lived. Quincy had none of the private and public institutions that characterized Jacksonville but was a town known for its flour mills, stove manufacturers and breweries.[1] About 20 miles north of Hannibal, Missouri, the town of Quincy was on the east bank of the Mississippi River 100 miles from the state capital in Springfield and nearly 250 miles from the Paris station where the Jaquess family had lived during the past year. The town of Quincy, its location in a county called Adams and its downtown park called John's Square all received their names from President John Quincy Adams. He had taken office in 1825 after the U.S. House of Representatives elected Adams, rather than Andrew Jackson, to the presidency.[2] According to a 19th-century history of the county, the residents who picked Adams as their county's name knew that the neighboring county of Morgan had chosen Jacksonville as its county seat and they wanted to see "in the struggle for position among the counties of the state ... who takes the lead Adams or Jackson."[3]

Unlike Jacksonville in Morgan County, the Adams County seat is on the edge of the county rather than in its middle. A pamphlet published by the City of Quincy tells another story to explain this unusual location. The three commissioners appointed to find a suitable central location for the county seat started out on horseback in the rainy season. After splashing through mud and marshy ground for three days, they came back to a village on the Mississippi River, chose it as the county seat and gave it the name of Quincy.[4] The town has had at least three nicknames over the years; originally, it was called the "Model City," then the "Jewel of the West" and finally the "Gem City," its name today. All of these names reflect the hope that a town located on fertile land next to an important waterway held the promise of economic success.

The U.S. Congress provided 160-acre bounties in the area between the Illinois and Mississippi rivers[5] for veterans of the War of 1812. Quincy, located within this triangle called the Illinois Military Tract, opened a land office early in 1831. After it sold only nineteen 80-acre tracts the first two years, there was such an increase in purchases that the Quincy Land District outdid all other Illinois Districts.[6] Although only 20 to 25 steamboats docked at Quincy's wharf in 1835, this number grew to between 1000 and 1200 by 1841. That year, Quincy shipped 95,000 bushels of corn, 50,000 bushels each of oats and potatoes and 5000 bushels of beans. Soon slaughterhouses appeared to prepare beef for shipping and packet boats began providing round-trip transportation to St. Louis and Warsaw for both freight and passengers.[7] Quincy had become a booming business community.

Although the towns of Quincy and Jacksonville differed in many ways, both had well-known state and national figures as their residents. Stephen A. Douglas, a Jacksonville resident during his early years in Illinois, joined the bar in Morgan County and served as its state's attorney. Later in his career he became justice of the Illinois Supreme Court's Fifth Judicial District located in Quincy. Also, citizens from both Quincy and Jacksonville served as governors of Illinois. Joseph Duncan, governor from 1834 to 1838, used his mansion, built in Jacksonville in 1835, as his office and a place for discussing politics and government business. His famous visitors included Daniel Webster, General John J. Hardin and Stephen A. Douglas. John Wood, who is usually considered Quincy's first settler, became governor for parts of 1860 and 1861 when Governor William Henry Bissell died in office. Wood's Greek Revival mansion in Quincy took three years to complete, from 1835 to 1838. (Today both the Duncan mansion and the Wood mansion remain in good condition and are open to the public for tours.) Another Jacksonville resident, Richard Yates, was the Civil War governor of Illinois and a friend of James F. Jaquess. Unfortunately, the Yates home has not survived and was probably torn down near the end of the 19th century when Our Savior's Hospital was built on this property on East State Street.

The sixth of the seven Lincoln-Douglas debates was held in Washington Square in Quincy on October 13, 1858. Boatloads of spectators from the nearby towns of Keokuk, Iowa and Hannibal, Missouri, swelled the crowd to somewhere between 8000 and 15,000.[8] Before the two debaters arrived at Washington Square, part of the poorly constructed railing around the speakers' platform collapsed and several people fell from the stage to the ground, which postponed the debate for an hour.[9] At the Quincy debate Abraham Lincoln proclaimed that slavery was wrong, reiterating what he had stated at the debate in Galesburg six days before.[10]

Quincy left its mark on history by providing shelter for the Mormons fleeing from Missouri in the winter of 1839 before they relocated in the town of Commerce, which they renamed Nauvoo. Mormon historian Richard E. Bennett maintains in his article "'Quincy—the Home of Our Adoption': A Study of the Mormons in Quincy, Illinois, 1838–40" that this town was an excellent place for the Mormons to stay because of its location, its size and the fact that "it was a city on the move, destined to double in size to forty-four hundred by 1840."[11] Nineteenth-century Quincy historian Henry Asbury, in *Reminiscences of Quincy Illinois*, also writes about the "suffering and destitution" of the Mormons and the willingness of Quincy to provide employment for those who wanted to work.[12] The Mormons began leaving Missouri in January 1839 ahead of the deadline set up by the governor of Missouri and received a warm welcome that cold winter from the residents of Quincy and the surrounding countryside. Quincy and the rest of Adams County provided assistance for about 5000 Mormon refugees.[13]

Although Jacksonville likes to think of itself as a major station on the Underground Railroad, this distinction does not belong to the seat of Morgan County but to the seat of Adams County, Quincy, on the Mississippi River. Owen W. Muelder in his recent book *The Underground Railroad in Western Illinois* refers to Jacksonville and Springfield as "spur lines" off the "major artery" from Alton north through a series of towns and finally to Chicago.[14] By contrast, he describes Quincy as "famous or infamous depending on which side one was on, as the 'jumping off point' on the western Illinois Underground Railroad."[15] Slaves escaped across the Mississippi River from Missouri and headed north on the "Quincy Line" through western Illinois.[16]

Henry Asbury, who lived in Quincy during the operation of the Underground Railroad, tells the story of abolitionist Dr. David Nelson, who fled from Missouri in 1836, with a mob from Palmyra in pursuit, and arrived covered with mud from top to bottom on the Quincy side of the Mississippi.[17] The following year, Nelson established a manual labor school near Quincy called the Mission Institute. Nelson, a medical doctor, trained young men to become ministers, missionaries and apparently Underground Railroad conductors who guided escaped slaves across the Mississippi from Missouri to Illinois. The Mission Institute provided shelter for the slaves until they began their journey north. Two students and one teacher from the Mission Institute spent several years in the Missouri State Penitentiary after they were caught in 1841, tried and found guilty of aiding slaves to escape. A mob from Missouri crossed the Mississippi River and burned down the Mission Institute in March 1843 but were never arrested for their crime of arson.[18]

Another Quincy physician involved with Underground Railroad activities was Richard Eels, whose home near the Mississippi is open to tours. An African American named Berryman Barnet brought word to the doctor that a runaway slave needed transportation to the Mission Institute. Eels had the slave put on dry clothes and leave his wet clothing in the doctor's house before they left for the institute. When he realized that there were slave catchers in hot pursuit, Eels brought his buggy close enough to a fence surrounding a field of corn for Barnet to jump out of his buggy and hide in the corn. Although a slave catcher captured the runaway before morning and brought him to jail, Dr. Eels managed to escape to Chicago. When he returned to Quincy, the authorities arrested him based on the evidence of the slave's soaked clothing found in his house. Later Judge Stephen A. Douglas found Dr. Eels guilty and fined him $300.[19]

Quincy had female as well as male abolitionists. The wives of the Reverend Dr. Foote, Willard Turner and Dr. Eels banded together sometime in the 1850s to trick the Quincy jailer and free a slave from the local jail. When they brought supper for the prisoner, the jailer allowed all three women to enter the cell. The jailer left them and remained at a distance until the women asked to leave. The following morning the jailer found that one of the women had spent the night in the cell and the prisoner had left with her two companions. He let her out of the cell and chose not to keep her; meanwhile the runaway slave was well on his way to freedom.[20]

Unlike the Illinois Female Academy in Jacksonville, the Quincy English and German Seminary was the first college founded in that town and remained the only one until the Franciscans opened a school in March 1860. Fifty German-speaking boys enrolled in the Roman Catholic school and the two priests who taught there had to struggle to master the German language.[21] This school survived over the years as St. Francis Solanus College, Quincy College, and, since 1993, Quincy University. Unlike the successful Catholic school, the Methodist college where James Jaquess served from 1856 to 1862 had a brief and somewhat checkered existence. From Quincy English and German Seminary, its name changed to Quincy College and then, for a brief time, to Johnson College when it merged with a school of that name. Finally, after receiving a gift from an Iowan named

Charles Chaddock, the school changed its name to Chaddock College. The coincidence that two different schools had the name of Quincy College, a Methodist one in the 19th century and a Catholic one from 1917 to 1993, has caused confusion even among the residents of Quincy.

The Methodist school not only changed its name but also changed its location several times. It began in a church basement and then occupied a large building constructed to house the school. Then in 1875, the college sold this building to the Quincy school board and bought the octagonal house of former governor John Wood for unpaid taxes. When threatened with foreclosure at the end of the 19th century, the college turned over this property to deaconesses who opened an orphanage in the home called Chaddock Boys School. When this school moved into buildings of its own, the John Wood house became a Catholic grade school. It was finally razed in 1949 so that a Methodist church could be constructed on the lot. Illinois Wesleyan received whatever records existed when Chaddock College closed its doors, but they were apparently lost in a major fire that destroyed Wesleyan's "Old Main" in 1943. For these reasons little information about this school has survived.[22]

The Methodist school in Quincy was founded on September 23, 1853, seven years after Illinois Conference Female Academy.[23] Like the Jacksonville school, the one in Quincy originally held classes in the basement of a church, Vermont Street Methodist Episcopal. According to the *Quincy Daily Whig*, the Reverend Jesse H. Moore, identified as "a gentleman of ability and extensive experience," became the school's principal and doubled as supply pastor for the Vermont Street congregation. This is the same minister who preceded Jaquess at the Methodist Church and Male and Female Seminary in Paris, Illinois. Classes began in March 1854,[24] but the Quincy school did not receive its charter as a seminary until February 5, 1855, nearly a year after classes began.[25] The designation of "seminary" in the school's name does not indicate that it provided theological education. At that time "seminary" meant the same thing as "academy," a school providing secondary education and often serving as a preparatory school for students planning to attend college.

During the first year of classes, the trustees of Quincy English and German Seminary started to raise funds to construct a building and purchased an acre of land on the corner of Fourth and Spring streets as the permanent location for the school.[26] The building erected there was advertised in the *Quincy Daily Whig* as a "most beautiful piece of Architecture ... situated in a retired part of the City."[27] Classes moved from the church basement to the new building when the fall term of 1856 began.[28] As the name suggests, the Methodists intended to meet the educational needs of all members of their denomination in Quincy, both those who spoke English and those who spoke German.

James, Sarah Jane, Margaret and Willie Jaquess moved in November 1856 from Paris to Quincy, the town that was the location of the meeting of the Illinois Conference that year. The academy trustees had elected James president in June[29] and the Illinois Conference ratified their decision at this meeting. The Jaquess family moved into their quarters in the new building, now completed according to its original plan.[30] As the Methodists had predicted at their annual meeting two years earlier, the new academy would, from its beginning, rank high among the schools of the Illinois Conference.[31]

The seminary building, advertised in Quincy newspapers as "well arranged for health, comfort and convenience," was similar in many ways to Main Hall at the Methodist college in Jacksonville. The seminary building housed the Jaquess family, members of the "Board of Instruction" who chose to live there and about fifty female pupils.[32] According to the 1860

Original building, Quincy English and German College, from 19th century catalog (Archives of United Methodist Great Rivers Church located at MacMurray College).

census, Isaac Newton Jaquess' daughter Laura,[33] who was the same age as James' daughter Margaret, was living with the president's family. The seminary building also had enough classrooms to accommodate three hundred students.[34]

Unlike most 19th-century academies, seminaries and colleges, the Quincy school enrolled both males and females. The primary classes included both boys and girls, but this arrangement appears not to have extended to preparatory classes. A page that has survived from the school's catalog identifies the Reverend Marshall M. Johnson as "Principal of Male Preparatory Department" and Miss Minerva E. Masters as "Preceptress of the Female Preparatory Classes and Teacher of Guitar Music." The males and females in the preparatory department, who would be called high school students today, appear not to have attended coeducational classes. However, because of the small number of students in the collegiate course, men and women did attend the same classes in the "Classical and Scientific" courses of study.[35] Although female students could live in the college building, male students were required to live at home or board with local families. From its beginning, the school expected male students to be "studious young Men and Boys" who would "study [in] their rooms at home, or their boarding places."[36] When there were no men in the first three graduating classes—1859, 1860 and 1861— President Jaquess "accounted for their absence partly by ascribing an earlier maturity to the female mind, and partly by the general laxity of home discipline as applied to boys."[37]

Also, unlike other Illinois schools, the Methodist college in Quincy provided classes for German-speaking as well as English-speaking students. The 1850 Census reported that 38.8 percent of the Quincy population had been born in Germany.[38] The first German Methodist Episcopal church, located at 514 Jersey Street, opened in 1854 and remained in operation until 1901.[39] Jaquess was comfortable working with these students because he was familiar with the Germans who had settled near his home in Posey County. These Rappites, founders of New Harmony, came originally from Germany where the Lutheran church and the government in Wurttemberg had persecuted them. The *Quincy Whig* apologized in 1857 for not calling attention to the German department at the Methodist seminary in an article about the school. The newspaper stressed that in Quincy, German boys and girls could be "thoroughly educated in their own native tongue ... without having to cross the Atlantic."[40]

Much of the seminary's curriculum resembled the courses of study at Mount Carmel Academy and the Illinois Conference Female Academy in its early days. In 1856, instruction in primary English or German cost

$4.00 a term, preparatory or higher English or German cost $6.00, and the collegiate course was $8.00. But, unlike the Mount Carmel and Jacksonville schools, the Quincy seminary also offered two courses of study leading directly to jobs: a commercial department for "young gentlemen wishing to qualify themselves in the useful Science of Book Keeping" and a teacher's class with a course of study "the same as that prescribed by the laws of the State of Illinois." There was also instruction in music, drawing and painting. The institution described its discipline as "parental — mild but strict" and claimed that its excellence rested on "the thoroughness of its instruction and moral discipline."[41]

Advertisements for the school claimed that it was "the object of the Institution ... to afford to both sexes an ample means of instruction in all the various departments of Science, from the first rudiments of Knowledge, up to the highest branches taught in our best Seminaries and Colleges."[42] Although the legislature did not approve changing the school's charter from a seminary to a college until 1863,[43] the school began calling itself a "college" as early as 1859 and started marketing its faculty, their degrees and their areas of expertise. President Jaquess taught "Mental and Moral Philosophy" as he had at Illinois Conference Female College, and Sarah Jane now taught "Rhetoric and History." There was "a full board of competent teachers" that offered classes "in the Latin, Greek, French and German languages" as well as "the different branches of Mathematics, Natural Science [and] Belle Lettres."[44]

Like most other 19th-century institutions of higher learning, Quincy College had literary societies intended to encourage its students in social as well as educational development. Quincy had separate societies for men and for women although these organizations held joint activities. A few programs from these "Exhibitions" have survived.[45] James' daughter, now called Maggie, and her future husband, Henry A. Castle, participated. Maggie was a member of the Opal Society and read an essay entitled "Desolation" at a joint exhibition with the Franklin Literary Society on March 19, 1861. Henry Castle, a Franklin Society member, debated a member of the Opal group on the topic "Are Modern Times Superior, as a Field for Eloquence, to Ancient." There is no record of who won.[46]

Most 19th-century schools eventually ran into financial difficulties, but the college in Quincy experienced money problems within six months of its founding. When contractors finished building schoolrooms in the basement of Vermont Street Church so that classes could begin there in March 1854, the board of trustees had no money to pay them for their work. Hoping to raise necessary funds to operate the school, the trustees decided to try a Perpetual Scholarship Plan similar to those adopted at Mount Carmel Academy and Illinois Conference Female College. The trustees set out to build a huge endowment by selling 300 scholarships at $100 each then changed their minds and stopped sale of the scholarships. A short time later they reversed themselves again and decided to sell 400, rather than 300, scholarships.[47]

When Jaquess became president in November 1856, the board of trustees immediately authorized him to borrow $10,000 in the name of the school. In late December he reported back to the board that he had not been successful. Then, on January 10, 1857, he decided to solve the problem by providing the $10,000 himself. Motivated by Jaquess' action, one trustee added $3000 and other trustees executed notes for smaller amounts until Quincy Seminary had $15,000 for operating the school. But this amount did not come from gifts but from loans that the school was responsible for repaying. The Quincy school was now $15,000 in debt with no means of paying this amount back to its president and trustees except by selling the school's only building that served as the guarantee for the loans. Then things went from bad to worse.[48]

Because he was not having much success in Quincy, Jaquess tried to persuade some of his wealthy Methodist contacts in Jacksonville to loan money to Quincy College. One individual that he approached was John C. Hamilton, a highly successful businessman who sometimes served as a local minister for the Methodist Episcopal Church.[49] Since the college building was already mortgaged, the trustees now had to mortgage 150 feet of the west portion of the seminary lot to secure these loans. Finally, in the fall of 1860, Quincy mayor Thomas Jasper[50] and President James F. Jaquess filed a joint suit for $10,000 against the president and trustees of Quincy English and German Academy. Their action led to a rash of other suits and countersuits that involved most of the board members.[51]

Meanwhile, life at Quincy College went on as usual but James Jaquess was now more outspoken on the topic of slavery than he had been when he was president of the Illinois Conference Female College in Jacksonville. Shortly after Abraham Lincoln took his presidential oath on March 4, 1861, the Confederates bombarded Fort Sumter near Charleston, South Carolina, on April 12, and captured this military installation the following day. The first Quincy residents who volunteered for the Union army left for Springfield on April 21, and the community held a public ceremony to honor these men in Washington Square. Orville Browning, the man who would soon take over the Senate seat of Stephen A. Douglas after Douglas' death, spoke to the crowd along with the Reverends Horatio

Foote and James Jaquess. Browning recorded in his diary that there were thousands present at the ceremony and "there was not a dry eye."⁵²

A letter from a displeased parishioner using the pseudonym "AJ" attacked Jaquess as an abolitionist in the *Quincy Herald*, on May 28, 1861. He stated that it was a good thing that Jaquess "has only a College and not the destinies of this country in his hands." Although he had "never heard him [Jaquess] dabble in politics in the pulpit heretofore," the letter writer claimed that this sermon failed to consider the important question of what is to become of the slaves if slavery was abolished. He maintained that the war that had just begun did not mean "that in fighting for the glorious flag of our fathers, we are fighting for the extinction of slavery."

Those who had heard Jaquess' sermons were not surprised when he announced that he was resigning as president effective at the close of Quincy College's commencement ceremonies on June 26, 1861, in order to join the Union army. The newspaper reporting this event speculated that the college trustees would work out a deal with Jaquess and rehire him as president.⁵³ The trustees executed deeds on the college property in the name of James F. Jaquess before he left for the battlefield to satisfy the school's immediate demands for money. Jaquess immediately transferred these papers to Thomas Jasper and entered the Union army as chaplain of the 6th Illinois Cavalry. Jasper foreclosed on the mortgage in January of the following year.⁵⁴

The *Quincy Whig Republican* had guessed correctly. Jaquess did agree to accept the Quincy College presidency for a second time but he also remained in the army. The newspaper referred to him as President Jaquess in its account of the college's commencement in 1862 and expected him to return to Quincy to preside at this ceremony. But it was Sarah Jane Jaquess who was in charge and awarded the degrees. The newspaper reported that she handled the ceremony "in a manner that could not have been surpassed by the most eloquent College President."⁵⁵ James Jaquess resigned from the school, this time permanently, shortly after the 1862 commencement. The board of trustees reorganized the college and appointed the Reverend Charles K. Vickers as the new president.⁵⁶

Things changed greatly at Quincy College after James Jaquess left the presidency. It is likely that Sarah Jane had to give up her teaching position and the family had to move from their rooms in the college building to a different location in Quincy. The trustees appointed agents to raise money to keep the school afloat and it continued to limp along. Faculty members no longer had salaries but instead received percentages of the tuition paid to the school. Such a small number of students enrolled in the fall of 1862 that, according to Marquis D. Hornbeck in his account of the college's financial history, there was not enough money from their tuitions to pay the present teachers "even a scanty living," and the school let several faculty members go.[57] Teachers ran ads in the local newspapers in an effort to attract students to enroll with them privately.[58] Thomas Jasper, who held the deeds executed in Jaquess' name, suggested that the board deed the school's property to Illinois to use as the location of a "military college," but the trustees rejected this idea. Finally, in March 1863, the federal government instructed Quartermaster Flagg to take possession of the college building to use as a hospital. The Quincy College building became Military Hospital #4 for wounded Union soldiers who arrived by boat up the Mississippi. Although there was discussion about returning to the place where the school had started and offering classes in the basement of Vermont Street Methodist Episcopal Church, there is no evidence that the college followed through on this idea.[59]

When the federal government took possession of the Quincy College building, the German Methodists left the English and German Seminary and established their own school in Warrenton, Missouri. The goals of the school were to care for Civil War orphans and to provide higher education for youth of the German Church of the West. They bought 32 acres in May 1864 and began classes that October. The school's original name was Western Orphan Asylum and Educational Institute; then, its name changed to Central Wesleyan College and Orphan Asylum five years later. The two parts of the institution were separated in 1884, and in 1939 the orphanage closed and the children were sent to a Methodist children's home in St. Louis.[60]

The college campus grew from one to several buildings, and the school suffered financial problems, fires, a tornado and anti–German feeling during World War I. Other German colleges merged with the school in Warrenton, but eventually the language of the college moved from German to English. The four-year school became a two-year junior college in 1930 and, finally, did not open in the fall of 1941. Six years later the college, now named Truman State University, bought the school's library; the contents that reside in the Truman State archives are almost entirely in the German language.[61]

Two years after Jaquess and Jasper filed their suit to obtain payment for their loans to the college, the chancery court of Adams County finally rendered its decision. The court ruled against the school and ordered the master of chancery to pay the college's debts to a number of different individuals, most of them trustees, the payments to include accrued interest, expenses and charges involved in filing their suits. If the college defaulted on these payments, the master of chancery would then sell the building and grounds of the college at an auction open to the public on the steps of the Adams County Courthouse. The chancery court called the money to be paid to the school's host of debtors "the debt of said James F. Jaquess" because the college's mortgage had been turned over to him by Thomas Jasper.[62] In an effort to raise funds for Quincy College, President Jaquess had been borrowing money in his own name and then loaning it to the school. A small ad placed by Jesse H. Balfour in the *Quincy Daily Whig Republican* gives a clue to what had been going on. The ad requests the return of Balfour's lost memorandum book that contains a note for $493 from James F. Jaquess.[63] This loan from Balfour to Jaquess did not enter the pockets of the president but helped to fill the coffers of Quincy College. If credit ratings had existed in the 1860s, Jaquess would have had a higher rating than Quincy College.

When the court auctioned Quincy College on August 15, 1863, the highest bidder was James F. Jaquess, represented by his agent. James was now Colonel Jaquess of the 73rd Illinois Volunteer Infantry Regiment. The amount of his bid was $22,000. When Jaquess failed to follow through with a cash payment, the master of chancery auctioned off the property a second time two months later. This time Porter Smith, identified by Henry Asbury as a carpenter who had moved to Quincy from Ohio in 1836,[64] purchased the college property for the lesser amount of $15,600. The same day, the president and trustees of Quincy College filed a petition in the circuit court of Adams County claiming that Jaquess was responsible for paying the difference of $6400 between the original sale amount and the amount paid by Smith.

The Illinois Supreme Court finally settled this case in the January 1864 term. The court ruled that the second auction of the Quincy College property was entirely legal because the master of chancery had failed to secure a judge's approval for the original sale to James F. Jaquess. Therefore, "rejection of the bid of Jacquess [sic], put an end to his liability thereof," and Quincy College could not sue Jaquess for the difference between his bid and the amount paid by the second bidder. The supreme court case noted that the "petitioners state that said Jaquess, so far as they know, and as they believe, has no property tangible to execution, or out of which he could be made to respond to damages for loss occasioned by his failure to complete his said bid and purchase, and that they believe said Jaquess to be insolvent."[65]

Jaquess reported personal assets of $25,000 in 1860.[66] A few years later, the Illinois Supreme Court referred to him as "insolvent" after he had lost these assets in an attempt to save Quincy College from closing its doors. He understood the academic side of operating a college and was beloved and respected by both faculty and students. However, he seems as ignorant of college finance as the men who sat on the college's board of trustees. James Jaquess came from a well-to-do family and had inherited, rather than accumulated, his sizeable assets. Like many other antebellum schools, Mount Carmel Academy and Quincy College disappeared because of poor management and the appearance of state institutions to replace church schools in providing education. Illinois Female College continued and became MacMurray College, but eventually this school had to become coeducational to remain successful. But Illinois Female College did not survive because of the leadership of Jaquess who resigned from the school when it was in dire financial difficulties. Keeping an institution viable, educationally and financially, was simply not a job for which James F. Jaquess was well suited. After the Civil War, he never returned to a career in education.

Chapter 4

Chaplain, 6th Illinois Cavalry

When James F. Jaquess joined the Union army on August 28, 1861, Governor Yates appointed him chaplain of the 6th Illinois Cavalry, a position that placed him in the regiment's headquarters. The governor knew Jaquess and his family well from their years as neighbors in Jacksonville and thought that this Methodist minister would make a fine chaplain, a position that received the same allowances and pay as an officer holding the rank of captain. Like most Civil War regiments, the 6th Illinois Cavalry wanted a unique nickname of its own. Such monikers usually told something about the background of the men in that regiment or an adventure that all of them had shared. The men of the 6th Illinois Cavalry decided to call themselves the "Governor's Legion" to advertise that Richard Yates had handpicked several of the unit's officers.

Shortly after formation of the 6th Cavalry, a regimental "civil war" broke out among the top officers. In addition to James Jaquess, the governor had appointed two other men from Jacksonville, Thomas H. Cavanaugh as colonel and Benjamin Grierson as major. The struggle for power within the regiment also involved another Yates appointee, Lieutenant Colonel John Olney from Shawneetown in Southern Illinois. All of these men received their positions because they shared the distinction of knowing the governor personally.[1]

Before they served together in the 6th Cavalry, Chaplain Jaquess and Colonel Cavanaugh were already friends from the minister's years in Jacksonville. The Cavanaugh family attended East Charge Church, close to the Methodist school, and two of Cavanaugh's daughters, Hannah and Ellen, attended the Illinois Conference Female Academy.[2] For a brief time in the 1850s, Cavanaugh owned a newspaper called the *Constitutionist*, a Whig publication with the motto "a weekly paper for people devoted to the best interests of Illinois." The *Constitutionist* grew from a weekly publication into the first daily newspaper in Jacksonville under the guidance of Cavanaugh's successor, John M. Taggart. Jaquess chose the *Constitutionist*'s job department to print the school's 1853 catalog[3] and possibly other catalogs as well.

Only a few days after the Civil War broke out, Cavanaugh wrote to the governor about a military appointment for his nineteen-year-old son, Thomas H. Cavanaugh, Jr., who had "the war-fever bad." Already past the age of 50, Cavanaugh described himself as "too old" to join the ranks of "the glorious old Union."[4] Yates ignored Cavanaugh's claim that he was too old to serve and appointed him colonel of the Governor's Legion; the governor also appointed Cavanaugh's son to help his father by filling the position of adjutant for the regiment.

Although their families lived only five blocks apart, there is no indication that Benjamin Grierson knew James Jaquess when they both lived in Jacksonville. Very likely, the main reason that Jaquess and Grierson did not cross paths was that they belonged to different social classes in terms of wealth and education. James and Sarah Jane had lived in Jacksonville for nearly three years before Benjamin H. Grierson arrived on the 4th of July in 1851. He bought one-third ownership, with his father and his brother, in a brick house at 852 East State Street.[5] Grierson was trying to support his family by giving music lessons but was having trouble making ends meet.

In the hope of bettering themselves, the Griersons moved north of Jacksonville to the river town of Meredosia and lived there for a brief time. Here Grierson became part owner of a grain and produce business and was able to buy his own home. But by the time Fort Sumter fell in April 1861 and war was declared, the Grierson family was back in Jacksonville, living in the family home. His business had failed and he had sold the house in Meredosia to help pay his debts. Grierson was teaching music again but still needed a more lucrative profession to support his family.[6]

Although he recruited soldiers in Jacksonville and helped organize Company I of the 10th Illinois Infantry, Grierson was reluctant to join himself. Governor Yates knew that Grierson was available to carry out a mission and sent him to Cairo, Illinois, to bring dispatches to Benjamin M. Prentiss, colonel of the 10th Illinois Infantry. Among the messages that Grierson delivered was notification of the appointment of Prentiss as brigadier general of all the Illinois troops. The governor may have known that Grierson was in search of a better job than teaching music and anticipated the offer that Prentiss made to Grierson. Prentiss and Grierson knew each other well from their days as Republican campaigners. On the basis of this friendship, Prentiss offered Grierson the position of aide-de-camp with the rank of lieutenant. Although no salary had been authorized for this position, Grierson accepted the job and trusted that Prentiss would find a way to see that he received a lieutenant's pay.[7]

All went well until John C. Fremont took command of the Union army's Department of the West, replacing General William S. Harney. Fremont believed that Prentiss outranked Ulysses S. Grant and made the error of placing him over Grant. When Fremont discovered that just the opposite was the case, he reversed his decision. But the mess that followed Fremont's mistake convinced Grierson that it was time for him to move on. He asked Governor Yates to help him find a suitable opening in another unit and, on October 24, 1861, Yates appointed him major in the 6th Illinois Cavalry where Cavanaugh was the colonel and Jaquess was the chaplain.[8]

John Olney, who later instigated a power struggle within the 6th Cavalry, caught the governor's attention after the fall of Fort Sumter. At that time Olney wrote the governor assuring him that, in spite of its proximity to Kentucky, much of the area in Southern Illinois called Little Egypt remained loyal to the Union. Olney was a lawyer who had been active in the Republican Party, both as a delegate to the party's 1858 convention and as an elector at the 1860 convention.[9] Like Grierson, Olney had experience in the army before becoming part of the 6th Cavalry. He originally joined the 18th Illinois Infantry when it was formed at Bird's Point, Missouri, and served as quartermaster and later as lieutenant. He understood from his previous military service what was expected of the commanding officer of a regiment. Governor Yates appointed John Olney lieutenant colonel of the 6th Cavalry, a rank that was higher than Grierson's and second in command to Colonel Cavanaugh.[10]

The Governor's Legion was organized at Camp Butler near Springfield on November 19, 1861, and arrived at Shawneetown about a week later. Both Grierson and Olney joined the unit there. As both officers saw immediately, Colonel Cavanaugh was allowing the men under his command to sit in their tents doing nothing rather than keeping them occupied with military drilling. The lack of discipline among the men was apparent, and both Grierson and Olney immediately questioned the competence of Cavanaugh as their superior officer. Grierson wrote in his diary that James Jaquess was Cavanaugh's only friend and referred to the chaplain as the colonel's Man Friday.[11] But John Olney did not confine his opinion of

Cavanaugh to diary entries and letters home. He publicly devoted himself to finding a way to force Cavanaugh to resign or be dismissed. Colonel Cavanaugh's response to a letter from General Ulysses S. Grant gave Olney an excellent opportunity to take action against the colonel and bring the men of the Sixth Cavalry along with him.

Before the 6th Illinois Cavalry was officially mustered in on January 9, 1862, General Grant and Colonel Cavanaugh had already exchanged correspondence about the trade in "Whiskey, Coffee, Tea and even Powder" between merchants in Shawneetown and Rebels on the Kentucky side of the Ohio River. Grant wanted Cavanaugh to see that delivery of these goods to the enemy stopped. The general said nothing about closing down the businesses of the men who were selling these items or preventing the men of the 6th Cavalry from patronizing these local merchants.[12] But Colonel Cavanaugh decided to solve the problem in precisely that way. He completely shut down those Shawneetown businesses that were providing the contraband and, as a result, his men, as well as the Rebels, no longer had access to whiskey. Both Jaquess and Cavanaugh belonged to the Methodist Church, a denomination that strongly opposed the consumption of alcohol.[13] But as Cavanaugh should have expected, the soldiers of the 6th Cavalry did not agree with this point of view. It was common for chaplains to face such problems with both officers and men who saw "a good and faithful chaplain ... [as] a standing reproof of their wicked conduct."[14] The regiment was furious with Cavanaugh for what he had done and wanted to continue enjoying their whiskey.

Selling whiskey to men in the ranks remained an issue throughout the war. Merchants called sutlers accompanied regiments as they moved from place to place and they sold goods not provided by the government to the soldiers. Sale of liquor by sutlers was supposed to be illegal, but most of the sutlers ignored these rules or found ways to circumvent them. One way of getting around the regulations was selling peaches pickled in whiskey rather than pickled in the usual way of vinegar and sugar. The sutlers also sold patent medicines laden with alcohol and bay rum hair tonic as substitutes for liquor.[15] The Union's Army of the Potomac issued General Orders No. 105, near the end of 1863, to clarify practices of registered sutlers. These rules included delivery of liquor and wine to officers and required sutlers to deliver a package of liquor to an officer within twenty-four hours of when he ordered it. Otherwise, the sutler would face accusation of keeping alcoholic beverages to sell in ways that the present military law did not approve.[16]

But a regiment without whiskey was a regiment ready to rebel, and

Lieutenant Colonel Olney used the men's anger to his advantage. As a native of Shawneetown, Olney knew the tavern owners that the colonel had put out of business and sympathized with their point of view. Also, because Colonel Cavanaugh did not attempt to drill the men in his regiment, the unhappy men of the 6th Cavalry just sat around with a lot to gripe about and almost nothing to keep them occupied. This situation made the officers' job of keeping the men in line that much harder. Major Grierson wrote in his diary that although Colonel Cavanaugh brought a man from Camp Butler to serve as drillmaster, the colonel's choice "spent his time in guzzling beer at the suttliers [sic] and talking loudly about what great things he expected to accomplish."[17] Colonel Cavanaugh reported the situation to Richard Yates, another member of East Charge Methodist Church in Jacksonville, and expected the governor to understand his point of view. The colonel claimed that the whiskey dealers that he had prevented from selling liquor to soldiers in his regiment were "'moving hell beneath and heaven above' to ruin" him and "the instrument they used in their attempts" was the officer second in command, Lieutenant Colonel John Olney.[18]

According to Major Grierson, Cavanaugh did not care that "neither the officers nor the men had any confidence" in him.[19] The colonel was more interested in trying to impress General Grant in an effort to advance his own career. Both Colonel Cavanaugh and Chaplain Jaquess had plans for themselves greater than their present positions. Cavanaugh wanted to command a brigade and Jaquess wanted to plan battle strategy for the brigade that Cavanaugh hoped to command. Their plan involved leaving the 6th Cavalry without its colonel and its chaplain and making personal visits to those individuals who had the necessary influence to make Cavanaugh's promotion possible.

Their first move was to visit General Grant in Cairo, Illinois. They lobbied him to support a promotion for Cavanaugh from colonel to brigadier-general, the appropriate rank for an officer in command of a brigade. James Jaquess brought along a battle plan that he had already designed for this as yet nonexistent brigade and showed it to Captain James B. Fry, chief of staff for General Don Carlos Buell. This plan involved the brigade's marching south to capture Memphis, Tennessee. Making battle plans was certainly not expected of a regimental chaplain, and Fry considered Jaquess' plan "in the highest degree absurd." After examining the chaplain's plan, Fry wrote a "Private and Unofficial" letter to General Richard Fuller, adjutant general of Illinois, stating his opinion of the chaplain's idea. Fry admitted that he forgave the chaplain's odd behavior and unusual ideas because Jaquess "was so full of military ardor" and excused him "for planning campaigns which could not be carried out."[20]

A visit to Governor Yates was the next stop for Jaquess and Cavanaugh on their journey to advance their careers. Cavanaugh could not command a brigade unless the governor took action to authorize the forming of one. Since Jaquess had greater influence with Yates than Cavanaugh did, it was the chaplain's job to convince the governor. He told Yates that Colonel Thomas A. Scott, the assistant secretary of war, had already authorized the governor to form a brigade of Illinois regiments and that General Buell had agreed to accept this brigade after it had been organized. There is no evidence that Scott or Buell had said or done any of the things that Jaquess reported to Yates as having already been decided. The governor believed what Jaquess told him and stated that he was most willing to oblige Colonel Scott by furnishing regiments for such a brigade. But the governor did not share the chaplain's opinion of who should lead this brigade and recommended that this command go to John M. Palmer, not Colonel Cavanaugh. A resident of Macoupin County, Palmer later served as governor of Illinois from 1869 to 1873.

When Yates contacted Scott about establishing the brigade, the assistant secretary of war replied that General Buell thought that forming such a brigade "could not be done at present without serious interference with other arrangements."[21] Cavanaugh still maintained that Yates had offered the position of brigade commander to him, making it is unclear whether the colonel actually believed this fantasy or merely hoped that he could persuade others to believe it. Cavanaugh wrote to Governor Yates from Cairo that General Grant had accepted the brigade as General Halleck's representative and he even speculated about what men he would appoint to his staff when he received command of this brigade. As might be expected, he planned to promote his son from adjutant of the 6th Illinois Cavalry to his father's aide de camp in the brigade.[22]

General Grant was beginning to question exactly what was going on and wrote to Captain J.C. Kelton at the Department of Missouri to clarify that he would send the troops necessary to form a brigade only if he received notice from headquarters that it would be accepted. Major General Henry W. Halleck answered Grant's letter himself and advised Grant to ignore "the wishes of politico-military officers" like Cavanaugh. He told the general not to "let any political applications about brigades and divisions trouble" him "a particle" since "all such applications & arrangements are sheer nonsense, & will not be regarded."[23]

Back at the camp at Shawneetown, Grierson and Olney heard the whole story about the machinations of Colonel Cavanaugh and Chaplain Jaquess. Major Grierson recorded in his diary that, in spite of all his politicking, Colonel Cavanaugh had "ingloriously failed to receive the appointment" and Governor Yates had given this post instead to Colonel John M. Palmer[24] from Carlinville, Illinois. Although Grierson was content with recording what Cavanaugh had been doing to promote his career, John Olney chose instead to use the colonel's absence as an excellent opportunity to organize a rebellion. Major Grierson was absent from camp on a visit to his sick mother in Jacksonville when Olney made his move. When he returned, Grierson recorded that there was now a war going on in the camp. Olney had drawn up a petition demanding that Cavanaugh resign as colonel of the 6th Cavalry and almost all of the commissioned officers in the regiment had signed the document. It is uncertain whether Grierson would have added his signature to Olney's petition if he had been in camp when other officers signed it but the lieutenant colonel had already forwarded the petition to Governor Yates before Major Grierson returned. Immediately after he reached camp, Cavanaugh and Jaquess locked Grierson in with them in the colonel's room and spent three hours telling him their version of what had taken place. In response to the petition sent to the governor, Colonel Cavanaugh ordered that a court of inquiry meet in camp on the 7th of February to discuss the problems between him and the lieutenant colonel.[25]

The U.S. Congress had established procedures for operating the volunteer army that included rules for a court of inquiry similar to a court-martial in the regular army. This law stated that "a military board or commission" should "examine the capacity, qualifications, propriety of conduct and efficiency of any commissioned officer." If possible, those sitting in judgment should include at least two individuals with a rank that was the same as that of the officer being brought before the court. A court examined Cavanaugh's behavior and acted on the differences between him and John Olney, the two highest ranking officers in the regiment. There is no indication that the court, as the law recommended, secured two officers with the rank of colonel from outside the 6th Illinois Cavalry to sit in judgment on Cavanaugh.[26]

On the day that the court convened, Cavanaugh tried to justify his management of the regiment in a long letter to Governor Yates. He said that Judge William Thomas, the Jacksonville friend of Jaquess and Yates, had advised him to resign voluntarily rather than risk being forced to resign. Cavanaugh's answer to this advice was, "*Never; so help me God.*" Cavanaugh suggested that the governor solve the whole situation by sending

Olney back to the 18th Illinois Infantry, the regiment from which he had come. The colonel promised Yates that he would send the results of the court of inquiry to the governor and to General Halleck and vowed that he would abide by the court's decision.²⁷ But when the court failed to exonerate him, a decision that he had not anticipated, Colonel Cavanaugh refused to carry out his promise.

Temporarily foiled by the colonel's refusal to accept the verdict of the court of inquiry, Olney drew up a second petition with a different approach that he hoped would persuade Cavanaugh to change his mind. This petition requested that Colonel Cavanaugh resign for "the good of the Service and of the regiment" not because of the verdict of the court. Thirty-seven commissioned officers signed this petition. As would be expected, the colonel's friend, James F. Jaquess, was not among them. Nor did Benjamin Grierson sign his name to this document, although this time he was present when Olney circulated it among the regimental officers.²⁸ Choosing not to sign this petition became a very wise move on Major Grierson's part.

Within a week of the abortive court of inquiry, Olney began to worry whether Governor Yates would make the right decision and replace Cavanaugh with him. The lieutenant colonel knew that Yates and Jaquess were friends and was afraid that the governor might decide to award Cavanaugh's position to the chaplain. Besides being the governor's friend, Jaquess had the advantage of not joining in Olney's efforts to force Cavanaugh to give up his post. In an effort to persuade Yates not to make such a serious error, Olney informed him that "at least forty of the Commissioned officers and a thousand of the men would regret exceedingly the appointment of Chaplain Jaquess as Colonel."²⁹ When a few weeks had passed and Cavanaugh still had not resigned after two petitions had told him to do so, Olney wrote to Yates again. This time Olney blamed the governor for appointing "an imbecile, malignant old man" like Thomas Cavanaugh to the position of colonel in the 6th Cavalry or any regiment and demanded that Yates undo his mistake.³⁰ It may have been this letter that persuaded the governor that Olney was not the man to assume Cavanaugh's job.

Finally, six weeks after the court of inquiry, Cavanaugh submitted an "unconditional resignation" to General Halleck. The reasons that he gave for resigning were "business matters of vital importance to myself and the future of my family" and "no immediate prospect of active service" for the regiment. He made no reference to the two petitions signed by the commissioned officers or the role of Lieutenant Colonel Olney in forcing him to resign. Although he intended to resign effective March 31, Colonel Cavanaugh had not received official notification of acceptance of his resignation by April 5, when he decided to write Halleck a second time. Meanwhile there was speculation among the men in the regiment about what was really going on. One theory was that Cavanaugh had tendered his resignation but General Halleck had refused to accept it.³¹ While the regiment awaited confirmation of Cavanaugh's resignation, there was maneuvering between Olney and Grierson, the two highest ranking officers, in an effort to become the one that Governor Yates would appoint to take Colonel Cavanaugh's place. Since he was the officer second in rank to Cavanaugh, Lieutenant Colonel Olney was sure that he was the officer that Yates would promote and give command of the regiment.

Although the 6th Cavalry had remained in Shawneetown from November 1861 to February 1862, the regiment finally moved on to Paducah and Columbus, Kentucky. Next the unit split into three parts, with 5 companies in Trenton, Tennessee; 5 companies in Memphis, Tennessee; and 2 companies in Paducah, Kentucky, and Bird's Point, Missouri.³² James F. Jaquess realized that he certainly could not perform the functions of regimental chaplain in three different locations and chose to remain in Paducah with the rest of the top officers and boarded there with his aunt. She belonged to the Methodist Episcopal Church, South, the group that had broken away from the national church in 1844. She was sympathetic to the Confederate cause and knowledgeable of their military plans. When he ate breakfast with his aunt on Friday, April 4, 1862, Jaquess continually teased her about her point of view concerning the war until "in her wrath she informed him that [Confederate] General Johnston planned to attack Grant Saturday with 50,000 men" at Pittsburg Landing, Tennessee.³³ Located on the west side of the Tennessee River, this landing received its name from an early settler called Pitts Tucker whose "trade was in hard liquor."³⁴

That morning Chaplain Jaquess left Paducah immediately by steamboat and arrived at Pittsburg Landing, Tennessee, on April 5. He told General Ulysses S. Grant that Confederate general Albert Sidney Johnston planned to attack the Union forces early the following morning. When Grant asked for the source of this information, Jaquess did not mention his aunt in Paducah but joked instead that "it was a revalation [sic] from the almighty." Grant knew that Jaquess was a friend of Colonel Cavanaugh, the officer who had caused so much dissent within the 6th Illinois Cavalry, and the chaplain's flippant answer angered him. General Grant told Chaplain Jaquess that he must forget this silliness and "report back to his regiment."³⁵

Grant's order did not daunt Jaquess, who located General Benjamin Prentiss next and told him about the attack planned for the following day. Prentiss told the chaplain "if the Rebels wanted to fight all that they have to do would be to pitch in and they would be accommodated." But unlike General Grant, General Prentiss decided to check into what Jaquess told him and sent Colonel David Moore with three companies from the 21st Missouri and Major James E. Powell with two companies from the 25th Missouri to look for Confederate troops in the vicinity. In *Shiloh: Bloody April*, Wiley Sword claims that although Moore reported that they had checked the area thoroughly, his reconnaissance was actually "a failed mission and a faked report." Believing what Moore told him, General Prentiss maintained that "everything was 'all right'" and told his "officers not to be alarmed."[36]

Earlier the same evening Chaplain Jaquess had repeated his aunt's claim to Thomas J. Bryant, a Methodist minister from the Illinois Conference, and joined a group of officers, chaplains and civilians gathered in Bryant's tent to enjoy a meal together. This time Jaquess told his listeners that his information about the Rebel attack came from "leading southern Methodists in Paducah." Although the chaplain's report had little or no effect on Grant and Prentiss, Captain Bryant stated that it "made a profound impression on the minds of the company present so that we were not surprised" when General Johnston attacked the Union forces at dawn the following morning, April 6.[37]

Although two generals ignored the chaplain's warning and his regiment was not present, Jaquess still made a name for himself at the Battle of Pittsburg Landing, often called the Battle of Shiloh because of a nearby church with this name. When Governor Yates wrote to President Lincoln in January 1864, he cited the chaplain's bravery during this bloody battle as one reason for promoting Jaquess to the rank of brigadier general of volunteers. The governor told Lincoln that Jaquess had risked his life "taking from the field, under fire, the wounded and providing Hospital accommodations and careing [sic] for the unfortunate sufferers of that trying engagement."[38] Of approximately 111,000 men who took part in this battle, more than 16,000 were injured.[39] Although each regiment had its own small field hospital, wounded soldiers needed to be moved as rapidly as possible to facilities away from the war zone. Union governors such as Yates of Illinois and Harvey of Wisconsin commandeered steamers, equipped them as floating hospitals and sent them down the Mississippi River with nurses, doctors and ministers.[40] The field and staff rolls in Jaquess' military file show that he was absent from the 6th Cavalry during both March and April of 1862 "at hospital."⁴¹ Since Jaquess himself was not ill or wounded, it is probable that he was providing spiritual care to Union soldiers in a military hospital or on a hospital boat.

There is an interesting but insufficiently documented story that one of the wounded men that Jaquess removed from the battlefield at Pittsburg Landing was George W. Johnson, Kentucky's first Confederate governor. Johnson was not the usual Civil War soldier since he was almost 50 years old and had a withered arm.⁴² When Union soldiers killed his horse on the first day of the battle at Pittsburg Landing, he "formally enlisted as a private in Company E., 4th Kentucky." Serving the Confederate cause as a foot soldier, Johnson was wounded both in his right thigh and in his abdomen and left dying on the field for almost 24 hours.⁴³ According to the story, Jaquess recognized Governor Johnson among the many wounded on the battlefield and took him to a hospital boat and stayed with him until his death.

Often soldiers lying dead on the battlefield could not be identified; those soldiers who were recognized "had rough head boards placed over them ... made from the sides of cracker boxes, barrel staves, and the like."⁴⁴ In *History of the Orphan Brigade*, Ed Porter Thompson states that George W. Johnson's "highest wish in life was to do right, and the next highest was to see his friends do right."⁴⁵ Johnson proved the truth of this statement while lying among dead and dying soldiers in a hospital. He did "do right" by identifying a dead Confederate soldier not as Captain Thomas W. Preston, who resembled General Johnston, but as General Johnston himself. This general was leader of all the Confederate forces at Shiloh and his death was a loss that the Union forces could celebrate.⁴⁶ According to the undocumented story, some Union friends, including James Jaquess, arranged for Governor George W. Johnson's body to be sent home to Scott County, Kentucky, where he was buried.

Immediately after the Battle of Pittsburg Landing, the Western Sanitary Commission commandeered several steamers in river towns and transformed them into floating hospitals. These boats carried bedding, medical supplies, doctors, nurses and chaplains down the Mississippi River to the Tennessee River and the scene of battle. The boats made return trips with wounded Union soldiers and the men and sometimes women who were caring for them. The *Black Hawk*, a steamer operated by Captain Brand between Hannibal and Quincy, made its first trip to Pittsburg Landing on April 10. The Chicago, Burlington and Quincy Railroad had offered this steamboat to Governor Yates. When the governor arrived, wounded soldiers were still lying on the battlefield among their dead comrades.⁴⁷

While Jaquess was removing wounded soldiers from the battlefield at Pittsburg Landing, Olney and Grierson occupied themselves by discussing who would be more likely to replace Cavanaugh and receive command of the 6th Illinois Cavalry. Citing foul weather as his reason for not continuing their face-to-face discussion, Olney gave his reply "with pen and ink" to a "proposition" made by Major Grierson. Although the content of Grierson's proposal is unknown, it appears that the major had called attention to Olney's previous statements that he did not want to command the regiment. Lieutenant Colonel Olney's letter now informed Grierson that he had changed his mind. Olney maintained that his only reason for having told Governor Yates that he did not want to command the regiment was Colonel Cavanaugh's claim that Olney "was actuated solely by the desire to get his place."[48]

The colonel's resignation had entirely changed this situation. Now Olney saw no "impropriety" in allowing his name to be considered. He was obviously concerned about still another petition signed by most of the regiment's officers and sent to the governor. These officers wanted Ben Grierson rather than John Olney to become their colonel. According to Olney, these officers had "signed it under a false impression and that they would not now do so." This "false impression" was that Olney still did not want to command the regiment.[49]

The rules established by Congress for volunteer military units also included the proper procedure for replacing officers. The rules stated that all the men in a company should vote to fill vacancies at the rank of captain or below but vacancies above the rank of captain should "be filled by the votes of the commissioned officers" only.[50] Lieutenant Colonel Olney objected to this rule and argued against it in a letter to General John W. Fuller. Olney maintained that the entire regiment, both officers and men, should elect their colonel because they all had "an interest, and should be allowed a voice."[51] No doubt Olney thought that he had a better chance of winning the election if every soldier could cast a ballot.

But there was no need for an election of any kind. Instead Governor Yates himself intervened to fill Cavanaugh's position by appointing a successor. Olney had written his letter to General Fuller on April 12, but Yates settled the matter before Fuller received it. On April 13, Major Grierson met with the governor on his steamboat docked near Paducah on its way to Pittsburg Landing. Yates began by offering Grierson command of an entirely different regiment, the 2nd Illinois Cavalry, but Grierson turned this position down. It is possible that Yates may have planned to award the 6th Illinois Cavalry to John Olney if Grierson accepted the governor's original proposal. But when his first solution did not work, Yates promoted Major Benjamin Grierson to the rank of colonel and gave him command of the 6th Illinois Cavalry.[52]

It is interesting to speculate why Yates bypassed Olney, the officer with the higher rank, and chose Grierson instead. The governor certainly knew Grierson, the music teacher from Jacksonville, better than he knew Olney. Also, Yates knew Cavanaugh as a Jacksonville newspaper publisher and fellow Methodist at East Charge Church and had appointed both Cavanaugh and his son to the regiment. But, most significant, Olney, the Shawneetown lawyer, was the man who had drawn up two petitions asking Cavanaugh to resign and encouraged his fellow officers to sign them. Benjamin Grierson had wisely ignored the struggle within the 6th Illinois Cavalry and avoided signing his name to either of Olney's documents.

Governor Yates had made a wise choice. President Lincoln affirmed the wisdom of this decision on June 3, 1863, when he appointed Ben Grierson to the rank of brigadier general of volunteers.[53] This promotion recognized the importance of Grierson's leadership in the famous raid of the 6th Illinois Cavalry that paved the way for Grant's successful siege of Vicksburg. When the Civil War was over, Grierson did not return to civilian life as a music teacher but became a career soldier. He won even greater fame after the Civil War as commander of the African American Buffalo, or Horse, Soldiers in the Indian Wars of the Southwest.

Although he had not received a promotion, Lieutenant Colonel John Olney remained with the 6th Illinois Cavalry until the end of the Civil War. He became seriously ill in 1862 after spending time in a Southern prison and was absent from the 6th Cavalry while recuperating at home.[54] He wrote to Governor Yates: "I think I can do more good by going into Southern Illinois and Raising a Regiment of Infantry than by anything I am likely to do as Lieut. Col. of a Cavalry Regiment."[55] When the Union army needed additional troops near the close of the war, he did return to Southern Illinois to recruit black soldiers.[56] John Olney remained with the 6th Illinois Cavalry until the end of the Civil War, was honorably discharged and resumed his law career.

Unlike Grierson, Olney and Jaquess, Colonel Cavanaugh disappeared shortly after his resignation from the 6th Cavalry. There is evidence that he tried one more time to receive a political appointment from Governor Yates. Cavanaugh asked for the position of authorized agent to the Illinois troops if the governor should decide to create such a position. If Cavanaugh had received this appointment, he would have procured supplies for the Illinois troops.[57]

Although Jaquess officially resigned from the 6th Illinois Cavalry on June 17, 1862, he was not properly mustered out. In an effort to correct this oversight, Governor Yates requested that John Loomis, the assistant adjutant general of Illinois, write to secretary of war Edwin M. Stanton and ask him to make the correction. Although Loomis made this request in March 1863, Stanton chose August 21, 1862, as the appropriate date. This was the date when members of the 73rd Illinois Infantry were mustered in with James F. Jaquess as colonel of the regiment.[58] His year as the chaplain of an Illinois regiment had not satisfied the desire of James F. Jaquess to serve his country. Virtually none of the men in the 6th Illinois Cavalry shared the Methodist point of view held by Chaplain Jaquess. His new position as colonel of a regiment of like-minded men suited James F. Jaquess far better. At last he had a chance to see some action and make a name for himself.

Chapter 5

Colonel, 73rd Illinois Infantry

When Abraham Lincoln called for 300,000 volunteers in July 1862,[1] James Jaquess persuaded Governor Yates to allow him to organize his own regiment and use his many contacts in the Methodist Episcopal Church to help him. To support Jaquess in filling his regiment, nine Methodist ministers persuaded some of their parishioners to follow them into the 73rd Illinois Volunteer Infantry. *A History of the Seventy-third Regiment of Illinois Infantry Volunteers* lists twelve clergymen who served as officers under Jaquess: Benjamin F. Northcott, William A. Presson, William E. Smith, Wilder B.M. Colt, Patterson McNutt, Thomas Motherspaw, Wilson Burroughs, George W. Montgomery, John Sutton, James I. Davidson, Peter Wallace and R.H. Laughlin. Six or seven licensed clergymen were also members of the regiment. In addition to the officers, most of the enlisted men came from prominent families in the Methodist Episcopal Church.[2] The 73rd Illinois, nicknamed the "Preachers Regiment," was mustered in at Camp Butler near Springfield on August 21, 1862.[3] As might be expected, the 73rd started out worshiping together whenever there was a chance and one of Methodist ministers was able to conduct the service. But after a few months, the regimental chaplain had to assume the entire job with occasional help from Colonel Jaquess.[4]

But having a preacher in command of a Civil War unit was, by no means, unique. The Reverend Jesse H. Moore became colonel of the 115th Illinois Infantry, a unit formed from the many Lutherans and Catholics who had originally volunteered for the 73rd. Moore and Jaquess had already crossed paths two times, at the Paris Station and then at Quincy English and German Seminary. After the Civil War, Moore was elected twice to the U.S. Congress and later was appointed U.S. consul in Peru, in 1881, where he contracted yellow fever and died in 1883.[5] Besides the 73rd and 115th Illinois, there were other Civil War regiments that had ministers as their leaders, such as the 7th Ohio and its "Fighting Parson" and the Reverend Perry and his "Saints" of the 48th New York. But the 73rd was the only regiment that was "A 'Real' Preachers Regiment."[6]

A few students from Quincy College and two members of the colonel's family also followed him into his regiment. Thirteen-year-old Willie Jaquess, the son born to James and Sarah Jane in Jacksonville, joined the 73rd as drummer boy of Company H. Isaac Newton Jaquess, the colonel's "half cousin" from Mount Carmel, was also mustered in as the new chaplain of the 73rd on February 24, 1864, to replace the Reverend John S. Barger from Jacksonville, who had been reassigned.[7]

A few months after its organization, the Preachers Regiment earned a second nickname. The men of the 73rd had such a fondness for ripe persimmons that they searched for a tree with fruit suitable to eat at the end of every day's hard march. According to the regimental history, Captain Bernard Laiboldt, commander of the brigade that included the 73rd, claimed that if there was "a persimmon-tree in the public square of Richmond," the 73rd would certainly "capture that city." The Preachers Regiment was now also the Persimmon Regiment.[8]

The battle of Perryville, Kentucky, fought on October 8, 1862, was the first Civil War battle for the men of the 73rd Illinois Volunteer Infantry. Sergeant-Major Henry A. Castle, described as a 6-foot 5-inch twenty-one-year-old student,[9] missed the regiment's "baptism of fire" because he had been hospitalized earlier with burnings and aches that announced the beginning of typhoid fever.[10] His situation was all too common among Civil War soldiers, as disease and infection became major killers of men in both the Union and Confederate armies. Castle, one of the recruits from Quincy College, became the colonel's son-in-law in April of 1865.

From the commander-in-chief to the men in the ranks, nearly everyone questioned the ability of West Point graduate General Don Carlos Buell to lead the Union army. Lincoln wanted to remove Buell from command before the battle took place at Perryville, but General George Thomas persuaded him not to act.[11] Buell had already lost the support of between twenty and thirty of his officers, who held a secret meeting in a house near Lebanon, Kentucky, on the night before the Confederate attack on Perryville. These officers prepared, but did not send, a dispatch to Lincoln asking the president to relieve Buell of his command because they had lost confidence in him.[12] The enlisted men also disliked Buell because the general showed little or no concern for them and, according to James Lee McDonough in *War in Kentucky from Shiloh to Perryville*, Buell expected his soldiers to exist on "half rations, hard marching, and tough work."[13]

In *Perryville: This Grand Havoc of Battle*, Kenneth W. Noe recounts the story of why General Buell missed the early hours of the battle at Perryville. On the day before the Confederate attack at Perryville, the general discovered men from the 75th Illinois "cleaning out a garden" and ordered them to stop pillaging and return to their unit. Then he "bore down on one particular back-talker" who grabbed the bridle of the general's horse to protect himself and jerked it very hard. The horse "reared and fell over backward with Buell still aboard." Although this fall did not injure him seriously, the general was not able to sit up or ride his horse.[14] These injuries confined the general to his tent on October 8, when the Battle of Perryville began. A strong wind blew the sounds of the conflict between the two armies away from Buell's tent.[15] He remained at his headquarters and did not realize that a battle was taking place until the middle of the afternoon.[16]

General Braxton Bragg's forces numbered about 20,000, while Buell's army had more than twice as many men.[17] But in spite of its greater numbers, the Union army was not victorious. While General Buell's soldiers enjoyed a delicious banquet that evening, the Confederate army slipped away from their encampment during the night and headed to Tennessee.[18] A few historians have referred to Perryville as a "strategic victory" for the Union forces because Bragg's army left Kentucky after that battle and never returned to this state again.

The regimental history describes Perryville as a battle full of misdirection and misunderstanding for the inexperienced Preachers Regiment. Initially, the 73rd "advanced in line of battle — and unsupported — across an open field, and for a very brief time held a position near a rebel battery preparing to open fire." The soldiers quickly realized the seriousness of their situation and withdrew "not a moment too soon." They never received any explanation for the "grievous blunder" that had placed them in this "exposed position." The Preachers Regiment then moved safely into its proper position in the front line to the right of the 44th Illinois with the 2nd Missouri and the 15th Missouri stationed immediately behind them to provide support.[19]

At this point in the fighting Colonel Jaquess received a message that he interpreted as an order to change his regiment's position and he commanded his men to retreat from their present location through the ranks of the units stationed behind them. The hardened veterans of the 2nd Missouri believed that the men of the 73rd had fallen back because of cowardice and "derisively cried out, 'Shame!'" Ordered to replace the retreating 73rd in their former position on the front line, the 2nd Missouri marched forward causing the two units to become "all mixed up." However, the two units soon started to fight together and gave the Rebels "'a double dose' of fire."[20] Victor Hicken, in *Illinois in the Civil War*, claims that the Battle of Perryville "did serve one purpose, however. It taught all of the new troops, including those of the 73rd Illinois (the 'Preachers Regiment'), that war had a startling definition all its own — it meant killing."[21]

Edna J. Shank Hunter's description of the first battle of the 125th Illinois in *One Flag, One Country, and Thirteen Greenbacks a Month* describes the "baptism of fire" of the Preachers Regiment equally well: "Perryville was a quick and brutal initiation of new Illinois regiments to warfare." It was "a stubborn and brutal fight" and "at the end of it, the ground was covered with the bodies of the slain."[22] The 73rd Illinois lost both enlisted men and officers as the result of the regiment's first engagement. One man was killed in battle and ten others, including Major William A. Presson, were wounded; six of these casualties died later of their wounds.[23]

The Battle of Perryville, sometimes referred to as the messiest encounter of the Civil War, ended inconclusively and unsatisfactorily from the viewpoint of the Union command. Although Buell obeyed the order to go after Bragg's army, his pursuit was half-hearted at best. Ignoring Secretary Stanton's orders, Buell gave up pursuing Bragg and directed the Union forces toward Nashville. While he was in Louisville collecting supplies for the Union army's march to Nashville, the general learned from a newspaper article that he had been "sacked" and would have to face a court-martial.[24] General William S. Rosecrans relieved Don Carlos Buell of his command. A military court of inquiry, known as the Buell Commission, met in Cincinnati for several months but failed to exonerate Buell. The major charge against him was that after the battle he had not pursued the army of General Braxton Bragg with sufficient vigor. Buell never returned to his command and left the service in May 1864.[25]

Because Jaquess had mistakenly ordered the men of the 73rd to retreat, the colonel and several other officers from his regiment had to face a court of inquiry concerning their leadership at Perryville. During the first year of the war the U.S. Congress had passed statutes establishing rules for examination of officers in the volunteer army before a military board. This board was similar to the Buell Commission that ruled on the general's actions at Perryville. The military board consisted of three to five officers from a regiment other than the regiment of the officers being judged. These judges had to hold the same rank or a higher rank than the officers appearing before them. The court that ruled against the colonel of the 6th Illinois Cavalry, Thomas H. Cavanaugh, had not followed these statutes. Although the Battle of Perryville took place early in October, officers of the 73rd did not appear before the military board at Nashville until December. Those officers found guilty of incompetence had the option of resigning from the volunteer army.[26]

If records of this military board survived, these documents have not yet appeared, but it is clear that the court's judgment was unfavorable. Rumors circulated among the enlisted men about what had happened during this examination of their officers. The regimental history states jokingly that "the crop of resignations [that followed] may have been slightly augmented by it."[27] About one-third of the 32 commissioned officers in the regiment resigned either in fearful anticipation of the hearing or as an honorable option after the military board passed judgment. Ten officers resigned between December 1, 1862, and January 16, 1863, and an eleventh officer received an honorable discharge on December 31, 1862.[28]

Unlike other officers of the 73rd Illinois, James Jaquess decided to fight rather than run and asked his friend Governor Richard Yates to request President Lincoln to intervene on his behalf. As a former Jacksonville neighbor of the governor, Jaquess realized that he would accomplish more if he talked to Yates face to face instead of writing to him. Colonel Jaquess sent personal letters from the camp on Mill Creek to two of his superiors expressing two different arguments for why he should be granted a leave of absence. One letter asked for twelve days of leave so that Jaquess could take care of his own personal business. This letter claimed that his attorney had informed Jaquess that his "personal presence and attention" were required in important business involving some $30,000.[29] His second letter focused instead on the colonel's desire to fulfill the needs of the men in his regiment. He spoke of 112 "enlisted men, left sick on line of march," who wanted to return to duty and also the regiment's need for certain items that his officers thought required his "immediate and personal attention."[30] One or possibly both of the colonel's arguments did the job, although the reasons given are spurious.

His superior officers granted Jaquess a leave of absence from his regiment, but the colonel did not devote his furlough to taking care of personal money matters or giving his attention to regimental needs. Instead he traveled to Springfield to share his problem with his friend Governor Yates. After listening to what Jaquess had to say, Governor Yates wrote two letters in the colonel's behalf on Christmas Eve. These letters, one to the secretary of war, Edwin M. Stanton, and the other to President Abraham Lincoln, say virtually the same thing. Yates emphasized by underlining that he was "satisfied beyond the possibility of a doubt that there is injustice." The governor emphasized that Colonel Jaquess was "a most capital officer" and he did not "want Col. Jaques[s] to resign or to leave the service" because he believed that there was "no better Colonel in the service."[31]

When Jaquess got back to his regiment in Nashville, he wrote a letter to Lyman Trumbull, U.S. senator from Illinois, probably following through on a suggestion from Yates. The colonel claimed that "at the instance of one who it is said owed us a grudge," the officers of the 73rd "were ordered before a board of examination" that "has reported unfavorable." Jaquess told Trumbull that although he had the option of resigning, he did not wish to follow this course because he believed that, given time, the 73rd would "equal the best." The colonel requested Trumbull to see President Lincoln in person and make certain that he and his officers did not have to resign.[32]

Trumbull may have seen Lincoln in person as Jaquess requested, but it was the letter from Yates that persuaded the president to take action. An endorsement on the governor's letter, written in Lincoln's hand, reads, "Secretary of War please watch for the report alluded to within, and when it arrives, take no action on it till you confer with me. A. Lincoln." Lincoln's message is dated January 2, 1863. Thanks to Yates and especially to Lincoln, Jaquess did not have to resign from the service but continued to serve as colonel of the 73rd Illinois Infantry until the end of the Civil War.[33]

After returning from his trip to Springfield, Jaquess remained with his regiment in Nashville while he waited to hear whether the governor of Illinois had convinced President Lincoln to intervene in his behalf. Because of the unfavorable decision of the military board, Jaquess could not lead the 73rd Illinois when the regiment fought its second Civil War battle, Stones River, from December 31, 1862, to January 2, 1863. Major William A. Presson, one of the regiment's Methodist ministers, commanded the regiment from December 26 to January 5 in the colonel's place.[34] Presson had served as drillmaster of the 73rd from the regiment's earliest days at Camp Butler. Although he had been wounded at Perryville, he was back in camp by December 10 and drilled the entire battalion two days later. According to the regimental history, the 73rd "seemed to awaken and take on a new life under the skillful handling which the major was able to give it."[35]

The 73rd Illinois was part of the Second Brigade of the Third Division of the Union army under the command of Brigadier General Philip H. Sheridan. As James A. McDonough recounts in *Stone's River— Bloody Winter in Tennessee*, Sheridan "personally visited each of his twelve regiments and saw that his orders were executed." He came "on foot and unattended" and ordered each commanding officer "to arouse his men quietly, have them breakfast and form in the line of battle at once."[36] Brigadier generals Jefferson C. Davis and Richard W. Johnson did not follow Sheridan's example and failed to warn the regiments in their divisions about what was about to take place.[37]

At the outset of the battle Colonel Frederick Schaefer, commander of the Second Brigade, which included both the 73rd and the 2nd Missouri, ordered Captain Brazell from the 2nd Missouri to take command of the right wing of the 73rd. As recounted in the regimental history, Major Presson spoke "a few apt and well-chosen words" to the 73rd telling them "to keep cool, take deliberate aim, and fire low, and adopt the motto, 'Murfreesboro or die.'"[38] During the fight that followed, Colonel Schaefer was killed by a "ball passing in at the lower part of the right ear and coming out at the left ear."[39] Lieutenant-Colonel Laibold of the 2nd Missouri then took over as brigade commander for the remainder of the conflict.

No Better Place to Die, the title of Peter Cozzens' book about the battle at Stones River,[40] accurately describes how the men of the 73rd Illinois remembered this bloody battle. Major Presson, who had recovered from his wound at Perryville, "was struck by a ball or piece of shell and knocked from his horse."[41] Henry A. Castle, whose "left hand was shattered by a rebel minnie ball," was eventually discharged for medical reasons the following April.

Henry A. Castle, sergeant-major of 73rd Regiment of Illinois Infantry from December 26, 1862, to April 17, 1863. James F. Jaquess officiated at the wedding of his daughter, Margaret, to Henry A. Castle on April 18, 1865, in Quincy (W.H. Newlin, David F. Lawler, John W. Sherrick. *A History of the Seventy-Third Regiment of Illinois Infantry Volunteers*, 1890).

Later he recruited men for another regiment, the 137th Illinois Volunteer Infantry, and served as their captain.[42] Sergeant William Newlin describes how the battlefield looked to those members of the 73rd who survived: "Many of our brave boys fell. Nine of them were lying cold in death near us, awaiting the simple, unceremonious burial accorded a soldier on the field of battle. Some of them looked as though they had just fallen asleep.... Others appeared as if their last moments had been spent in pain."[43] Twelve members of the 73rd were killed in action, including one officer, Captain Edwin Alsop, and 5 others died later of their wounds.[44] The losses for the Union army were 100 officers and 1620 enlisted men killed and a total of 7714 wounded.[45] An even bloodier battle was to come later that year at Chickamauga.

When Colonel Jaquess was absent with leave during parts of April and from early June until September 14 of 1863,[46] William A. Presson, who had become lieutenant colonel in January, commanded the 73rd. He had drilled the men during their early days at Camp Butler and the regiment considered itself fortunate to have Presson, who, as described in the regimental history, excelled in "matters of drill and strictly military maneuvers and movements."[47] Then, on August 10, General Sheridan gave Presson the choice of resigning from the army or facing the possibility of a court-martial. The lieutenant colonel, one of the Methodist ministers, chose the option of submitting his resignation and departed without any indication of what had caused Sheridan to provide this choice. Still another Methodist minister, Major James I. Davidson, was promoted to lieutenant colonel and served as commander the 73rd until Colonel Jaquess took charge of the regiment three days before the Battle of Chickamauga.[48]

When James Jaquess spoke to the men of the 73rd at their annual reunion in 1890, he reminded them: "Comrades, we were never so near heaven as we were on that terrible occasion, and will not be again, till caught up to meet the Lord in the air."[49] The colonel's account of what happened to the 73rd at Chickamauga is a fair description of what all the Union forces suffered in this bloody battle. After the encounter at Perryville, General Bragg had marched the Confederate forces to Chattanooga, where they remained virtually invulnerable. General William Rosecrans, now the leader of the Union troops, needed a plan to entice the Rebels to come out to fight. He decided to divide his troops and send them marching in different directions so that Bragg would decide to leave his stronghold in order to pursue them. The strategy of General Rosecrans succeeded and Bragg's army evacuated Chattanooga and made a stand at Chickamauga Creek.[50]

Following orders from Rosecrans, Colonel Bernard Laiboldt's brigade, which included the 73rd Illinois, crossed the Tennessee River on September 2 and marched a long distance from the rest of Union forces before receiving orders to return. It took Laiboldt's brigade until Saturday, September 19, to retrace their steps and join the rest of their comrades. Near daybreak the following day, Laiboldt's Brigade, with the rest of Major Philip H. Sheridan's Third Division, took a position on a hill near the road to Chattanooga. They were then ordered to move to the center of the action in order to provide support for the Union army's First Division under the command of Brigadier General Jefferson Columbus Davis. However, by the time Laiboldt's men reached this new position, the Confederates had routed the First Division.[51]

The most significant combat for the Preachers Regiment took place on the final day at Chickamauga. Colonel Laiboldt reported to his superiors that after being "thrown in confusion by the fleeing troops and finally exposed to the scathing fire of the enemy in front," his "troops gave way." He explained that he rallied "them once more" but because they were unable "to hold a position," he let his troops, including the 73rd, retreat to the mountains, where, after about three-quarters of an hour, he managed to round up all of the rest of his men.[52] Blame fell on General Rosecrans for the order that led to this confusion and the loss of the battle to the Confederate army. When Ulysses S. Grant took command of all the armies in the West, he replaced Rosecrans with General George H. Thomas.

The men of the 73rd Illinois had decidedly more graphic recollections of Chickamauga than those mentioned in Laiboldt's account. Private Chauncey H. Castle from Company I, the younger brother of Henry A. Castle, recalled in a talk at an annual reunion of the 73rd: "I saw my friends falling dead or wounded all about and near me.... I could not observe what was going on at any distance, as I was twice knocked down, being shot first in the right and next in the left leg."[53] The regimental history recalls with pride that at Chickamauga "amid all the hurry, excitement, and confusion, our regimental colors were not suffered to trail in the dust." Although the color-bearer was shot down, Captain Thomas H. Kyger of Company C rescued the flag before it could touch the ground and removed it safely from the battlefield.[54]

From the distance of more than forty years, at a reunion of the 73rd, Comrade Jack recalled that "the field of Chickamauga where amid the awful roar of musketry and the thunder of the artillery the terrible battle of September 19th and 20th thinned our ranks down to almost one-half of our number."[55] Although a great many men and horses died at Chickamauga, Comrade Jack's statement is certainly exaggerated. Twelve soldiers were killed outright and 11 more died of their wounds. Also, for the first time, members of the 73rd were taken prisoners; only one soldier had been captured earlier in the war.[56] These losses later motivated Colonel Jaquess to ask Governor Yates to permit him to recruit replacements for his regiment. It is not clear whether Jaquess received this permission, but at least 15 new recruits were added during the next few months.[57]

Although Willie Jaquess, like his father, was absent from the 73rd for long periods of time, he was definitely with the regiment at the battle of Chickamauga.[58] Willie's account of this battle, printed in a publication of the Southwestern Indiana Historical Society, is the most memorable among the recollections of survivors of the 73rd. This thirteen-year-old boy returned to the Union lines in an army ambulance that passed "through the battlefield where the fighting was heaviest, and though about ten days since the battle, the ground for nearly two miles ... was literally covered with dead men and horses." The ambulance would go a short distance and then stop for a few minutes, so that the whole trip took nearly two hours. He recalled that the smell was terrible "but we had to stand it; there was no help for it."[59] Writing about his youthful experiences as an elderly man, Willie explained: "It would be hard for any one, not an actual witness of the scenes of such a battle as Chickamauga, to realize conditions. But, in places, it seemed that I could have walked upon dead bodies without touching the ground."[60]

Writing of an event that happened more than 65 years before, William G. Jaquess clearly recalled his boyhood experience of being taken prisoner at Chickamauga. Before the worst of the fighting began, Colonel Jaquess had ordered Willie and several other members of the band to take their instruments and go back to Craw Fish Spring at the rear of the army, the location of the Union hospital. Confederate soldiers had already captured the hospital before Willie and the others arrived and the Rebels made them prisoners. Willie worked in the hospital, where he made friends with surgeon Major Hurlburt, the Confederate doctor who was now in charge. Willie shared with him how anxious he was to return to his regiment. When the doctor heard about a plan for prisoner exchange, he told Willie about an agreement between General Bragg and General Rosecrans to exchange "a sound confederate for a wounded federal."[61]

With Hurlburt's help, Willie hid in one of the ambulances that was returning wounded Federal soldiers and made it safely across the Union lines. As soon as they saw the ambulances, Union soldiers lined up on both sides of the road and inquired about men missing from their units. When someone asked about survivors of the 42nd Indiana, Willie realized that they must be in that regiment's camp. The commander of the 42nd Indiana, Lieutenant Colonel William McIntyre, was Willie's uncle. McIntyre had married Rachel Jaquess, the younger sister of Colonel Jaquess, who had lived with the family while she attended Illinois Conference Female College. Since he doubted that he could find his own regiment in the dark, Willie jumped out of the ambulance and located his uncle's tent. Willie and his uncle found Colonel Jaquess the following day. A soldier had reported to the colonel that he recognized Willie lying dead and Willie's father feared that this report was true. When Willie reappeared after a ten days' absence, James Jaquess was thrilled to see his only son unharmed.[62]

Author James Gilmore (pen name Edmund Kirke) published a juvenile romance about this incident titled "The Boy of Chickamauga," in the November 1865 issue of *Our Young Folks*, an illustrated magazine for boys and girls. The plot and characters in Gilmore's story closely resemble the events and people in William Jaquess' personal account of his experience published in 1929. Gilmore calls the boy in his story Willie; identifies his father, the Colonel, as a clergyman; and includes a character called Captain Pratt, the name of a member of Company B of the 73rd. The author also mentions Colonel McIntyre but incorrectly identifies him as Willie's "mother's own brother." There is little doubt that those parents who read "The Boy of Chickamauga" to their children in 1865 recognized the identity of the father from a widely publicized trip of James F. Jaquess and the story's author to Richmond the previous year.[63]

The colonel's participation in the Battle of Chickamauga remained significant to him until the end of his life. The Rebels shot two horses from under Colonel Jaquess during this battle. The regimental history, "The Boy of Chickamauga" and "Narrative of Chickamauga and Chattanooga," written by the colonel's son, all mention this event. Several years later, Jaquess filed a claim with the federal government for reimbursement of his expense in replacing these horses. Finally, in the last years of his life, the colonel cited injuries that he received at Chickamauga when the horses fell from beneath him to support his application for an "Invalid Pension."[64]

Jaquess was almost the only officer in the Third Division left with his regiment when the Battle of Chickamauga ended. Commanders of seventeen other regiments had been killed or wounded. Major-General Sheridan cited Colonel James F. Jaquess and several other officers for their leadership at this battle. Sheridan described the colonel as "especially distinguished for skill and great personal courage" during the battle.[65] The Battle of Chickamauga proved that Colonel Jaquess had become the "capital officer" that Governor Yates had promised Lincoln in his letter to the president on Christmas Day 1862.

Although Colonel Jaquess was absent from the 73rd on "detached service" beginning October 17, 1863,[66] he returned in time to lead his regiment at the Battle of Missionary Ridge, sometimes called the Third Battle of Chattanooga. As he did other times during the war, the colonel had served as a member of a military court similar to the one that had examined him and his officers after the Battle of Perrysville. The severe Union losses at Chickamauga had led to the consolidation of the 73rd and other regiments from the First and Second brigades into a new First Brigade of nine regiments under Colonel Francis T. Sherman. This brigade was part of General Philip H. Sheridan's Division.[67]

The Union forces had achieved their stated objective of capturing Confederate rifle pits on the slope of Missionary Ridge by four o'clock on November 25. In "The Preachers Regiment at Chickamauga and Missionary Ridge," Lester L. Swift explains: "What happened next was not scheduled. It might have been called out and out disobedience of their orders." The Preachers Regiment and several other units decided not to stop partway up the hill, and, ignoring official orders as well as "a withering hail of grape shot, canister and minnie balls raining down on them," they continued to march upward.[68] Because they did not act on orders from above them, their independent decision could have been court-martial material.

Steven E. Woodworth in *Six Armies in Tennessee: The Chickamauga and Chattanooga Campaigns*, describes what actually took place: "The fiery Sheridan urged them on vigorously. Recognizing the Seventy-third Illinois, longtime members of his division, he called out, 'I know you, fix bayonets and go ahead.'"[69] As explained in the regimental history, the Union "forces outnumbered those of the enemy; but for defensive purposes, the position held by Bragg's army on Missionary Ridge was vastly superior to that held by Rosecrans's army at Chickamauga."[70] The Union regiments expected a pitched battle when they reached the top of the ridge, but by the time they arrived, the Rebels were already scurrying down the other side of the mountain. Thanks to a few regiments ignoring orders, Missionary Ridge now belonged to the Union army.

At the reunion of the 73rd in 1890, Colonel Jaquess looked back lightheartedly on the 73rd's march up Missionary Ridge. He joked about the regiment's response to their orders to halt on the way up the ridge: "Our

Planting the U.S. flag on Missionary Ridge (W.H. Newlin, David F. Lawler, John W. Sherrick. *A History of the Seventy-Third Regiment of Illinois Infantry Volunteers*, 1890).

orders were to halt — but, for what purpose, or for what length of time ... was not named ... we did halt — came to a dead halt — a perfect standstill of a halt ... which lasted, as near as I could guess, all of five seconds — when the march up the ascent of the Ridge was resumed."[71] Then he added a bit more seriously, "Had our forward movement at Missionary Ridge resulted in disaster to ourselves, and others, who followed our lead, someone had been court-martialed and cashiered."[72]

The previous year Jaquess had written a letter to the 73rd about another event that happened during the battle at Missionary Ridge. This reminiscence, printed in the regimental history, mentions that a soldier from the Preachers Regiment captured a gray horse for the colonel during this battle. Jaquess had told his men, "I want you to capture, besides many prisoners, one horse — a good one — for me. They — the rebs — got both of my fine horses at Chickamauga, as you know, and I want one now in return, and another later on." In answer to the colonel's challenge, "William Carmine, rushed out a few steps in advance of the line and caught a beautiful gray horse by the bridal; several of the boys aimed their guns at the rider, and resistance on his part would have been useless." A few minutes later Jaquess presented this horse to General Sheridan, who knew that it "was captured by one of the 73d boys." According to Jaquess, the "powerful gray pacing horse, called Breckinridge" that the general often rode was the same animal that the colonel had presented to him.[73]

There are several other accounts of the Preachers Regiment at Missionary Ridge. Willie Jaquess, along with other band members, observed what took place from a distance. In "Narrative of Chickamauga and Chattanooga," he explains that "It would be hard for any one who did not witness the battle of Missionary Ridge to appreciate its grandeur.... For one to be able to see practically all the men engaged on both sides was a sight never to be forgotten, nor ever paralleled."[74] The regimental history questions whether the 73rd arrived first at the top of the ridge because it was "next to impossible for any regiment to fully and satisfactorily establish a claim to having planted its flag on top of Missionary Ridge *before* any other regiment." But the flag of the Preachers Regiment was certainly "among the first flags."[75] James Jaquess' official report of the 73rd's casualties at Missionary Ridge provides inflated figures about the casualties in his regiment: "3 privates killed. 1 officer — Lieutenant-Colonel Davidson — wounded, 23 privates wounded, some 2 or 3 of them mortally." The colonel also maintains that the 73rd Illinois "captured more prisoners in number than there were men in the regiment."[76] In contrast, the official report included in the regimental history provides much smaller numbers: "3 killed and 3 wounded of which one died of his wounds."[77] This battle was memorable not only because few comrades died or received wounds but also because the 73rd could celebrate a memorable victory after the disaster at Chickamauga. Missionary Ridge was also memorable because it was the last battle of the Preachers Regiment with Colonel Jaquess as their leader. The regimental history states that Colonel Jaquess left his regiment on June 5, 1864, and did not return to camp until April 27 the following year.⁷⁸ He was absent from the 73rd on a different kind of government business, as an agent of President Lincoln.

Beginning with the battle at Resaca, Georgia, on May 14 and 15, 1864, another officer commanded in Jaquess' place. Major Thomas W. Motherspaw, also a Methodist preacher, led the regiment not only at Resaca but also at Adairsville (May 17), Kennesaw Mountain (June 27), and Peach Tree Creek (July 20). Major Motherspaw also mentioned the regiment's engagements "before Atlanta from July 22 to August 26, and at Jonesborough, Ga., on September 1" in his report to Colonel Emerson Opdycke, commander of the First Brigade, which included the 73rd Illinois.⁷⁹ Motherspaw continued to lead the 73rd into combat until Captain Wilson Burroughs, still another Methodist minister, took over from him on December 3. Motherspaw had been wounded during a night battle at Franklin, Tennessee, on November 30 and died from those injuries on December 18, 1864.⁸⁰

Four officers and 48 enlisted men of the 73rd Illinois were killed in combat during the course of the Civil War. There were also 112 soldiers wounded in combat, of which 45 died of their wounds. Additionally, 16 men died in prison, and another 102 died as the result of disease. The 73rd lost a total of 215 individuals to death for one reason or another.⁸¹ According to the regimental history, when Jaquess and his son finally returned to their regiment near the end of April 1865, the colonel told the assembled men of the 73rd that "he expected to remain ... until we were mustered out of service." He added that he "had no doubt but that our faces would soon be turned homeward."⁸² The entire regiment was officially mustered out of the Union army on June 12, 1865.⁸³

Shortly after the Battle of Missionary Ridge, both William Thomas, the prominent Jacksonville attorney who served as a trustee of Illinois Conference Female College, and Illinois governor Richard Yates wrote laudatory letters about James Jaquess to President Lincoln. Writing on the day after this battle, Judge Thomas called attention to the colonel's outstanding personal qualities: "Talented, Educated, Brave, Honest, and Reliable." He also reminded the president that Jaquess was Lincoln's "friend personally and politically."⁸⁴ The governor sent a one-sentence note to Lincoln on December 10, 1863: "No man in the army is more worthy of promotion than Col Jaques[s]."⁸⁵ He then wrote a longer letter two months later citing Jaquess' bravery as a chaplain at Pittsburg Landing as well as his gallant leadership of the 73rd at Perryville, Chickamauga and Missionary Ridge.⁸⁶

The purpose of these letters was to obtain a promotion for the colonel to the rank of brigadier general in the volunteer army. But in spite of the pleas of two highly influential men from Illinois, Lincoln did not promote Jaquess. The president did not need Jaquess to become commander of a brigade. Lincoln was considering entirely different plans for the colonel that would not involve leading men on the battlefield but would still require the all the personal qualities that Judge Thomas so highly praised. Jaquess was going to be become a private agent for President Lincoln.

Chapter 6

Private Agent for President Lincoln

Colonel Jaquess was absent from the 73rd Illinois for long periods of time in 1863 and then was away for nearly 11 consecutive months from June 5, 1864, to April 27, 1865. When Jaquess was gone, other officers took his place and led the regiment into all the battles after the engagement at Missionary Ridge. The regimental history recounts these instances but provides no explanation of why Jaquess was absent or what he was doing when he was away. Although the colonel's military file also shows periods of time when he was gone from the 73rd, it provides few clues about his activities during these absences. It became evident several years after the Civil War ended that Colonel Jaquess was absent from his regiment because he was carrying out missions for President Lincoln and many of his assignments were intentionally kept secret. Like some presidents before him, Lincoln enlisted private individuals to handle unofficial negotiations and to discover and report enemy plans. Lincoln sent his personal agents to the Confederate states, Canada and Europe on secret missions. He paid these agents from a private fund and they reported directly to him.

Although Lincoln's agents were often successful, sometimes their secret missions failed to remain that way. Shortly after the South seceded, Lincoln asked George Ashmun, a friend from their days in the U.S. House of Representatives, to undertake a mission to Canada at the salary of $10 a day and expenses. His assignment was to persuade the Canadian government to take the "right" position with regard to the South. Someone leaked Ashmun's mission a few days after his appointment and the United States government had to recall him officially.[1]

In contrast to Ashmun, Thurlow Weed, known as the "Wizard of the

Lobby," succeeded in the task that Lincoln assigned to him. He was a great political organizer whose mission was to secure pledges of $1000 each from 15 corporations and individuals. Lincoln wanted this money to finance efforts to defeat Peace Democrats in the Connecticut and New Hampshire elections. Weed was successful in raising the money, but it remains unclear just how the Republican Party spent it.[2]

Another personal agent, William Lloyd, came closer to fulfilling the modern idea of a spy. He crossed into Rebel territory and remained there throughout the Civil War. The president promised him a salary to report what he learned about the location of Confederate fortifications and forts and the ability of the Confederate army to wage war. After Lincoln's assassination, the federal government reimbursed Lloyd for his expenses but refused to pay his salary.[3] The Supreme Court finally ruled in 1875 that the oral contract between Lincoln and the now deceased spy Lloyd was not enforceable "because it might do harm to make public the details of the enterprise and embarrass the government."[4]

The Allen Pinkerton National Detective Agency also employed private individuals who worked as federal spies. They reported to Pinkerton, who then passed their information on to General George B. McClellan, commander of the Army of the Potomac. One of these spies, Timothy Webster, was working as a double agent in the South. Pryce Lewis, who had just completed a dangerous undercover mission in the South in 1861, and John Scully, an inexperienced young man, joined Webster and all three were arrested in Richmond in February 1862. Webster was executed as a double agent and the other two men spent nineteen months in prison until they were exchanged for Confederate prisoners. After the treatment of Pinkerton's men, private individuals no longer crossed into the South but worked instead in counterintelligence. President Lincoln, who wanted agents to report directly to him rather than to Pinkerton, chose Union soldiers such as Colonel Jaquess as federal spies. Probably in 1863 and certainly in 1864, Abraham Lincoln invited James F. Jaquess, the friend of Yates and Harlan, to join his cadre of private agents.[5]

Traveling alone, James Jaquess crossed enemy lines into the Confederacy for the first time in the summer of 1863. It remains uncertain whether Jaquess served as a private agent for Lincoln and the federal government on this mission or made this trip only for reasons of his own. The colonel had become convinced by the spring of 1863 that clergy in the Methodist Episcopal Church, South (MECS) were growing weary of fighting their brothers in the North. As a Methodist clergyman with the gift of persuasion, Jaquess believed that he could convince his fellow preachers in the MECS to pressure Confederate leaders to end the conflict.

Congregations of the Methodist Episcopal Church (MEC) located in Southern states had seceded from the national body at a contentious session in New York in 1844. The congregations from the South then met in Louisville in 1845, where they adopted their own constitution. One year later the new denomination held its first general conference in Petersburg, Virginia. The basic difference between the two denominations was each one's position on slavery.[6] As Robert Bray points out in *Peter Cartwright, Legendary Frontier Preacher*, the Methodist split was "an eerie foreshadowing in miniature of what the United States would face in 1860–61."[7]

The MEC, like the federal government, decided to ignore the presence of slavery in the border states of Kentucky, Missouri, Delaware and Maryland, which had not seceded from the Union. Then the "radicals" within the MEC drafted a proposal in 1860 to alter the denomination's *Discipline* to state that all members of this denomination could not buy, sell or hold individuals in order to make them slaves. The general conference barely defeated this proposal. If it had passed, the new *Discipline* would have forced MEC members in the border states to either free their slaves without any remuneration or face excommunication.[8] Colonel Jaquess believed that clergy of the MECS "most ardently desire[d] peace, and the privilege of returning to their allegiance to church and state" and that he had the ability to negotiate terms of peace that would be acceptable on both sides of the Mason-Dixon Line.[9]

In May 1863, Colonel Jaquess wrote to James A. Garfield, chief of staff for General Rosecrans, presenting these ideas and requesting permission to make a trip to the Confederacy.[10] Rosecrans first sent a telegram and then a letter to President Lincoln recommending that Lincoln allow Jaquess to carry out his plan. Rosecrans referred to Jaquess as "a man of high character & great influence in the Methodist Church." Although he thought that Jaquess would not be able to accomplish what he expected, the general still believed that the colonel's mission would generate "a moral force" that would "compensate us for his temporary absence from his Regiment." General Rosecrans enclosed the colonel's request in his letter to Lincoln and suggested that the president let him send Jaquess to Washington to explain his proposal in person.[11]

Lincoln replied that "for certain reasons it is thought best for Rev. Dr. Jaques[s] not to come here" and suggested that the colonel write a letter to him instead.[12] Jaquess did as Lincoln had requested[13] and asked James R. Gilmore to deliver his letter to the president on a trip that he was making to Washington City. A popular freelance author who wrote under the pen name of Edmund Kirke, Gilmore had visited the Union camp to talk with General Rosecrans about whether he was planning to run as the Democratic candidate for president the following year. Gilmore became the colonel's partner on a second trip to the Confederacy in the summer of 1864 and would later describe their adventures in several magazine articles and books.

When Gilmore reached the Willard Hotel in the capital, he sent a letter of his own to Lincoln and enclosed the one from Jaquess. He wrote that he needed "to lay another matter of *great importance* before the President in a *private* interview" and asked that the president "oblige him by naming some hour *today*."[14] Gilmore had published *Among the Pines, or South in Secession-Time* the previous year and was considered something of an expert on the South. He was bringing information that he had learned on a recent trip to the Confederate states. Unlike Jaquess, Gilmore had no trouble getting Lincoln to grant exactly what he had requested. His information of "great importance" was a plan to persuade the slaves to make a unified rebellion throughout the Confederacy during the night of August 1. The Confederates captured a letter outlining this plan and the proposed insurrection never took place.[15]

Nine days passed before President Lincoln replied to General Rosecrans concerning the colonel's request to make a trip to the Confederacy. The president claimed that he had "but a slight personal acquaintance with Col. Jaquess" although he knew "him very well by character." Lincoln pointed out that Jaquess could not go to the Confederacy with "any government authority whatsoever" and might risk being "condemned, and executed as a spy" if he were taken prisoner. The president suggested that Rosecrans give the colonel a furlough and decide on "any length of time" that suited him.[16] Jaquess submitted a formal request for his furlough on June 4,[17] but did not cross into enemy territory until July 13.[18] Although he reached his destination of Petersburg, Virginia, there is no evidence that he was able to broker a peace settlement of any kind with the help of clergy in the UMCS. However, Stephen F. Knott maintains in *Secret and Sanctioned* that Lincoln may have looked at the colonel's trip as a way of driving "a wedge between members of the Southern Methodist Church and the Confederate government" and for that reason "controversial enough to require him to deny its existence."[19]

The colonel was back at Barnum's Hotel in Baltimore on July 22, when he sent a letter to Lincoln. He informed the president that he had "obtained *valuable* information for *peace* through the channel I proposed."[20] Then, after waiting two weeks for a reply from Lincoln that never came, Jaquess left Baltimore without being granted an audience with the president. The colonel's whereabouts are unknown from the time he left Baltimore until he took command of his regiment on September 14, shortly before the bloody battle of Chickamauga.

Probably the president did not see the letter from Jaquess and no reply from Lincoln to the colonel has ever appeared. In his book *Personal Recollections of Abraham Lincoln and the Civil War*, published in 1898, Gilmore claims that Lincoln expressed concern about not hearing from Jaquess. The president "feared some evil had befallen" the colonel and "regretted having let him go."[21] But Gilmore was remembering events that occurred more than thirty years earlier and he often strayed from accuracy when reporting them.

If the president did not receive the colonel's letter, it is probably because of his two secretaries, John Nicolay and John Hay, who both came from Pittsfield, Illinois. They certainly had little or no use for James F. Jaquess and labeled him a fanatic because of his uncritical opinion of his own abilities as a diplomat. They may have decided that giving the colonel's letter to Lincoln would be a waste of the president's valuable time. In their book *Abraham Lincoln: A History*, they compliment the president for not listening to a report from Jaquess because "it was preposterous to suppose that in the brief space of a single week he could have gathered any considerable information concerning public sentiment." Nicolay and Hay devoted several pages of their Lincoln biography to ranting against Colonel Jaquess, who, in their opinion, would "do better service as a soldier than as a diplomat."[22]

In a letter to James Gilmore written in Chattanooga on November 4, Jaquess expresses his disappointment in not seeing the president after the colonel's trip to the Confederacy. He tells Gilmore that he cannot understand why Lincoln "should *decline* any communication with me" when I had "*most valuable information*" to report. Jaquess points out that he succeeded "perfectly clear on the other side of the line," where he "met a most cordial reception" and "was most strongly urged not to cease" in his "efforts." According to the colonel, his "only trouble [was] on this side,"[23] probably a reference to Nicolay and Hay and their decision to see that Lincoln did not receive the colonel's letter.

Nearly thirty years later, Colonel Jaquess revealed the nature of the valuable information that he had been unable to deliver to Lincoln in 1863. In a speech at the 1890 reunion of the 73rd Illinois, Jaquess called his inability to communicate with Lincoln "an incident of the war veiled in mystery, and attended with fearful consequences to General Rosecranz [*sic*], and his brave army of the Cumberland." The colonel claimed that during his time in the South he heard rumors about plans to increase the size of General Braxton Bragg's army.[24] Although Confederate general Armistead Lindsay Long proposed such an increase in May, there was nothing done about his recommendation until three months later. The official decision took place in August after Jaquess had already returned to Union soil.

But if the colonel heard such rumors, he would certainly have wanted to share them with Lincoln because any information about increasing the size of the Rebel army might motivate the federal government to provide more soldiers for General Rosecrans. With the presence of a larger Union army, the Battle of Chickamauga might have concluded with fewer Northern soldiers killed, wounded or captured. Stephen F. Knott argues that the colonel's mission in 1863 was a failure not because he was unable to report to the president but because he failed to achieve what he had expected to accomplish. Jaquess did not discover "any great shift of sentiment within the Southern Methodist Church" and failed to make connections with "a peace faction in the Confederate government."[25] When Colonel Jaquess appeared before a congressional committee in 1870 to request reimbursement for missions that he had undertaken for President Lincoln in 1864 and 1865, he told this committee that the sum he was requesting did not include the 1863 mission because Lincoln had already reimbursed him for that trip.[26] This statement certainly suggests that Jaquess had acted as a private agent for Lincoln on his first trip to the South, and after he returned, the president had paid him accordingly.

Whether the colonel's trip in 1863 was a mission for the president or a personal effort to reach preachers in the Methodist Episcopal Church, South, only a handful of people knew anything about the trip. Ervin Chapman maintains in *Latest Light on Lincoln* that the president "insisted that knowledge of the proposition should be limited to, and held in strict confidence by the only persons who had any information respecting it." He identifies "President Lincoln, Generals Rosecrans, Thomas and Garfield, Colonel Jaquess and Mr. Gilmore" as the only ones who "had any knowledge or intimation of the existence of this unique mission."[27] The general public first learned about the 1863 trip a year after it had taken place when James Gilmore included it in *Down in Tennessee*, a book published in 1864.

Although called the Second Peace Mission, the trip to the Confederacy made by Jaquess and Gilmore in the summer of 1864 was actually a political mission, not a mission to negotiate peace. Between 1864 and 1898, James

R. Gilmore published three articles and two books that mention this mission. Later authors have relied heavily on these accounts although they are often more fiction than fact. Gilmore's first magazine article, "Our Visit to Richmond," which appeared in the September 1864 issue of the *Atlantic Monthly*, is closest to the actual event and probably nearest to the facts. Confederate accounts of the 1864 interview with President Davis tend to confirm the accuracy of Gilmore's original version.[28]

President Lincoln had a strong political purpose for the Jaquess-Gilmore mission and a real stake in its outcome. Lincoln wanted to save the Union but, above all, he wanted to be reelected president in 1864 so that he could achieve this goal. As early as 1862, President Lincoln and Horace Greeley, the powerful editor of the *New York Tribune*, had exchanged letters about the real goal of the Civil War. In a letter to Greeley that appeared in the *Tribune*, Lincoln had made it clear that his "paramount object in this struggle" was "to save the Union, and ... *not* either to save or to destroy slavery." He had written: "If I could save the Union without freeing *any* slave I would do it, and if I could save it by freeing *all* of the slaves I would do it, and if I could save it by freeing some and leaving others alone, I would also do that."[29]

By 1864 Greeley and many other Northerners firmly believed that the war was accomplishing nothing and must end, no matter what the cost, including destruction of the Union. There were residents from the Confederate states meeting in Canada who claimed that the South wanted peace. Greeley believed that these men were official representatives of the Confederate government who reflected the viewpoint of Jefferson Davis. He urged Lincoln "to submit overtures of pacification to the Southern insurgents."[30] Lincoln was counting on Jaquess and Gilmore to bring back proof that Greeley was wrong and such peace negotiations would be fruitless.

The president chose as his emissaries two men who could guarantee that what Jefferson Davis said would be spread throughout the North. James Jaquess was an excellent public speaker and James Gilmore was a well-known journalist, the right combination to repeat the words of Jefferson Davis both orally and in print. Lincoln needed to send two unofficial representatives to talk with President Davis because sending officially sanctioned peacemakers would have indicated that he recognized the Confederacy as a separate sovereign nation and not as a part of the United States in rebellion. The colonel's first trip focused on promoting reconciliation between the North and South through the influence of ministers in the MECS. The purpose of the 1864 trip with James Gilmore was entirely different. Lincoln sent Gilmore and Jaquess to bring back proof that peace was not possible under present circumstances. To achieve peace, the North must either allow the South to become an independent nation or defeat the South and force the Confederacy back into the Union.[31]

James Gilmore planned the 1864 trip with Lincoln's help although the President's two secretaries maintained that Gilmore did not decide to join Colonel Jaquess until "the last moment." Because Hay and Nicolay considered this undertaking "as visionary as might be expected from the joint effort of a preacher and a novelist," they decided that Jaquess, the chaplain who had once tried to plan battle strategy, must have proposed this ridiculous idea.[32] What the two secretaries did not realize was the extent of Lincoln's involvement in this trip or the president's hope that Jaquess and Gilmore would bring back evidence that the Union could not be restored until the North had won the war.

Gilmore's first step in planning the 1864 trip to Richmond was obtaining a leave of absence for Jaquess from his duties as colonel of 73rd Illinois. In the middle of May, Gilmore obtained a note from President Lincoln approving an extended "leave of absence until further orders" for Colonel Jaquess. He sent a copy of this note in a letter to Major General George H. Thomas, commander of the Army of the Cumberland that included the colonel's regiment.[33] Although Gilmore also wrote to Jaquess explaining what he and the president had in mind, this letter appears not to have survived. But a brief note sent by the Colonel on June 10 from the battlefield in Georgia confirms that he had received this letter.[34] Gilmore shared the colonel's reply with the president[35] while Jaquess traveled from the Union camp to a hotel in Baltimore. He arrived there by June 28, when he wrote to the Department of the Cumberland asking for an extension of his furlough. The result of this request is that his leave is "extended indefinitely."[36] Jaquess also sent a telegram to James R. Gilmore telling him that "it is important" for the writer to join him in Baltimore.[37]

How very different the 1864 trip was from the one that Jaquess had made alone the year before. In 1863 Lincoln was not directly involved and allowed others to make the decisions about the colonel's trip. He let General Rosecrans decide whether Jaquess got a furlough and Major General Robert Schenck determine whether he would be sent on to Fortress Monroe in order to enter the Confederacy. But in 1864, Abraham Lincoln worked out all the details in advance. The president wrote a pass for Gilmore and Jaquess: "Allow J.R. Gilmore & friend to pass, with ordinary baggage, to Gen. Grant, at his Head Quarters."[38] Jaquess explained that he was referred to as "friend" because "he had come into the Confederacy a year ago and had visited Petersburg on a similar errand; and that it was feared if his name should become known ... some of those [people who] had formerly met him in Petersburg would conjecture that the purpose for which he now came"[39] was the same as in 1863.

Ulysses S. Grant then wrote to General Robert E. Lee on July 8, asking that Gilmore and Jaquess "be allowed to meet [Confederate] Col Robt. Ould ... at such place between the lines of the two Armies as you may designate."[40] Ould replied that he would be waiting for Jaquess and Gilmore "at some convenient point between Deep Bottom and Chaffin's bluff" at 1:00 P.M. on July 14.[41] Two days passed while the Confederate War Department reviewed this request, and Jaquess and Gilmore did not cross into Rebel territory until July 16. They met Ould and other Confederate officials including Charles Javins, provost-guard of Richmond, who remained with them throughout their stay.

That night they traveled the three-hour journey to Richmond in a horse-drawn ambulance behind a carriage that displayed a flag of truce. Ould led them to a room in the Spotswood Hotel containing beds for Jaquess, Gilmore and Javins. They learned that the landlord assumed that the two unknown men had come to Richmond from Georgia because "no one but a Georgian would call for cornbread at this time of night." When a servant brought their dinner a short time later, Gilmore and Jaquess maintained their supposed identities by discussing events in Georgia with an appropriate accent while the servant was in their room. This account may be Gilmore's effort to insert a bit of comedy.

The following morning they wrote a note to the Confederate secretary of state, Judah Benjamin, requesting permission to meet with President Davis. Ould delivered the note and then escorted Gilmore and Jaquess to a building that had been the United States Custom House but now served as Benjamin's office. After questioning them closely, Benjamin told them to return at 9:00 P.M., when Jefferson Davis would meet with them.

There are no official records of this meeting, but unofficial Union and Rebel accounts are fundamentally the same.[42] Gilmore's "Our Visit to Richmond" portrays the meeting as a discussion between President Davis and Colonel Jaquess with an occasional comment from Gilmore. However, Judah Benjamin's version presents Gilmore as the one who does most of the talking. As recounted by Gilmore, Jaquess stressed to Jefferson Davis that Lincoln and the people of the North wanted to end this bloody war and many Southerners were also anxious for peace. The colonel then told him, "But we cannot let you alone so long as you repudiate the Union." Jefferson Davis answered with the words that Lincoln expected Gilmore and Jaquess to hear: "We are not fighting for slavery. We are fighting for independence — and *that*, or extermination, we will have." As they were leaving, Jefferson Davis told them, "Say to Mr. Lincoln from me that I shall at any time be pleased to receive proposals for peace on the basis of our Independence." As Robert S. Harper suggests in *Lincoln and the Press*, Jefferson Davis' "explicit exposition of the aims of the Confederacy emasculated the peace group in the North and did much to ensure a term for Lincoln."[43] After visiting prisons and hospitals the following day, Jaquess and Gilmore crossed back through the Rebel lines at sundown on July 18.

An article identified as "A Special Dispatch from Washington" appeared in both the *Philadelphia Enquirer* and the *New York Times* a few days after Gilmore and Jaquess returned. It described how Colonel Jaquess had "fared sumptuously, being fed on chicken, turkey, mutton and all the viands of a well-appointed hotel, and entertained with fine brandies and costly wines" but said nothing about the purpose or outcome of the visit.[44] James Gilmore wrote to Lincoln immediately to let the president know that he was "very much surprised and mortified to see the absurd and ridiculous reports of Col Jaquess and my visit to Richmond." He assured Lincoln that he "had no hand or part in it."[45] On the same day, Colonel Jaquess wrote to Gilmore from Washington, D.C., claiming that he was "thunder struck at finding a statement of our trip in a Philad Paper."[46]

However, there was also an account of an entirely different peace mission on the front page of the same issue of the *Times* that mentioned the Jaquess-Gilmore mission. It concerned the peace meetings involving Confederate representatives at Clifton House in Canada that Horace Greeley had praised to President Lincoln and the rest of the nation in his newspaper, the *New York Tribune*. According to the *New York Times*, these meetings had come to nothing and the Confederate commissioners were now preparing a letter to the Chicago convention of the Democratic Party scheduled in August. The commissioners promised that their letter would include "strong assurances of the Union under Democratic auspices," implying that the Peace Democrats and the Confederacy were in cahoots.[47]

The *New York Times* was a Republican newspaper that supported Lincoln and his administration. Its owner and editor, Henry J. Raymond, became chairman of the Republican National Committee for the 1864 election. Unfavorable comments about the Niagara Peace Conference and the Peace Democrats were normal in a Republican newspaper. But what about the article reporting the Jaquess-Gilmore mission to Richmond? The *New York Times* did not recount much about what took place except that "Col. Jaques[s] met with considerable success in impressing his views upon Mr.

Davis." The *Times* probably printed all it knew about the trip, which was little or nothing. However, this Republican paper needed a way to convince its readers that all was not lost. The meetings in Canada had failed but there was a recent peace mission to Richmond that might actually accomplish something. A few days later, James Gilmore published an article in the *Boston Transcript* that was picked up by the *New York Times*. He denied any connection with the "Sander-Greeley negotiation that is said to be going on at Niagara Falls" and concluded with a plug for an article on his trip with Jaquess to Richmond that was to appear in the September issue of the *Atlantic Monthly*.[48]

In his brief message to Gilmore sent on July 21, the colonel reported that he would be informing Lincoln about their trip to Richmond at 8:00 P.M. that evening. This meeting did not take place at the White House but at the "Soldier's Home" to which the president had moved the week before to escape the summer heat of Washington.[49] There was a clerk present at the interview to record what Jaquess reported orally. Given the title "Rebel Terms of Peace," this report was distributed as Republican campaign literature during the 1864 campaign. Jaquess stated that this written report was given to the treasurer of the Republican Congressional Committee, his friend from Indiana Asbury, Senator James Harlan. "Rebel Terms of Peace" begins with a letter from Harlan dated September 5 and a reply from Jaquess dated two days later. Harlan referred to their "long and intimate acquaintance" and asked the colonel to give his personal version of the interview with Davis. The document presents a lengthy conversation between President Davis and the colonel but mentions Gilmore only in the title and in the colonel's letter to Harlan.[50]

Although the colonel's account is much the same as Gilmore's article in the *Atlantic Monthly*, "Rebel Terms of Peace" definitely has the ring of a propaganda piece. There is a touch of humor when Colonel Jaquess tells Jefferson Davis that "some of your friends, and I may say admirers, have asked me this question, 'Do you know that you look precisely like Jeff Davis?'" The colonel's last name is misspelled "Jacques" in the title and "Jaques" in his letter to Harlan. Obviously, the colonel did not proofread "Rebel Terms," or possibly even see it, before its publication by the Union Congressional Committee, and it is very likely not an accurate record of what he said to Lincoln the evening of July 21.[51]

On the evening when Jaquess told the president about his trip with James Gilmore to Richmond, Lincoln engaged the colonel to undertake several additional missions as the president's private agent. There is evidence in several sources that Jaquess was absent from his regiment for a long period of time during 1864 and 1865. The regimental history states that when "Colonel James F. Jaquess rejoined the regiment" on the afternoon of April 27, 1865, he had been absent "since June 5, 1864."[52] The field and staff muster rolls in the colonel's military file also show absences during March, April, May and June of 1864 as the result of several different "Special Field Orders." Then for nine consecutive months, from late July 1864 to April 1865, the colonel was "absent with Leave per S.O. [Special Order] No. 248 War Department, [issued] July 25, 1864."[53] This furlough began only a few days after the colonel's meeting with Lincoln to make a report on the trip to Richmond. Finally, the official records of the Union and Confederate armies during the Civil War indicate that Thomas W. Motherspaw or Wilson Burroughs led the 73rd in all military encounters after the battle at Missionary Ridge.[54] However, none of these sources explains where Colonel Jaquess was or what he was doing when he was not with his regiment.

When Jaquess reported to Lincoln after his trip to the Confederacy in 1864, the president sent him immediately on two consecutive trips to Niagara.[55] His assignment was to assess what was presently going on there between Confederate peace commissioners and United States citizens who had crossed into Canada to meet with them to discuss ending the war. Jaquess talked with two of the peace commissioners, Clement C. Clay and Jacob Thompson. Clay had served as governor of Alabama, then as U.S. senator from that state and finally senator in the congress of the Confederacy. Thompson, from Mississippi, who served as U.S. secretary of the interior under President James Buchanan, resigned this post as soon as the Civil War broke out. Although he reported the outcome of both trips to Lincoln, Jaquess does not mention what Lincoln replied.[56]

Publication of Jefferson Davis' statement that the South would have "independence" or "extermination" had not stopped the Peace Democrats from clamoring for official negotiations. Because things had been going badly for the Union army, making peace with the South became a major topic of discussion in July and August of 1864. Horace Greeley finally pressured Lincoln into negotiating with the Confederate delegation that had been meeting at Niagara. Lincoln agreed to give these Southerners safe conduct to Washington, D.C., so that he could talk with them, only to discover that these men had no official standing with the Confederate government after all.

Later, in August 1864, the chair of the National Executive Committee of the Union Republican Party urged Lincoln to appoint an *official* United States commissioner to talk with President Davis about conditions for making peace. Lincoln was beginning to fear that he would lose the election and the North might lose the war if he did not make some official move toward peace. After all, the previous efforts of Jaquess and Gilmore had no *official* sanction from the U.S. government. Lincoln and his cabinet discussed the Union Republican Party's proposal of official negotiation with the South but decided against carrying it out. Then, after being a hot topic of discussion for much of the summer of 1864, the need to negotiate an acceptable peace no longer held center stage. When Confederate general John Bell Hood surrendered Atlanta to General Sherman on September 1, the chances for a Union army victory became favorable at last.

Next Lincoln sent Jaquess to Niagara on a third and different kind of mission, this time as a "working member" of what the colonel referred to as "a sort of convention of rebel leaders and sympathizers and spies, with some persons from the United States who went over to confer with them." Jaquess began by visiting ex-president Buchanan, Lincoln's Democratic predecessor in office, at his residence in Lancaster, Pennsylvania, for advice on how to become an official delegate to this "convention." Jaquess claimed that when he was with Buchanan, the ex-president drank "more liquor ... than I ever drank in my life." He also maintained that Buchanan was a confidante of the pro–Confederacy group at Niagara, possibly because of his previous connection to Jacob Thompson. The colonel became the representative for a part of Southern Illinois and most likely used an assumed name. He agreed with Lincoln's assertion to Abram Wakeman, a New Yorker who promoted the president's reelection in 1864, that the real purpose of the Niagara meeting was not to pursue peace between North and South but "to assist in selecting and arranging a candidate, and a platform for the Chicago Convention" of the Democratic Party to be held on August 29.[57]

As the Chicago convention grew near, Lincoln became more and more convinced that it was "exceedingly probable" that he would "not be reelected." The transition between the Buchanan administration and the Lincoln presidency had been more difficult than any that had preceded it. Believing that he should behave better than his predecessor had, Lincoln was determined to cooperate with whomever was elected president in 1864. He asked his cabinet to sign but not to read a memorandum that he had drafted that stated his willingness "to so co-operate with the President elect, as to save the Union between the election and the inauguration."[58]

On his third mission to Canada, Jaquess met a disaffected Southerner who told him about a Confederate plot to burn Northern cities and shipping. From this Southerner Jaquess learned the identity of the Rebel chemist who was making the incendiary bombs and where the colonel could locate him. This information motivated Jaquess to smuggle himself through enemy lines on a third trip to the Confederacy. When he talked with the Confederate chemist, Jaquess learned that this man had become "opposed to the whole thing" and believed that the weapon that he was creating was "not sanctioned by the laws of War." Colonel Jaquess, who had taught chemistry during his presidency at Illinois Conference Female College, worked with the unnamed chemist to alter the chemical ingredients of the bombs. Together they created a formula that would catch fire when exposed to the air, burn brightly for a short time, and then extinguish itself. The Colonel spent between $1200 and $1300 out of his own pocket on the ingredients for the new bomb formula.

After he returned from helping the Southern chemist to create a self-extinguishing bomb, James Jaquess spoke for the reelection of President Lincoln at eight Union Republican meetings in the states of New York and New Jersey. Unlike his earlier missions, his campaigning for Lincoln was certainly not secret and the dates and locations of the colonel's speeches appeared in newspapers. Usually he had support from other speakers such as Governor John A. Andrew of Massachusetts and Governor John Brough of Ohio, but on two occasions he was the only featured speaker. James Jaquess was an outstanding public speaker, in political meetings as well as in the pulpit, and his well-known support of Lincoln's candidacy certainly contributed to the president's reelection. His next assignments from Lincoln came after the president's successful reelection.[59]

When Confederate spies tried to burn New York City on November 23, 1864, the day before Thanksgiving,[60] they might have failed because of the self-extinguishing bomb Jaquess helped to create. Historians often claim that this unsuccessful effort was supposed to be a payback to General William Tecumseh Sherman and his troops for burning Atlanta eight days earlier. Jaquess claimed that the Confederate plot to destroy New York failed because the bombs they used simply did not work. He maintained that the fires went out because the new chemical formula that he and the Southern chemist created included a means of "self-extinguishment." One claim at the time was that the fires in several hotels and the Barnum Museum died because they were set in closed areas with insufficient oxygen. Another explanation was that those individuals who accidentally discovered the fires simply put them out.

John W. Headley, one of the Confederate spies who tried to burn New York, agreed that the bombs did not work properly. He explained in *Confederate Operations in Canada and New York*: "It seemed to us that there was something wrong with our Greek fire.... We came to the conclusion that [the] manufacturing chemist had put up a job on us."[61] But two contemporary authors have a somewhat different point of view. In *The Man Who Tried to Burn New York*, Nat Brandt identifies Greek fire as "a mixture of phosphorus in bisulfide of carbon commonly used in hand grenades." He points out that this mixture failed to work at St. Louis and St. Albans, Vermont, as well as in New York and blames all these failures on the Southern chemist who did not explain how to use his formula properly.[62] Clint Johnson takes a similar position in *"A Vast and Fiendish Plot": The Confederate Attack on New York* and argues that the Confederate spies did not practice using the Greek fire "under the same conditions that they would have inside an enclosed hotel room." He argues that the Confederate plan would have succeeded if the Southern spies had piled up the hotel room furniture, poured on bottles of Greek fire and opened the room's window so that there was enough oxygen to feed the fire. He points out that contemporary articles in two New York newspapers agree with this explanation.[63]

The colonel's private service to the president concluded with some fence-mending missions following Lincoln's reelection in November 1864. Jaquess visited Horace Greeley twice but Greeley "was not willing to be reconciled" and continued to claim that "Mr. Lincoln lied to him." However, Jaquess was more successful with Governor Horatio Seymour, a Democrat from New York, and Governor John A. Andrew of Massachusetts. Seymour was a major critic of Lincoln's first administration, while Republican Andrew was a strong supporter of the Northern cause. Jaquess claimed that he brokered a meeting between the two of them in New York City and paid their expenses himself.

Colonel Jaquess presented details of his service as a private agent to the Senate Committee on Military Affairs in 1870. Although Lincoln had reimbursed Jaquess for his trip South in 1863, the president had not repaid him for any other expenses. Jaquess explained that Lincoln had tried to pay him before the colonel left for New York to talk to Horace Greeley and Horatio Seymour, but Jaquess did not want to take such a large sum with him on this trip. Then he missed connections with the president when Lincoln left on March 23, 1865, aboard the *River Queen* to visit the Union troops. Lincoln did not return to Washington until April 9.[64] By that date, Colonel Jaquess had already headed west to Quincy, Illinois, to officiate at his daughter Margaret's marriage to Captain Henry A. Castle. When the Reverend Jaquess performed their wedding on April 18,[65] President Lincoln had been dead since 7:22 A.M. on April 15. When the senate committee questioned Jaquess about why he had waited until 1870 to present his case, he explained that secretary of war Edwin M. Stanton told him not to try to submit his claim while President Andrew Johnson was in office, and the colonel had followed his advice.

The Committee on Military Affairs did not question the accuracy of what Jaquess told them and authorized the secretary of the treasury to pay Colonel James F. Jaquess his full request of $6719 "for services performed and money expended by said Jaquess during the recent rebellion, under the direction of the late President Abraham Lincoln." One of the colonel's friends since college, Senator James Harlan, proposed this legislation as Senate Bill 886. Congress did not pass the legislation to pay the $6719 until February 12, 1873, the 64th anniversary of Lincoln's birth. In justifying approval of the payment to Colonel Jaquess, the committee said that they "looked upon the claim as one of a sacred character, growing out of the intimate and confidential relations of Colonel Jaques[s] with the president."[66]

Chapter 7

Trial for Murder by Abortion

General Robert E. Lee surrendered to General Ulysses S. Grant at Appomattox, Virginia, on April 9, 1865. Only 8000 armed men remained from the original 28,000 men that had made up Lee's army, and all the Confederate soldiers in his command "were suffering from reduced rations and scant clothing, exposed to battle, cold, hail, and sleet." Confederate forces in North Carolina, South Carolina, Georgia, Florida, Alabama and Mississippi surrendered shortly thereafter, but the Civil War did not end until more than a month later when General E. Kirby Smith surrendered his men west of the Mississippi on May 26.[1]

After officiating at his daughter's wedding to Captain Henry A. Castle in Quincy,[2] the colonel and his son, Willie, returned to the camp of the 73rd Illinois on April 27. Although he had promised to remain with his regiment until it disbanded,[3] Jaquess was no longer with them when the officers and men of the 73rd were mustered out at Camp Butler on June 27. Most members of the 73rd headed back to their hometowns; Jaquess remained in Nashville, where he said he was serving "on Special duty."

The colonel did not want to return to his wife and family in Quincy and he had no desire to return to a Methodist pulpit. His experiences as a college president in Jacksonville and Quincy had also convinced him that this job was not a suitable one for him. Colonel Jaquess wanted a position that would match his abilities and also provide a legitimate excuse for staying in Nashville or somewhere close by. For these reasons Jaquess wrote to General Clinton B. Fisk, senior officer in the Tennessee and Kentucky Bureau of Refugees, Freedmen and Abandoned Lands, on the same day that the men of the 73rd Illinois returned to civilian life.[4]

General Clinton Bowen Fisk, who strongly supported the rights of emancipated Negroes, was well suited for his position with the Freedmen's

Bureau. At the conclusion of the war he allowed a newly formed school for blacks to use empty Union barracks in Nashville, Tennessee, and gave this school a personal gift of $30,000. This "school for Negroes" that opened on January 9, 1866, became Fisk School, the predecessor of today's Fisk University.[5] When he told Jaquess the plans for Camp Nelson, they represented the orders of his superiors more than his own opinions.

The colonel's letter to Fisk asked to become part of the general's "important mission" of helping former slaves to adjust to life as freedmen. Jaquess wrote that since he had not yet been mustered out, he would prefer to retain his military rank but was willing to accept any assignment that Fisk gave him: "feeding the hungry, clothing the destitute, superintending the education of the people under your care or any such work." Rather than sending this letter in the usual manner, Jaquess asked his second in command, Lieutenant Colonel James I. Davidson, to deliver the letter in person to Fisk at Refugee House in Nashville.[6]

Jaquess remained in Nashville for nearly two months waiting for the general's reply. When Fisk finally answered the colonel's request, he no longer remembered Jaquess' first name or initials and addressed his letter to Colonel D.C. Jaquess. He informed the colonel that he had assigned him to the position of superintendent of the Lexington Kentucky Sub-District of the Freedmen's Bureau with headquarters at Camp Nelson about 20 miles away from the city of Lexington. The colonel's chief responsibility was "the supervision and entire Control of the Colored Refugee Home" located there.[7] When Fisk placed Jaquess in charge of operations at Camp Nelson, Jaquess had achieved his goal of remaining near Nashville but his new job was certainly not an enviable one.

As Ross Webb explains in "Kentucky: 'Pariah among the Elect,'" citizens of a border state, like Kentucky, that had remained in the Union considered the presence of the Freedmen's Bureau "an insult and injury to both the loyalty and sovereignty of Kentucky and charged [the Bureau] with gross violations of the rights of white Kentuckians."[8] As an employee of the Freedmen's Bureau, Colonel Jaquess could not expect to be well received in Kentucky. Originally an army facility, the camp had become a haven for runaway slaves seeking shelter and education during the final years of the Civil War. Fisk informed Jaquess that, now that the Civil War was over, the general's "superiors [wanted] to close out the Camp at the earliest practicable day." He told Jaquess not to "receive into the [Colored Refugees] Home another individual old or young except humanity evidently demands it" and to "get rid of the families there now — before the winter sets in."[9]

Fisk warned Jaquess that the colonel's subordinates would strongly oppose these orders. The Reverend John G. Fee, assistant superintendent Lester Williams and all the teachers in the school for former slaves would "make every possible effort to continue a big establishment — as the larger it is kept the more flourishing the schools congregations hospitals &c." General Fisk required Jaquess to submit a progress report every five days so that he could make sure that the colonel was carrying out his orders. From what the general told him, Jaquess realized that his staff would make it difficult to carry out the tasks assigned by Fisk[10] and, when he succeeded, Jaquess would have put himself out of a job.

Although Camp Nelson now served as a haven for black refugees, it had originally been built in 1863 as a supply depot in central Kentucky from which Major General Ambrose E. Burnside could support a campaign to free from Confederate rule the citizens of East Tennessee who had remained loyal to the Union. When this plan proved unworkable, the United States Sanitary Commission opened a soldiers home at the camp in the winter of 1863-1864. But it was the Union army's need to recruit black soldiers that turned Camp Nelson into a huge refugee facility for the families of these soldiers.[11]

Kentuckians were strongly opposed to the U.S. government buying their slaves and freeing them so that they could enlist as Union soldiers. These white Kentuckians greatly feared what might happen if the army put guns in the hands of former slaves. They also maintained that they were economically disadvantaged by not having these slaves to continue working for them. The Emancipation Proclamation had not applied to border states like Kentucky and the federal government had been careful to keep things this way to insure Kentucky's continued loyalty. However, by the beginning of 1864, the Union forces desperately needed black soldiers to swell their ranks. The army decided to use Camp Nelson as the location for a school for black soldiers as well as a separate training facility for white recruits.[12]

It was typical for the families of black soldiers to follow them to army camps. This practice posed a special problem in Kentucky because the women and children who showed up at Camp Nelson were still slaves, making it illegal to give them sanctuary. Families of black soldiers recruited in Kentucky were sometimes beaten as a surrogate punishment for the men who had left to become soldiers. Other slave owners simply turned out the women and children when the men joined the army. Escaped and expelled slave families flooded into Camp Nelson. Many of them died there, chiefly because they had previously lived in isolation from common communicable diseases. At its highest point, Camp Nelson housed thousands of refugees in hundreds of buildings staffed by hundreds of workers. When the war ended, the federal government no longer needed to train black soldiers and care for their families. The Freedmen's Bureau took over Camp Nelson and instructed General Fisk to empty the facility as soon as possible. After visiting the camp in person, Fisk placed Colonel Jaquess in charge and gave him the difficult job of shutting the place down.[13]

Jaquess wrote to Fisk on August 23, to let the general know that he had "come, and seen, and hope[d] to conquer" the monumental task of emptying the camp. He was particularly anxious to receive authority to remove African Americans from the camp by providing them with transportation.[14] Major John H. Cochrane replied the following day that General Fisk had authorized the transportation requested by Jaquess, provided that the refugees could prove that they would not be "a charge upon the Government."[15] Nevertheless, transportation, or the lack of it, remained the colonel's chief problem during his brief tenure as superintendent.

Jaquess quickly realized that the Reverend John Gregg Fee, a Presbyterian minister sent by the American Missionary Association, would be his greatest problem. Fee had founded Berea College, the first racially integrated school in Kentucky. Four different times mobs had attacked him because he preached abolitionist principles. Fee had come to Camp Nelson in July 1864 to oversee the school for black refugees. At first, the Presbyterian minister expressed little concern about the appointment of Jaquess because Fee expected to remain head of the school.[16] However, Jaquess soon spotted Fee as a troublemaker who constantly quarreled with his staff of teachers.[17]

W.W. Wheeler, the farm superintendent at Camp Nelson, identified the reason for this friction in a letter to the Reverend George Whipple, secretary of the American Missionary Association. Wheeler explained that Fee had upset his staff by hiring an educated young black woman named Belle Mitchell to teach in the same school with white teachers. According to Wheeler, the rest of the teachers did not accept Belle Mitchell because she was "colored" and disregarded her "correct christian [sic] deportment and unexceptionable personal habits." He pointed out that Belle did not even look "colored" and Fee had explained to his staff in advance that "her features are good European her complexion but little darker than yours or mine and her hair of 'the most straightest sect.'" However, as Wheeler told the Reverend Whipple, almost all of the female teachers walked out of the dining room when Belle Mitchell sat down to eat at the same table as the rest of the staff.[18]

When Fee informed Jaquess about hiring this young lady, the colonel failed to anticipate how white staff members would react. He did not realize that, although most white Kentuckians were strongly committed to the United States, they could not accept the idea of Negroes as free persons. Although Kentuckians fought on the Union side, they still held more than 65,000 blacks in slavery at the close of the Civil War.[19] When the ruckus began, Jaquess tried to solve the problem by removing Belle from the teachers' dining room and sending her to eat with the black residents at the soldiers home. But Fee refused to accept this solution. Wheeler explained that Jaquess became angry because Fee would not cooperate with him and "flew right around and said I will have nothing to do with it. I will leave it with the mess." Obviously, the colonel also left the situation "in a mess" when he decided to leave Belle's fate in the hands of those who would have to work and eat with her. Wheeler compared Jaquess to Pontius Pilate because he washed "his hands as Pilate did, of old and with about as much effect in clearing his skirts of guilt." Without any further discussion of the problem, Jaquess left Camp Nelson for Louisville on what he referred to as "business."[20]

Rather than trust Jaquess to give the general a true account of what had happened, the Reverend Fee decided to write to Fisk himself and explain the incident from his own point of view. Fee claimed that the Reverend Lester Williams, the Baptist minister who was superintendent of the Refugee Home, was to blame for Belle's mistreatment. Fee maintained that "if there had not been some ungodly young men boarding at the table & Bro Williams had not 'sided' with them, there would have been little or no opposition" from the rest of the staff. The following day, Fee wrote a second letter to General Fisk to report that after Jaquess left, the staff had staged a "demonstration" to protest Belle's presence.[21] When the colonel returned to Camp Nelson and evaluated the situation, he informed General Fisk that he "found it necessary to remove Rev. Fee from all connection with the day school."[22]

Meanwhile enmity was increasing among the Camp Nelson staff. Claiming that she had authority from Colonel Jaquess, the wife of Lester Williams refused to allow Mary Colton and Mrs. William Scofield to continue teaching in the school because they were friends of the Reverend Fee.[23] When the Reverend Fee returned to Camp Nelson after spending a week in Berea, he discovered that Colonel Jaquess had brought the conflict among the staff to an end by ordering Belle Mitchell to leave Camp Nelson.[24]

The colonel's decision to remove Belle Mitchell from the Camp Nelson staff did not end her career as a teacher. She went on to a position at another school operated by the American Missionary Association, this time in Lexington, Kentucky.[25] The daughter of Mary and Monroe Mitchell, who had bought themselves out of slavery, she became a well-known teacher in Fayette County. Belle Mitchell also helped to found the African American Orphan Industrial Home and was an active member of the colored women's club. She died in 1942 at the age of 93 or 94.[26]

Education of newly emancipated African Americans was the goal of the nearly eighty northern aid societies that provided both teachers and financial support.[27] As Linda B. Selleck points out, the head of the Freedmen's Bureau, General O.O. Howard, maintained that "education was absolutely essential to the blacks to prepare them for their new duties and responsibilities."[28] Established in March 1865, the Freedmen's Bureau was within five years operating 4239 schools with 9300 teachers who taught more than 247,000 students at the cost of five million dollars by 1871. Most of the teachers in the bureau's schools as well as those operated by various religious denominations were women, both black and white. Northern Quakers furnished the money and materials to hire black teachers and also opened their own Quaker schools to black children.[29] African Americans also maintained schools of their own, providing both the staff and the money for their operation.[30] Although the emphasis was on teaching the basic skills of reading, writing and arithmetic, the Quakers established a small orphanage for black children in Helena, Arkansas, that later became Southland College, a school that operated for more than 60 years.[31]

But the colonel's chief worry was not the Belle Mitchell incident, his suspension of Fee or the future of education for blacks. His greatest concern was an order from the quartermaster general in Washington, D.C., stating that officers of the Freedmen's Bureau could receive supplies, means of transportation and any other necessities only by means of requisitions first approved by the commissioner of the Freemen's Bureau and then by the secretary of war. Jaquess realized that this bureaucratic requirement would make it nearly impossible to accomplish within a short time everything that Fisk had ordered. He explained to Fisk that he had to "get this kink out of this piece of red tape" if he was ever to succeed in emptying Camp Nelson in a timely manner. Jaquess claimed that he had several hundred refugees ready to be transported and he could "clean out this camp on the double quick" if he only had the necessary transportation.[32]

Before two weeks had passed, Jaquess faced an entirely different problem, one far greater than transportation of freedmen and bureaucratic red tape. Louisa C. Williams, from Nashville, who was now in Louisville, was pregnant with a child that very likely was the colonel's. It was his affair with this woman that had motivated Jaquess to seek a job with the Freedmen's Bureau in or near Nashville rather than return to civilian life in Quincy. The colonel's last letter from Camp Nelson dated September 11 said nothing about Louisa Williams but told General Fisk that he had to leave for his home in Quincy immediately. The reason that he gave was similar to the ones that he had used to obtain furloughs from his regiment: "money matters, to the amount of several thousand dollars" that required his "immediate attention and presence." Jaquess had previously told Fisk that he wanted to make this trip on September 20.[33] The next report of the colonel's whereabouts appeared in the *Louisville Journal* and the *Louisville Democrat* on September 23. The papers stated that he had been arrested in Louisville on the charge of murder by abortion as Louisa Williams had died from the procedure. The *Louisville Democrat* called him Dr. "J.T. Jacques" and referred to him as a physician who was once a preacher in Illinois.[34]

The national attitude toward abortion was different in 1865 than it has become in the United States since the beginning of the 20th century. As James C. Mohr explains in *Abortion in America: The Origins and Evolution of National Policy*, females who received abortions between 1840 and 1880 were often "white, married, Protestant, native-born women of the middle and upper classes who either wished to delay their childbearing or already had all the children they wanted."[35] He also points out that beginning in 1840 "abortion became, for all intents and purposes, a business" and "abortion-related advertisements appeared in both urban dailies and rural weeklies."[36] After its founding in 1847, the American Medical Association became an important force in pushing for antiabortion laws.[37] But antiabortion did not become an American policy until laws were passed between 1880 and 1900.[38] By 1900 every state except one had on its books some kind of antiabortion law. It is significant that the only state without this legislation was Kentucky.[39] The purpose of the trial of Colonel Jaquess was to publicly humiliate a Northerner who had led a regiment in the Union army and now worked for the Freedmen's Bureau Although he had very likely fathered the baby and paid the fee of the abortionist, Jaquess certainly had not broken any law in Kentucky because none existed.

Early in 1865, President Lincoln had placed General John M. Palmer from Carlinville, Illinois, in charge of the Military Department of Kentucky located in Louisville. Palmer had a long-time acquaintance with Jaquess, and when he read about the colonel's arrest, he visited Jaquess, who was being held in the Louisville jail. Palmer knew that the most influential person to contact in the colonel's behalf was former Governor Yates, now U.S. Senator Yates, and sent a telegram to his home in Jacksonville: "Col Jaquess is in great trouble and desires you to come here [Louisville] immediately."[40] There is no evidence that Yates responded to Jaquess' cry for help and traveled to Louisville or even that he was at home in Jacksonville and received Palmer's telegram.

There were widely different reactions to the news of the colonel's arrest among those who knew him. Judge William Thomas from Jacksonville, the trustee from Illinois Conference Female College who had urged Lincoln to promote Jaquess, wrote: "I cannot believe a word of the charge."[41] General Palmer wrote to his wife that he did not believe that Jaquess had advised the abortion that resulted in the murder charge. He added that he hoped Jaquess was "innocent of the authorship of the woman's trouble," but feared that the colonel "was guilty of that."[42] Back at Camp Nelson, the Reverend Fee, certainly not a friend of Jaquess, had also read a newspaper account of the arrest. He referred to the woman who had died as the colonel's "paramour or 'mistress.'" He also claimed that Jaquess had lied to his staff at Camp Nelson about making a business trip to Quincy and had gone straight to Louisville to procure this woman's abortion.[43] Even although he was extremely angry with Jaquess for dismissing Belle Mitchell, the Reverend Fee's opinion of what happened in Louisville is closest to the truth.

Accounts of what happened in Louisville tend to reflect the politics of the newspapers rather than the facts of what actually took place. The account of a Union officer, abortion and murder was bound to make a shocking story. As presented shortly after the Civil War by all three Louisville papers, this story became absolutely sensational.

Explaining the viewpoints of all the Louisville newspapers in *The Civil War and Readjustment in Kentucky*, E. Merton Coulter points out that the *Louisville Courier* had been a pro–Southern paper while Kentucky maintained its neutrality, but when Kentucky gave up this position and supported the Union, the federal government issued an order "excluding it [*Louisville Courier*] from the mails, 'as an advocate of treason,' and later on the same day it was suppressed by Military force." Coulter also explains that although the *Louisville Journal* opposed the secession of Southern states, the paper referred to Lincoln's "call for troops as 'unworthy not merely of a statesman but of a man.'" He adds that although the *Louisville Democrat* was originally less radical than the other two papers, "with the coming of the Emancipation Proclamation ... it became more critical of the National administration than the *Journal*."[44] Not only Louisville newspapers but almost all 19th-century papers followed this biased style of presentation. By contrast, there is only one mention of Jaquess and the Louisville scandal in any of the newspapers published in the colonel's hometown of Quincy. This article is a reprint of a brief account in the *Louisville Democrat*.⁴⁵ Either Louisville news did not travel that far or, more likely, those who knew James F. Jaquess as a Methodist minister and college president dismissed what happened in Louisville as the work of Rebels and copperheads.

There was an exchange of correspondence among those who knew Jaquess when the colonel's arrest became widely known. As soon as General Fisk read an account of Jaquess' arrest in a Nashville paper, he wanted to know what was going on and immediately telegraphed General Palmer to find out whether this article was actually true. Palmer replied to Fisk by telegram: "Col. Jaquess is in Jail here [Louisville] charged as stated in newspapers."⁴⁶

Jaquess himself presented his version of what had taken place in a long letter to General Fisk written from the Louisville jail on September 30. To assure the general that Mrs. Jaquess was supporting him, the colonel made certain that Fisk knew that Sarah Jane was now in Louisville. The colonel admitted that he was acquainted with Mrs. Louisa C. Williams, the woman whose death had resulted in a charge of murder, but stated that he was not her lover as claimed in the newspapers. He explained that he had met her in Nashville through Lieutenant Colonel James I. Davidson and other officers and called her "a most worthy lady tho very poor and drawing rations." Jaquess told Fisk that he had "secured for her an agency in selling Sewing Machines" so that she could support herself. She had come from Nashville to Louisville to search for the man who had fathered her child but "found no trace of him."⁴⁷

Jaquess recounted to General Fisk the trips that placed him in Louisville on several different dates. He reported passing through Louisville on September 6 on his way back to Camp Nelson after meeting with Fisk in Nashville. Next he mentioned a trip to Quincy on September 11 that took him through Louisville on September 12 and again on September 20, when he was on his way back to Camp Nelson. He stated that when he arrived at his Louisville hotel on the return trip, he found a note from Mrs. Williams that had been delivered to the hotel a few days earlier. He visited her that day and found her very ill. When he saw her the following day, she told him that her doctor now said that she should be well enough to travel back to Nashville the next day. However, when he returned on Friday, September 22, Jaquess "found her in a dying condition" and spent the day looking for medical assistance. He came back that "evening to administer to her such comfort" as he could, but "she died in a few minutes." Jaquess concluded by telling Fisk that "the prosecution will do all they can to convict me," but "I feel that God is on my side and I will not fear what man can do."[48]

Colonel Jaquess made his initial court appearance on October 6. Mrs. Rebecca Dockins, the woman who was boarding Louisa C. Williams when she died, appeared with him at police court. Dr. Hermann Rosengarten, an abortionist with many aliases, was not present on October 6 but appeared at a later date. The court was packed with spectators interested in the colonel's case.[49] Jaquess had asked General Palmer to contact several people to appear in his behalf including "eminent citizens and clergymen of the States of Illinois and Ohio [probably Indiana], who had been the friends and associates of Colonel Jacquess [sic]." General Palmer himself also testified in the colonel's behalf.[50] Late on Saturday, October 8, both Jaquess and Mrs. Dockins were released on bonds of $2000, to insure their appearance at the next session of the circuit court.[51]

About a week later, the *Louisville Daily Journal* reprinted a letter from Mrs. Henry A. Castle, the colonel's daughter, Margaret, which had been previously published in the *Chicago Tribune*. She claimed that her father had been acquitted, an outcome that she wanted the colonel's "many friends throughout Indiana, Illinois and New York States" to know. The Louisville paper corrected this misinformation and repeated that Jaquess had not been acquitted, only released on bail. The newspaper concluded by promising that Colonel Jaquess "will soon have the opportunity of establishing his innocence" in circuit court.[52] The opportunity did not come for another six months.

Colonel Jaquess made his first appearance before Judge George W. Johnston in the Jefferson County Circuit Court on December 8. His case was third on the docket for that day. The first defendant to come before Judge Johnston was none other than Major General Palmer himself on the charge that he had aided Ellen, the slave of S.R. Womack, to escape from her owner. The judge quashed this indictment on the grounds that since the requisite number of states had passed the 13th Amendment, slavery no longer existed and "the rights of the master to the services of the slave must fall with slavery." However, the very fact that Palmer's indictment came before the court says much about the attitude in Kentucky toward Union army officers and the Freedmen's Bureau. James Jaquess was a representative of both. The second case concerned a woman charged with murdering her father by poisoning his dinner. Although this case was certainly sensational, it was the indictment against Jaquess that had attracted the crowd. After the jury was seated, the clerk read a sixteen-page indictment to which Jaquess pleaded not guilty. One witness for the prosecution had given his testimony and a second witness had begun to testify when the court adjourned until the following morning. The reason for ending testimony was that one of the defense attorneys had been taken very ill.[53] The colonel's case was not called again until a month later, when it was postponed until the next term of the court because of the absence of some material witnesses.[54]

The case alleging the "murder" of Louisa Williams next appeared in court on May 10, 1866. Although the colonel, Mrs. Dockins and Dr. Rosengarten appeared together, the judge intended to try them individually.[55] One newspaper identified Jaquess as "a minister of the Gospel, and afterwards one of the peace commissions to Richmond, and then a Colonel of one of the Illinois regiments,"[56] three accomplishments that were likely to turn a Kentucky jury against him. The judge heard the colonel's case before those of Rebecca Dockins and Hermann Rosengarten, and Jaquess was arraigned on three charges: "1st. Producing an abortion on Mrs. L.C. Williams, alias Wilson. 2d. Being accessory before the fact in procuring the death of Mrs. L.C. Williams. 3d. For being accessory before the fact in procuring the death of the child which Mrs. L.C. Williams gave birth to." Judge George W. Johnston was still presiding over the colonel's case but a second jury had to be seated. It took five hours to select this jury because nearly everyone had "already formed and expressed an opinion."[57]

On the first day of the trial, James C. Gill and Dr. Henry Miller gave evidence for the prosecution. After identifying himself as coroner of Jefferson County, Gill testified that the year before on September 23 he had received the report of a woman's death and summoned Dr. Miller to join him at a house on the Point, a part of Louisville located on the Ohio River. Gill ordered that the dead body be moved to the front room of the house where the physician could examine the body while he gathered evidence in the back bedrooms. Gill "brought away a small basket containing medicines" and "two Common-sense sewing machines, sold by Messrs. Bliss & Co." located in Louisville. Next Dr. Miller, a "practising [sic] physician in this city for thirty years" testified that the dead woman was three or four, but not more than five months, pregnant at the time of the abortion, which could "have been produced by the insertion of a probe or even a lead pencil" or by a drug called Ergot often used to cause abortions.[58]

When one juror was too ill to be in court the following day, the Jaquess trial did not resume until May 14. The defense immediately moved that newspapers be prohibited from publishing any accounts of the testimony of witnesses. Judge Johnston approved this motion and warned reporters that "further publication of the evidence by the city papers would result in their prosecution for contempt."[59] After Dr. Miller completed the testimony that he had begun on May 10, a second physician, Dr. A.B. Cook, gave additional evidence. Both doctors indicated that all signs pointed to Mrs. Williams having died from a botched abortion rather than some other cause. The defense cross-examined Dr. Cook about a passage from Beck's *Medical Jurisprudence* that stated that "signs after the expulsion of a mole or blasted ovum resembled so closely those of a premature delivery that even physicians might be deceived." Next the colonel's attorney read a second passage from another authority, Taylor's *Medical Jurisprudence*, stating that a "mole" closely resembles an "impregnated ovum or even placenta." But Dr. Cook did not waiver and continued to maintain "that he was confident that what he found in the womb of the deceased was a portion of a veritable placenta, that had not been expelled."[60] It is not surprising that with such salacious information to tell their readers, Louisville newspapers ignored the judge's warning and continued to publish reports regularly.

Testimony followed from witnesses who claimed that they had seen James F. Jaquess at the residence of Rebecca Dockins or walking nearby in the company of Louisa C. Williams. Tirzeh Murphy stated that he visited Mrs. Dockins' boarding house "at the request of Policeman Turner, who thought something wrong and wicked was going on there." Murphy said that he pretended to be interested in buying one of the sewing machines that Mrs. Williams was selling. Nancy and George Morrison, who lived next door to Mrs. Dockins, both testified that they first saw Jaquess in the neighborhood on a Sunday morning (probably September 17).[61] Their testimony certainly did not agree with Jaquess' explanation to Fisk that he stopped in Louisville on Wednesday, June 20, and found a note from Mrs. Williams at his hotel.

The following day several additional witnesses from the neighborhood of Mrs. Dockins' house testified to seeing Jaquess nearby. Jerry Edwards, who identified himself as a watchman at nearby Ferguson's Mill, testified that he saw Jaquess coming out of the schoolhouse privy across the street from Rebecca Dockins' residence on the morning of the day when Jaquess was arrested. Several others also placed Jaquess in that neighborhood, one of them claiming to have seen him there at least two weeks before Mrs. Williams' death. C.H. Bliss, who was in the sewing machine business, addressed the issue of Mrs. Williams' selling these machines to earn income. He stated that Jaquess had come to his place of business five or six weeks before Mrs. Williams died and bought a machine that Bliss sent to a Mrs. Williams in Nashville. He said that he sold "nine machines altogether to Colonel Jacques[s]."[62]

When witnesses for the prosecution had completed their testimony, an attorney for the commonwealth moved that *nolle prosequi* be entered in the case of Hermann Rosengarten (alias Dr. Miller) in order to introduce him as their witness. *Nolle prosequi* is a Latin phrase meaning "we shall no longer prosecute." If approved, this motion would allow Rosengarten to avoid prosecution at this time but would not guarantee that he could not be indicted later. Apparently, the commonwealth attorneys believed that the jury would find Jaquess guilty if Dr. Rosengarten could testify, without fear of prosecution, that the colonel had hired him to perform Mrs. Williams' abortion. The defense objected to the prosecution's request because most of the charges brought by the commonwealth stated that Rosengarten was the principal in the indictment while Jaquess was only an accessory before the fact. The arguments concerning the commonwealth's motion continued the following day. When Judge Johnston at last overruled the prosecution's motion concerning Rosengarten, the commonwealth attorney said that they had no additional witnesses to present and the defense announced that they had no witnesses to call. The judge instructed the jury that the commonwealth had presented insufficient evidence to convict Jaquess and instructed the jury to enter the verdict of "not guilty." Without leaving the jury box, they immediately rendered a verdict of honorable acquittal and Jaquess was released. Motions followed to enter *nolle prosequi* in the cases of Dockins and Rosengarten and both of them were also discharged. But in the words of the *Daily Courier*, "another most foul murder has to go unpunished, although the principal author of it was on trial."[63]

Although the *Louisville Daily Journal* had predicted in October 1865 that Jaquess would have a speedy trial, six months went by before he was found not guilty and released. By that time all the refugees and freedmen had gone elsewhere and Camp Nelson no longer existed. Because of General Fisk's orders to close Camp Nelson as quickly as possible, he had replaced Colonel Jaquess with Brevet General Wallace W. Barrett on the same day that Palmer's telegram confirmed that Jaquess was in jail.[64] A short time later, a civilian named R.E. Farwell succeeded Barrett in this position. Both men held titles suggesting that they were not, like Colonel Jaquess, superintendents of the Lexington Kentucky Sub-District of the Freedmen's Bureau but only superintendents of Camp Nelson. Farwell arrived at Camp Nelson on October 12 and filed his final report with Fisk six months and two days later. At one point Farwell received orders to speed up the process of closing Camp Nelson by making it such an unpleasant place that the refugees would decide to leave on their own.[65] Records indicate that John Ely took over Colonel Jaquess' remaining duties and became chief superintendent and chief sub-assistant of the Lexington office of the Freedmen's Bureau in February 1866.[66] Shortly after the Louisville judge dismissed his father-in-law's case, Henry A. Castle, a practicing lawyer in Quincy,[67] explained the colonel's financial problems in a letter to the editor in the *Quincy Daily Herald*. Castle explained that "the facts are, that by neglect of business, caused by absence in the army, he lost all his property, which had been invested in the college here" in Quincy. Although there were no longer any charges pending against him, Colonel Jaquess was now desperately in need of money "to defray the heavy cost of his trial."[68]

The Reverend James F. Jaquess was certainly not the only, or for that matter the most widely known, 19th century clergyman to end up in criminal court on charges of illegal behavior involving a woman. The most widely known trial was that of the Reverend Henry Ward Beecher, referred to as "the most famous man in America" in a recent biography by Debby Applegate.[69] Beecher was charged with adultery, a crime in New York State in 1875. Although Jaquess could be tried today on the charge of murder, the prosecution would have to prove that it was the colonel himself who had performed the abortion that led to Mrs. Williams' death.

Henry Ward Beecher appeared on August 13, 1874, before a committee from the church where he served as preacher to answer to the charge of adultery.[70] The committee exonerated him and a huge crowd had formed at Plymouth Church on the evening of August 28, 1874, to find out whether the committee had found him guilty or not guilty.[71] There was a criminal trial on the same charge the following year. Elizabeth Tilton's husband was the source of the accusations against Beecher. She wanted to testify at Beecher's trial but because of her "many confessions and retractions" in the past, neither the prosecution nor the defense wanted her to testify since they could not anticipate what she might say under oath.[72] Finally, "after six months of testimony, eight days of debate, and fifty-two ballots, worn down by exhaustion and ill health, the jury finally gave up." Because the jurors were unable to reach a verdict, the case was dismissed and Beecher was never tried on the same charge again.[73] Using information from numerous letters and diary entries of Beecher, Elizabeth Tilton and others, Debby Applegate is able to demonstrate beyond the shadow of a doubt that "the most famous man in America" was also an inveterate philanderer.

There is no known collection of similar materials about the love life of James F. Jaquess. Reaching a conclusion about the colonel's guilt or innocence is more a matter of logic. Judge Johnston ordered the jury to reach the verdict that Jaquess was "not guilty," but this does not indicate that the colonel was not the father of Mrs. Williams' unborn child. There must have been a pressing reason that the colonel wanted to work for the Freedman's Bureau in Tennessee and Kentucky rather than returning to Sarah Jane in Quincy, and it certainly was not "feeding the hungry, clothing the destitute, [and] superintending the education" of former slaves under General Fisk's "care."[74] Also, the letter sent to Fisk by Jacuess after the colonel's arrest offers a confused and unconvincing explanation of his trips back and forth to Louisville.[75] Although there is no way to prove that Jaquess fathered Mrs. Williams' child, the statement of General Palmer from Carlinville that the colonel "was guilty" of "authorship of the woman's trouble" is based on knowing Jaquess and his behavior over a long period of time.[76]

After the colonel's trial in Louisville, several contemporary newspapers printed stories that reflected the politics of the journal more than what had actually happened. When the *Mount Carmel Democrat* commented on the Jaquess trial on May 31, 1866, its name provided a clear indication of its opinion: "The trial of Col. Jaquess showed that the woman in whose death he was implicated was his paramour, that she was the victim of criminal practices and that he was present at her death, holding her in his arms." This article also stated that "superior guilt [was] upon Jaquess as it was he who brought her to the city, he was an associate, provider, advisor and friend, and it was through him that Rosengarten and Mrs. Dockins were involved in the guilty transaction."[77] Yet these statements are in some ways surprising. Jaquess lived in Mount Carmel briefly, taught at the Mount Carmel Academy and buried his first wife in a Mount Carmel cemetery. His half cousin, Isaac N. Jaquess, was a well-respected resident of Mount Carmel but then he was also a successful Republican politician. In contrast, a Danville, Illinois, paper published a piece that expressed an entirely different viewpoint. It was an interview with Lieutenant Colonel James I. Davidson, second in command of the 73rd Illinois Infantry, who was now the Reverend Davidson of Springfield. He had attended the colonel's entire trial and rejoiced at the jury's decision: "Thus endeth the attempt to ruin the prospects of a man of national reputation, whose popularity has ever been greatest where he is best known, who has rendered distinguished services to his country in her perils. and who is an exception among men for his gentlemanly and fine traits of character."[78]

But the strongest proof of the colonel's ability to retain the support of his friends and colleagues even in the worst of circumstances is the position taken by the Illinois Conference of the Methodist Episcopal Church at its annual meeting in the fall of 1866. The Methodists sometimes held trials to examine the behavior of wayward ministers, behavior that included inappropriate sexual behavior, and reprimanded or removed those pastors who had strayed from the path. Their annual reports often listed the names of those whom the church had found wanting. But in the case of the Reverend James F. Jaquess, they passed a resolution of support: "Resolved, That we tender to our beloved brother, Rev. J.F. Jaquess, our heartfelt sympathy with him in the persecution he has endured through the bitter hatred of copperheads and rebels; that we rejoice that he has passed through the fiery ordeal unscathed, with his character triumphantly vindicated; that we welcome him to our midst; and assure him that in his trials and triumph our hearts have been and still are with him."[79]

Although some accounts of the colonel's life mention that he held an important post in the Freedmen's Bureau, they fail to state that he held this position for less than two months and much of this time was spent in Louisville rather than at Camp Butler. In spite of all the bad publicity in Louisville papers that the Quincy papers sometimes reprinted, James F. Jaquess and his reputation survived this episode and he went on relatively unscathed to pursue a new career.

Chapter 8

Carpetbagger in Arkansas and Mississippi

When the police arrested Colonel Jaquess in Louisville on a charge of murder by abortion, he realized that moving back to Quincy, Illinois, was no longer an option. Even if a jury found him not guilty, the sensational trial leading to this decision was bound to tarnish his reputation. He knew that Sarah Jane would not welcome him back since the strict principles of her Christian upbringing would certainly stand in the way of her forgiving him. Jaquess needed to move someplace where the Louisville trial would not appear on the front page of a local newspaper and he could find a way to earn the money needed to cover his legal costs.

When the police court released the colonel on bond in October 1865,[1] he traveled to Helena, Arkansas, where no one was likely to know him or what was taking place in Louisville. He found a job as manager of a cotton plantation located between Helena and the Mississippi River. The success of this plantation depended on money provided by others since Jaquess himself no longer had any funds to invest.[2] The *Louisville Democrat* claimed that Jaquess owned not only this property but also a second plantation across the Mississippi River from Helena.[3] But tax rolls published in the *Helena Clarion* indicate that James Jaquess did not own property of any kind in Philips County, Arkansas. The plantation across the Mississippi River near the town of Tunica was not the colonel's property but belonged to another Jaquess, the colonel's younger brother Dr. George Jaquess.[4] In the fall of 1866, the Reverend Jaquess informed the Illinois Conference of the Methodist Church that he was now living in Helena, Arkansas, and he continued to report this address for the next two years.[5]

Although the Louisville jury had found Jaquess not guilty of murder by abortion, his daughter, Margaret, and her husband felt uncomfortable about remaining in Quincy and moved to St. Paul, Minnesota, shortly after the trial concluded. Henry Castle left behind his law practice specializing in U.S. military claims[6] and his political connections with the Union Party, which had picked him as their candidate for city attorney.[7] St. Paul became the permanent residence of Henry and Margaret Castle except for the years of 1897 to 1904 when they relocated to Washington, D.C., while Henry served as auditor for the U.S. Post Office Department.[8]

After severing her ties with Quincy College, Sarah Jane Jaquess served as secretary of the Freedmen's Relief Society of Quincy, an organization associated with the Methodist Episcopal Church. This group was formed in 1864 and remained active for several years. Part of Sarah Jane's job was writing accounts of the activities of the Freedmen's Relief Society for placement in Quincy newspapers. She reported on February 15, 1865, that about 1500 Negro women and children who depended on the federal government or on the Freedmen's Relief Society resided in Quincy.[9] Many were the wives and children of African Americans serving as soldiers in the U.S. Army, while others were the widows and orphans of black Union soldiers who had died in battle. The treatment of blacks in Quincy, as described by Sarah Jane, was worse than in Kentucky, since Quincy "authorities refuse[d] even to bury the dead of colored paupers."[10] When the Castles left Quincy, Sarah Jane moved with them to St. Paul and continued living there.

William G. Jaquess at age 53. The photograph was taken in Tunica, Mississippi (Minutes of Proceedings of the Twentieth Annual Reunion of Survivors Seventy-Third Regiment of Illinois, October 6, 1906, Abraham Lincoln Presidential Library).

When James and Sarah Jane's son, Willie, returned home from the 73rd Regiment, he enrolled in Quincy College for one more year. The school reopened in 1865 as the property of the Illinois Conference of the Methodist Episcopal Church when it was no longer needed as a military hospital.[11] When his classes recessed in the summer of 1866, William moved from Quincy to Mississippi with the purpose of living there permanently.[12] He chose to live near his father and his uncle George rather than his mother, sister and brother-in-law and was a resident of Tunica County, Mississippi, when he celebrated his seventeenth birthday that October.

Three years later, William bought 64 acres for himself at the "rock bottom" price of $68.65.[13] Eventually, his land holdings grew to 900 acres, of which 300 were under cultivation.[14] The residents of Tunica gave him the honorary title of "Colonel"[15] and elected him to a variety of public offices, including treasurer, sheriff, clerk of the circuit court and chancery court, and superintendent of education.[16] His obituary in the *New York Times* called him "one of Mississippi's most popular 'Southern gentlemen.'"[17] His marriage in 1871 to Mattie A. Nelson, the daughter of Dr. J.C. Nelson, had its material rewards. Deed records show that William and his father-in-law made several land purchases together.[18]

After Mattie's death in 1888, William married Maud Webber, a talented musician who had moved to Tunica from West Virginia. She taught music and was also the composer of waltzes, polkas and mazurkas.[19] The little village of Maud in Tunica County derives its name from her.[20] Drawing on his youthful experience as drummer boy of Company H of the 73rd Illinois, William played his drum in local parades and performed at community events including a patriotic pageant during World War I.[21] Tunica County residents particularly remember William Jaquess for preserving local history in a series of articles published in the *Tunica Times Democrat*.[22]

In *With Fire and Sword: Arkansas, 1861–1874*, Thomas A. DeBlack identifies Colonel Jaquess' new home in Helena, Arkansas, as the town that Union soldiers named "Hell-in Arkansas" because "the health and sanitary conditions were so deplorable and disease so rampant."[23] But managing a plantation near Helena was much easier than it might have been in other parts of Arkansas, especially when the new manager had served as a colonel in the Union army. One duty of the local Freedmen's Bureau agent was negotiating an agreement between the plantation owner, or a plantation manager such as Jaquess, and the former slaves who were now a work force of free persons. As DeBlack points out, unlike many others holding this job the agent in Helena, Henry Sweeney, "so adroitly navigated the complexities of the position that both his black constituents and local whites praised him."[24] One reason that Sweeney did an outstanding job was his previous experience working with blacks as lieutenant and later as captain of U.S. Colored Troops during the Civil War.[25]

Local agents received little or no guidance from Washington about what to include in contracts between the plantation owners and the freed persons who would for the first time receive pay for their labor. Depending on the county, monthly wages in Arkansas varied from $5 to $60 for men and from $5 to $30 for women. Unfortunately, some freed persons toiled all year without receiving any wages, only something to eat. A better arrangement than being paid for their work was sharecropping, a system in which a landowner allowed a tenant to use the land in return for a share of the crop.[26] Sweeney protected the workers in his territory from being cheated by making the requirement that the workers not sell their cotton until he had given them coupons.[27]

The U.S. Congress, in March 1867, passed its own Reconstruction Acts, which placed all Confederate states, except Tennessee, in five military districts. The acts excluded Tennessee because this state had been restored to the Union the previous year. The Fourth Military District, established on March 11, included the states of Arkansas and Mississippi with the central office located in Vicksburg. Major General Edward Otho Cresap Ord served as military commander of this district. Under the provisions of Congressional Reconstruction, local officials elected or appointed during the Confederacy could no longer continue in office.[28]

Although Arkansas had already begun its own plan of reconstruction and elected a postwar legislature, General Ord refused to allow these officials to continue to serve and did not permit the recently elected Arkansas legislature to reconvene. Instead Ord called for a constitutional convention in Arkansas to consider the changes that the U.S. Congress had proscribed and ordered that boards be formed to give the prescribed oath to those wishing to vote and then to register them as voters.[29] For the first time in Arkansas, voter registration included black males as well as white males.

Voter registration continued in Arkansas until September 1867. An election followed in November to establish rules for a constitutional convention and select delegates to attend. As described in Carl H. Moneyhon's *The Impact of the Civil War and Reconstruction on Arkansas: Persistence in the Midst of Ruin*, conservative newspapers opposed this convention, claiming that it was "the first step toward black domination" of the state. They preferred having Arkansas under military rule rather than establishing "a restored civil government run by blacks or carpetbaggers." They tried to prevent blacks from registering by spreading rumors that "registration was actually a Yankee trick to get blacks drafted into the army or to tax them." Conservatives also maintained that the carpetbaggers like James Jaquess had "no real interest in the complete freedom of blacks."

Finally, these white Arkansas natives "resorted to violence against Republican organizers, attacking them and driving them from counties."[30]

Near the end of 1867, James Jaquess informed a Chicago newspaper of his great displeasure with what was happening in Arkansas. The *Quincy Daily Herald* reprinted his comment with a Chicago byline: "Col. Jaquess says no man's life is safe in Arkansas, and is on his way to Washington to represent affairs to government officials."[31] There is no evidence that he presented his concerns to a congressional committee, but it is probable that he talked with his friends Richard Yates and James Harlan, who were both U.S. senators. Arkansas, like other Southern states, was suffering the great turmoil of Congressional Reconstruction.

A convention met between January 7 and February 14, 1868, and proposed a constitution to be presented to the voters. Now Conservatives concentrated their efforts on preventing ratification of this constitution. Their motto was a "WHITE MAN'S government in a WHITE MAN'S COUNTRY."[32] Brevet General Alvan C. Gillem, Ord's successor as commander of the Fourth Military District, reported that the Arkansas constitution had been adopted by a vote of 25,600 in favor to 22,994 against,[33] but both sides had cheated in numerous ways.[34] The newly elected Arkansas general assembly ratified the Fourteenth Amendment and elected U.S. senators to represent their state. President Andrew Johnson, a strong opponent of Congressional Reconstruction, vetoed the Arkansas constitution, but the U.S. House of Representatives overrode his veto. The House then voted Arkansas back into the Union on June 20; the U.S. Senate followed on June 22.[35] Arkansas was now officially one of the United States but the violence in Arkansas did not stop.[36]

James Jaquess' brother George relocated to Helena the same year that the colonel moved across the river to Austin, Mississippi.[37] After graduating in 1848 from the medical school at Transylvania University in Lexington, Kentucky, Dr. George D. Jaquess had practiced medicine in Petersburg, Indiana. During the Civil War, he served as surgeon of the 80th Indiana Volunteer Infantry.[38] His name appears on the Helena tax rolls as owner of a business referred to as "G.D. Jaquess & Co." valued at $6870.[39] Like many 19th-century physicians, George Jaquess was also a pharmacist who made and sold his own medications. As was typical of that time, George Jaquess' residence and business were located in the same building.

Congressional Reconstruction happened more slowly in Mississippi than it had in Arkansas, and the colonel's new residence was in one of the last Mississippi counties to undergo the process. Tunica was one of twelve counties formed from the Chickasaw Cession of 1832. Organized on February 9, 1836, the county called itself Tunica after an Indian tribe named Tunica, meaning "the people." Tunica County is the place Hernando de Soto was when he discovered the Mississippi River. Located in northwest Mississippi in the Yazoo and Mississippi Delta, Tunica's main source of income came from growing and selling cotton. At the time of the Civil War, its population consisted mostly of slaves.[40]

Since Tunica's creation as a county, three different towns have served as its county seat. Originally, the center of government was a town called Commerce, next to the Mississippi River, until a flood destroyed its entire business district.[41] When the board of police (later called the county board of supervisors) received free land from Judge Austin Miller in 1848, they made it the new county seat and gave it his first name. The first courthouse in Austin was a log structure fronting the town square. On June 26, 1863, the Union gunboat *Diana* landed at the Austin wharf and Union troops, under Brigadier General Ellet, burned the downtown and destroyed the courthouse. The board hired contractors to build a new courthouse in its place and moved the Tunica County government into its new home on Christmas Eve in 1866. The board issued a warrant for $29,650 to pay the contractors and then immediately stopped the sheriff from collecting taxes to pay the cost. Fifteen years passed before these contractors finally received payment by suing the board of supervisors of Tunica County. In the 1880s the board moved the courthouse, for the third and, so far, final time, to the town of Tunica. In 1890 the man who had donated property for the Austin courthouse, Judge Austin Miller, sued to get his land back but did not win his case.[42]

Just as Congressional Reconstruction started later and moved more slowly in Mississippi than it had in Arkansas, voter registration followed the same process as it had in Arkansas, with specially appointed boards registering all males who took the required oath of allegiance to the federal government. The purpose of this registration was to create an electorate to vote on calling a state constitutional convention to reestablish civil government and to restore Mississippi to the Union. Three months after Major General Ord took command of the Fourth Military District, all the counties in Mississippi, except three, had completed voter registration. One of the counties still without registered voters was Tunica.[43]

Rumors in Tunica were much the same as those spread by Conservatives in Arkansas. Many blacks would not register because of widespread fear that registering them was a way to ensure that the government could make them pay taxes and force them into military service.[44] There was also another rumor rampant in Tunica County that affected both blacks and plantation owners. This rumor claimed that land was going to be distributed to former slaves at Christmas 1867 so it was unnecessary to sign contracts with planters, since by the next year former slaves would have land of their own.[45]

Before Colonel Jaquess moved across the river to Mississippi, he and his brothers had organized a company of "partners in trade under the firm name and style of Jaquess Brothers" for the purpose of buying land in Tunica County.[46] In addition to "J.F.," there were three other Jaquess brothers in the organization, identified by the initials J.S., T.C. and G.D. Jonathan (J.S.), the oldest of the four, was a merchant in Evansville, Indiana, and, at one time, a partner there with William E. French in the dry goods business.[47] Thomas Coke (T.C.), although identified as a resident of Mississippi in the Index to Deeds, was also from Indiana, where he served in the state legislature from 1867 to 1871.[48] Of course, G.D. referred to Dr. George Jaquess. The "Jaquess Brothers" made their first purchase on January 25, 1869: 1300 acres, including animals and implements, for $28,000, with only half of the acres under cultivation.[49]

As a business venture, the purchase was far from a success. The Jaquess brothers paid $4000 in cash and signed four notes for $6000 each to be paid on January 1 of 1870, 1871, 1872 and 1873. They also had to pay 6 percent interest per annum on the unpaid part of the original price. The Jaquess Brothers paid the first $6000 note on January 1, 1870, and then sold the property twenty-five days later to George B. Peters for $11,920 plus an agreement that he would be responsible for making the three remaining payments of $6000. The Jaquess Brothers made only $480 from their first business venture plus whatever they may have received if they sold the implements, animals and the cotton crop that was in the ground when they bought the property. When the new owner failed to pay the original owner the remaining $18,000, there was another suit filed that eventually ended up in the U.S. Supreme Court. The court ruled that Peters, not the Jaquess brothers, was the party liable for the unpaid amount.[50]

The Jaquess Brothers, now called the Jaquess Company, made a second real estate purchase on February 6, 1869. This time they bought land located in Austin, the town where James Jaquess was residing. This property extended to the Mississippi River and included stone structures. The cost for the land and buildings was $800.[51] Property next to the river was an excellent location for buying and selling cotton and the stone buildings provided a suitable place to handle and store cotton. James Jaquess operated a commercial enterprise at this location "buying and selling and getting gain ... for about eighteen months or two years."[52]

Colonel Jaquess was hoping that he could give up his unsuccessful venture in buying and selling property and earn the money that he badly needed by obtaining a good political appointment after Ulysses S. Grant replaced Andrew Johnson as president on March 4, 1869. After all, Grant was a fellow Republican and a resident of Illinois. Four days after Grant's inauguration, the colonel wrote to his two friends and old stand-bys, Richard Yates and James Harlan, asking them to use their influence to persuade Grant to appoint him to the position of marshal of Mississippi, a federal law enforcement officer.[53] If Yates and Harlan did lobby for Jaquess, President Grant ignored their recommendations and chose instead two other men, one as marshal for the northern district and another as marshal for the southern district of Mississippi.[54]

Jaquess did receive other political appointments in 1869 that may have substituted as his "consolation prize" for not becoming a marshal of Mississippi. As Congressional Reconstruction stated that officials elected or appointed during the Confederacy could not continue in office, there were so many positions to fill by appointment that it became difficult to find enough suitable individuals. For this reason, the Fourth Military District appointed James Jaquess to fill simultaneously two or possibly three county offices in Tunica County. Jaquess became clerk of the probate court on April 24 and also clerk of the circuit court on May 22, 1869. He may also have served as clerk of the chancery court during 1870. All of these offices ended in January 1871, when newly elected officials took over.[55] It is doubtful that the people of Tunica County welcomed a former Union officer as their probate clerk, an influential position at that time,[56] but the colonel found a way to win the acceptance and affection of Tunica citizens. He gave income earned from his appointments to a Confederate soldier who had been disabled in the war.[57] According to attorney and local historian John W. Dulaney, Jr., in his book *Tunica County Scraps of History*, Jaquess was obviously a carpetbagger, but he "eased the pain of reconstruction" in Tunica County and "brought order ... much sooner than in other counties in the state."[58]

When the colonel became probate clerk of Tunica County, he gained the great advantage of having inside knowledge about what property would become available at the small cost of paying the back taxes. The Jaquess Company's next land purchase, on August 18, 1869, was a town lot in Austin on Cole Wales Street for $500. This property was one quarter of a section, or 160 acres. James Jaquess and his brothers may have intended this purchase for development of city lots rather than farmland. The price of about $3.12 per acre was not a bargain but was certainly more reasonable than their initial purchase.[59] The colonel purchased 640 acres on his own on October 6, at the cost only $113.82, or about 18 cents an acre, which certainly was a bargain. On the same day, his brother T.C. Jaquess bought his own 640 acres at the cost of $57.23, or about 9 cents per acre. This sale sounds like a "real steal."[60]

The 1870 census provides information about where members of the James Jaquess family were residing that year. These records indicate that both James Jaquess and his son, William Jaquess, were residents of Tunica County but lived in different locations.[61] James reported assets of $6000 in real property and $5000 in personal property, while William resided in a boardinghouse. Sarah Jane's name appears in St. Paul, Minnesota, where she was still living with Margaret and Henry Castle, but the colonel's name also appears at this address. Since the 1870 census did not take place at the same time in Mississippi and Minnesota, listing the colonel's name in both states suggests that he was visiting in St. Paul when that census taker came by. His annual report to the Illinois Conference of the Methodist Church in 1870 gave his address as Austin, Mississippi.[62]

Realizing that his personal finances were not growing as he had hoped, the colonel decided to approach the federal government about reimbursing him for his personal expenditures as Lincoln's agent during the Civil War. With the support of his friend Senator James Harlan, Colonel Jaquess asked the Military Affairs Committee of the U.S. Senate to reimburse him for trips that he had made for President Lincoln in 1864 and 1865. Although Harlan was not a committee member, he was present for the colonel's testimony and assured his fellow senators that he trusted the word of Jaquess "as implicitly as I would any man." The colonel asked for $6719 to cover his personal expenses for all missions except his visit to Petersburg, Virginia, in 1863, a trip for which Lincoln had already paid him. His request included reimbursement for the visit to Richmond with James Gilmore, three trips to Niagara Falls, the meeting with a Confederate chemist and talks with several politicians after Lincoln's reelection. Although the Military Affairs Committee approved the colonel's request shortly after his appearance in 1870, Jaquess was not paid until 1873.[63]

In addition to his request for $6719, Colonel Jaquess filed a claim with the United States War Department for reimbursement of the $300 that he had spent purchasing horses to replace the two mounts shot from under him during the Battle of Chickamauga. Although he requested a relatively small amount, the War Department still required him to complete numerous government forms. Because the animals that he bought had died in a later battle, he had nothing to show for his $300 purchase. The War Department did not give James Jaquess full reimbursement but, after a long wait, awarded him a small amount for his trouble, a treasury certificate for $100.[64]

Jaquess had still another idea for improving his finances and filed an application with the United States Patent Office for an agricultural implement that he had invented. On January 25, 1871, the patent office sent a letter to James F. Jaquess at an address in Commerce where he had moved from Austin after he had completed his jobs at the Tunica County Courthouse. Commerce is the community that lost its downtown, including the county's first courthouse, to the Mississippi River. Patent No. 111, 125 identifies Jaquess as the inventor of an implement consisting of "a center-draft detached head for harrows and cultivators" intended "to greatly increase the efficiency and usefulness of these implements of husbandry." Jaquess was hoping to increase his bankroll by manufacturing and selling this "IMPROVEMENT IN HARROWS AND CULTIVATOR."[65]

The connection between the Reverend James F. Jaquess and the Methodist Episcopal Church was coming to an end after he had faithfully reported to the Illinois Conference from 1866 through 1870. The church had classified him as "supernumerary," the denomination's term for a minister who "by reason of impaired health" is "temporarily unable to perform effective work." Then, during 1871 and 1872, the Methodists changed the colonel's designation from "supernumerary" to "superannuated" and no longer listed Jaquess' place of residence. "Superannuated" was a classification indicating that "through age, infirmity, or afflictions, [the minister has] become permanently disabled for ministerial labor." Probably the injuries that Jaquess received at Chickamauga prevented his serving as an active Methodist clergyman if his appointment required riding horseback on a circuit of several congregations. In 1873 the Methodist Church listed his residence as St. Paul, Minnesota, and returned him to the classification of "supernumerary." Then, the next year the church reported him as "located" and permanently removed him from the Methodist rolls.[66]

Unlike his son, William, and his brother George, James had no interest in becoming a permanent resident of the South. He had come as a carpetbagger anxious to replenish his coffers after losing money in an effort to save Quincy College and acquiring a large legal bill from his trial in Louisville. He remained in Arkansas and Mississippi while he managed a plantation, filled various positions in Tunica County government until an election could be held and bought and sold cotton at his place of business in Austin. Although he traveled to Washington, D.C., St. Paul and other places, he lived in the South until he relocated in Minnesota in 1873. By then he and his brother Jonathan had already discovered a new money-making venture and introduced it to relatives and friends in Evansville, Indiana. James Jaquess soon became the center of this scheme that was one of the great scandals of the Gilded Age. While pursuing this pot of gold, he made and then lost a fortune and seriously damaged his reputation in the process. After his careers as Methodist minister, college president, Civil War officer, private agent for President Lincoln, and carpetbagger in Arkansas and Mississippi, Jaquess had discovered what looked like an unbeatable road to wealth.

Chapter 9

Townley Fortune in England

"There's millions in it — millions!" is the repeated cry of Colonel Sellers, a memorable character in *The Gilded Age*, the initial attempt at writing fiction by Mark Twain (Samuel Clemens), with Charles Dudley Warner as his co-author. This book, published in 1873, gave a lasting name to the decades between the conclusion of the Civil War and the beginning of the twentieth century. The weak plot was Warner's contribution, while Twain created Colonel Sellers,[1] a character Twain maintained was based on his mother's cousin James Lampton, who expected to get rich quick through a variety of land schemes.[2] Colonel Sellers is Twain's characterization of many Americans during the Gilded Age who believed that a fortune was waiting for them in every scheme they tried.

A well-known English fortune supposedly waiting to be claimed was the Jennens estate on which Charles Dickens based the case of *Jardyce v. Jardyce* in his novel *Bleak House* published in 1853. By 1875 the Jennens fortune had attracted hopefuls from the United States, Australia, the Cape Colony, and India, although the only claims in the courts at that time were either British or American.[3] William Jennens, whose estate in Suffolk was worth over one million British pounds, had died on June 19, 1799, at the age of 97. He had remained a bachelor all his life and had outlived almost all members of his generation.[4] He served a luxurious table and sixteen servants sat down at his table even near the end of his life.[5] The dispute about who was the rightful heir to his wealth did not begin immediately after his death but started in 1810 when three Yorkshire men filed a claim.[6]

By the end of the 1840s, there were 235 agents who had crossed the ocean to file claims for their American clients.[7] Then the question of the rightful heir quieted down for about 30 years until Mrs. Elizabeth Barnett filed her claim for the estate as an American relative of Jennens. Although her claim was quickly ruled out, she stated in 1943 that she would be back in court after World War II was over. After the British court had dismissed claims to the Jennens fortune for 110 years, no British or American claimants have appeared since Mrs. Barnett.[8]

Great Britain was the main location for property and wealth sought by Americans both before and after the Civil War. American claimants had little or no understanding of how the British court system worked, while attorneys on both sides of the ocean behaved like Mr. Vholes, the lawyer in *Bleak House*, and encouraged their clients not to give up but failed to provide them with an opinion of their chances of succeeding.[9] Although there is some likeness between the Jardyce case in *Bleak House* and the cases of Jennens claimants, there is also a definite difference. In the Dickens novel the various Jardyce claims are stuck in court year after year while the Jardyce fortune diminishes until everything is lost because of court costs. As Patrick Polden explains in part 2 of his article "Stranger Than Fiction" in the *Common Law World Review*, the Jardyce claim in the Dickens novel "has the characteristics of an administrative suit, with a fund trapped in court and relentlessly eaten away in costs until entirely consumed." But the Jennens claims involved "no such fund, no ongoing case and the deadly refrain of 'costs in the cause' did not echo down the years."[10]

Over a period of 20 years, the *New York Times* published articles with headlines such as "Lunar Estates" and "Estates in the Moon" to warn Americans against investing in schemes promising riches from unclaimed British estates.[11] These articles advised Americans to avoid the bogus British American Claim Agency and warned them against the Hyde Estate, the Sandys Estate, and the Shreve Estate in England and the Vandersmith Estate in Germany.

A British estate usually had its own story explaining why the family in possession of this estate had to leave England for America. The two Hyde brothers, John and William, came to the United States when they were forced to leave their home because they had read Thomas Paine's *Rights of Man* and promoted its liberal ideas.[12] The story of the Sandys Estate differs in that the Crown supposedly confiscated this property from the rightful owners in 1533 and it remained in the possession of the Crown for 250 years.[13] In all of the accounts, there were supposedly legitimate heirs living in the United States who lacked the funds to pay British attorneys to pursue their claims and needed financial assistance from their fellow Americans.

By the summer of 1871 the Jaquess brothers realized that they would never become rich buying and selling land in Mississippi and looked into a scheme similar to what the *New York Times* had warned its readers against. James and his older brother Jonathan decided to make a trip to New York State to examine the details of the Lawrence-Townley[14] Estate as an investment possibility. The heir to this estate fell in the category of a legitimate descendent living in the United States who was too poor to hire a British attorney and needed others to invest their money to help him prove his right to a fortune in England. When he won his case, the American investors would get back their money with generous interest. The colonel had very likely learned about this money-making opportunity from the New York friends that his daughter, Margaret, mentioned in her letter defending her father after his arrest in Louisville.[15]

The two Jaquess brothers traveled by train to Buffalo, New York, at the invitation of Corydon Karr, attorney for William and Jasiel Lawrence. These brothers were too poor to pursue their claim to the Townley Estate in England unless they had monetary help from others. James and Jonathan carried a genealogical chart, probably created and provided by Karr, showing that the Lawrence brothers were definitely the rightful heirs to the Townley fortune.[16] James and Jonathan considered the bonds being sold to support the Lawrences a relatively inexpensive investment with the promise of paying excellent dividends. The colonel was expecting to receive the $6719 approved the previous year by the Committee on Military Affairs of the United States Senate and thought that the Lawrence-Townley bonds might be a good investment for these funds. After his limited success in making money in the South, James certainly needed whatever money he might be able to make.

A few weeks after the visit of James and Jonathan to Buffalo, attorney Karr came to Indiana to sell bonds to their friends and relatives. The two invited more than twenty potential investors, including their brothers and at least one of their uncles, to a meeting with Karr at Jonathan's office in Evansville. The colonel gave a talk about the Lawrence-Townley bonds and assured his audience that they would certainly make money from these investments. James Jaquess, a charismatic speaker who had enthralled Methodist congregations and persuaded voters to reelect Abraham Lincoln, soon convinced almost everyone present to buy Lawrence-Townley bonds. Since these bonds cost 10 cents on the dollar, the Evansville buyers paid $100 for a $1000 bond that would be paid out when the Lawrence brothers won the Townley fortune in the British courts. Actually, the Evansville buyers paid only 20 percent of the $100 at this meeting and signed notes for the remaining 80 percent of the bond's cost.[17] The colonel collected the money while Karr did the paperwork, and each buyer received a contract signed by Jonathan Jaquess, James Jaquess and Corydon Karr. Jonathan placed all the signed documents in a tin box and put the box in his office safe. No one ever collected the remaining $80 from the men who had bought bonds and their signed notes eventually disappeared.[18]

When Jaquess convinced members of his family and their friends to buy Lawrence-Townley bonds in 1871, he believed the truth of what he was telling them. If there was a "confidence man" involved in this transaction, it was attorney Corydon Karr. The designation "confidence man" had first appeared in an article published in the *New York Herald* on July 8, 1849, and applied to William Thompson, who was arrested for tricking New Yorkers into loaning him their watches, which, of course, were never returned.[19] Then in 1857 Herman Melville published a book entitled *The Confidence-Man: His Masquerade*. It recounted the trip made by passengers down the Mississippi on April Fool's Day and how a confidence man tricked them.[20] It is very doubtful that in the summer of 1871 James Jaquess was a confidence man who deliberately tricked members of his family and their friends. The Jaquess family had always been close to one another, as illustrated by the communal experiment of his father and uncles called the Jaquess Settlement and the business corporation named the Jaquess Brothers that bought Mississippi property. Colonel Jaquess believed that he was telling the truth about the wealth waiting for them in the Lawrence-Townley estate when he presented this investment to Southern Indiana buyers.

But the Lawrence brothers were not the only Americans who claimed that they were the legitimate heirs to the Townley fortune; at least one other group, the Chase family, also believed that they were the rightful Townley heirs.[21] Just as many 21st-century Americans believe that wealth awaits them in state lotteries, gambling casinos and investments that are actually Ponzi schemes, their Gilded Age ancestors expected to become rich through investing in schemes to recover unclaimed fortunes waiting in England. The very names of Lawrence-Townley Estate or Chase-Townley Estate contributed to these popular delusions although American newspapers repeatedly warned that there was no property in England with these names and there certainly was not. Instead there was property called the Townley Estate that was located in the counties of Lancaster, York and Durham in Northern England and included a residence called Townley Hall. The prefix Lawrence or Chase supposedly proved that Americans with these surnames were the true heirs to the Townley property and wealth.

The story of why the American Lawrences were the legitimate heirs to the Townley property and money begins in the 1690s. During this tumultuous time in English history, the Glorious Revolution had removed Catholic King James II from the English throne. Protestant rulers, William of Orange and James' elder daughter, Mary, replaced James on the throne. Because the Protestants were now in power, Mary, the daughter and only heir of Catholic Sir Richard Townley, eloped to America with a son of the Lawrence family. The reason for their elopement was that the Catholic Townleys would not allow Mary to marry a Protestant. Supposedly, when Mary Townley eloped, her right to the fabulous Townley Estate went with her.

But the Townley Estate was not just waiting in England for the arrival of the true heir from America. The Townley descendents who remained in England had long ago claimed the estate as their own and disputed the truth of poor Mary's story. The only way for an American heir to prove rightful ownership of the Townley estate was by presenting evidence in a British court, but such a great undertaking was too expensive for the financial means of one person. For this reason, the American heir had to raise sufficient funds by selling Lawrence-Townley bonds to a large number of investors.[22] When the American heir won the court case, the investors would receive the full amount stated on their Lawrence-Townley bonds.

Of greater interest to American investors, the Lawrence-Townley inheritance was supposed to contain much more than land. Promoters asserted that years of earnings from the estate, worth millions in American dollars, waited in the Bank of England to be claimed. Investing was open to anyone able to purchase relatively inexpensive Lawrence-Townley bonds, which sold for only a few cents on the dollar. Often the cost was not printed on the face of the bond, so the seller was free to quote any price that pleased the buyer. The name of a bank also appeared on some bonds to convince buyers that the certificate was entirely valid because a bank had issued it. Investors trusted promises that they would receive rich rewards when the Lawrence-Townley case was won.

Americans who believed that they were descendents of the Townley-Lawrence marriage sometimes formed associations similar to today's investment clubs. Two well-known groups were the Townley and Lawrence Association of Cincinnati, Ohio, and the Western Townley and Lawrence Association of Dayton, Ohio. These associations sometimes published names of their board members to give the appearance of being legitimate corporations, but the people listed on these boards often had no idea that their names were being used. Associations argued over the legitimacy of their genealogical charts and insisted that their claims were valid while those of other groups were entirely wrong.[23]

The New York Lawrences had claimed heirship to the Townley Estate for at least fifteen years before James Jaquess became involved. Evidence that the Lawrences sold bonds to finance their claims begins with John Austin Lawrence from Troy, New York, who was the eldest son of Lebbius Lawrence, who died in 1818. John Austin sold bonds called "Lawrence Scrip." There is one surviving piece of Lawrence Scrip, dated January 30, 1856, with John Austin Lawrence's signature, in the archives of the New York State Library in Albany. This piece of scrip promises that an investment of $5 will give the bearer $500 "out of first moneys received from the Estate."[24] When John Austin died in 1857, he left one son, Norman Lawrence, who died five years later without any surviving children. A new heir to the Townley millions had to be found.

At this point a war broke out between two Lawrence descendents, William Townley Lawrence, the second son of Lebbius, and Jasiel[25] Lawrence, a nephew of Lebbius, who both claimed to be the rightful heir to the land and money waiting in England. Several bonds of different designs and sizes, in the name of Jasiel Lawrence of Watson, New York, survive from 1869. There are small certificates from the Clark National Bank of Rochester, New York, and a large, fancy one from the First National Bank of Washington, D.C. The large certificate called "one share" was worth $1000 and cost $20. Prices had gone up since John Austin Lawrence had sold bonds at $1 per $100.

Jasiel Lawrence and William T. Lawrence settled the rift between them and began issuing bonds together in 1871. Corydon Karr signed for William, who supposedly was paralyzed, while Jasiel signed the bonds himself. These are the bonds sold at the meeting in Evansville, Indiana.[26] Then in 1875, an anonymous author published a fifty-six page book about Jasiel's claim to the Townley fortune called *The "Lawrence Townley" Estate of England and Heirship of William Townley Lawrence of Troy, N.Y.* The purpose of this book was to prove that Jasiel had cheated his cousin William, who was the only legitimate heir. According to the book, Jasiel had traveled to London in 1868 to put forward his cousin's case and had taken the evidence of William's heirship with him. Instead of helping William, Jasiel used William's papers to support his own claim. Jasiel stated that his uncle Lebbius had no living children at the time of his death and Jasiel himself was now the rightful heir. The existence of Lebbius' son William must have slipped Jasiel's mind during his ocean voyage to England.[27]

Although Jaquess definitely sold bonds in New York and Indiana,[28]

Front of Lawrence-Townley stock certificate (from the collection of Sherry Jones).

he has received blame for bilking citizens in several other states as well. Although the colonel's name never appeared on any Lawrence-Townley bonds issued during the years when he was selling them, there were bonds sold in Beloit, Wisconsin, in 1887 and 1891 that identify "J.F. Jaques [sic] as Attorney for the heirs." The spelling of the colonel's name is incorrect, he was never a practicing attorney and he was in England for much of the time during these years. A seller of bonds in Woodville, New York, in 1893 and 1894 identified himself as an "Agent for James F. Jacquess [sic]." This is another misspelling, and the House of Lords had already settled the Lawrence case in 1890. There was also an enterprise called the "Reconstruction Company of the Lawrence-Townley Estate" established after the turn of the century in Utica, New York. There is no mention of James F. Jaquess as attorney or claimant on bonds sold by this company in 1907 and 1908, but Jaquess had been dead for ten years by then. Because the colonel's name was familiar to potential buyers, other agents used it on bonds they sold. It is evident that Jaquess received blame not only for what he did but also for what others did while using his name.

Genealogy, and Decree of Chancery

It is now certain that Jasiel Lawrence, of Watson, Lewis County, New York, is the SOLE HEIR to the Lawrence-Townley Estate. The Lawrence family in different parts of the country have expended large sums of money in investigating their claims to this estate, but in vain,—all of them having failed to prove their heirship to this immense fortune, as the pure blood of MARY TOWNLEY, through whom the estate is derived, did not flow in their veins.

This Mary Townley was married in England to John Lawrence, the ancestor of the present Jasiel Lawrence. This marriage of John Lawrence and Mary Townley is found in the English Records. They emigrated to this country in 1716. The said John Lawrence, and Mary Townley, his wife, had only one son, named Jonathan, who was the great-grandfather of Jasiel Lawrence, the present heir-at-law of this estate. This Jonathan Lawrence married Hannah Robbins, of Walpole, Massachusetts, in 1738, by whom he had two sons, Jonathan, Jr., and William. Jonathan Lawrence, Jr., was the eldest son, and next heir to the estate, according to the laws of England. He was born in Walpole, Mass., in 1739. He married Rachael Smith, of Easton, Mass., in 1762. This fact is proved by the town records of Easton, and by other official documents in the possession of the present Jasiel Lawrence. This Jonathan Lawrence, Jr., and Rachael, his wife, had two sons. Libbeus and Jasiel. Libbeus was born in Nova Scotia, in 1765, and died in Lansingburg, N. Y., in 1818, leaving one son, John A. Lawrence, who died in Troy, N. Y., June 10th, 1857, leaving one son, Norman J. Lawrence, who died in 1862, without heirs. He was a soldier in the United States Army, and was shot while driving an ambulance. This closed the line of heirship of Libbeus Lawrence. Jasiel Lawrence, Sr., only brother of Libbeus, was born in Easton, Mass., in 1772, and died at Durhamville, Oneida Co., N. Y., in 1842, leaving Jasiel Lawrence, Jr., of Watson, Lewis Co., N. Y., who was born September 20th, 1808, and is the oldest surviving son, and only heir to the estate, according to the law of England.

The Court of Chancery of England, ordered by the House of Commons, Feb. 23d, 1865, decided: That "The Lawrence-Townley Estate remains unsettled, and as yet subject to a claimant," and there is marked on the Chancery books,—"Heirs gone to America." The Court also passed the following decree: That "The Estate belongs to the heirs of Mary Townley, who, having married a Lawrence, settled in America, and her descendants are the legal heirs to the Estate."

Back of Lawrence-Townley stock certificate showing genealogy and decree of chancery (from the collection of Sherry Jones).

After his success in 1871 when he convinced his family and their Evansville friends to buy Lawrence-Townley bonds, Jaquess became the official agent for William Townley Lawrence. There is no indication that he ever represented Jasiel Lawrence, who really had no claim as long as William was alive and had a son to follow in his footsteps. On a bond-selling trip to the East a few years later, Jaquess met an attractive widow named Anna Marie Peregoy Meixsel,[29] who was fifteen years younger than his wife, Sarah Jane. James and Sarah Jane had hardly seen one another since the scandal in Louisville in 1865. She lived in St. Paul while he lived in Arkansas and Mississippi, and when he later located in St. Paul, she joined their son, William, in Mississippi. Anna Marie had been a widow since 1866, and although James was 55 and she was 40, a romantic affair began between them.

When Anna Marie met James Jaquess, she had already lived in poverty for several years. Her late husband, Howard Meixsel, had earned his living as a cigar maker, and when the Civil War began he joined and fought with the Pennsylvania Militia. He received an injury at the Battle of Gettysburg in 1863, and when he died three years later, his military service was given as the cause of his death. After Meixsel's death, Anna Marie did not have enough money to support herself and their three children, and the four Meixsels lived with another woman and her children in Philadelphia.[30] She had so little money for herself and her family that in October 1872, she placed her two sons, thirteen-year-old Caleb and nine-year-old Howard, with the Shaker community in Mount Lebanon, New York,[31] while her daughter, Emma, remained with her. The following year, she tried to obtain a widow's pension based on her husband's war-related death, but the federal government turned her down because Meixsel had served in a state militia regiment, not in a regiment that was part of the United States Army. Anna Marie's sons left the Shakers in 1874 or 1875,[32] a sign that their mother's financial situation was improving because of her blossoming relationship with James.

There is no clear evidence that Anna Marie and James ever married. According to her application for a widow's pension after the colonel's death, their marriage took place on June 27, 1878, in a town called Smithville with a minister named Livingston officiating. Because of her poor handwriting, it is difficult to determine whether the abbreviation for the state is N.C. or N.J. and both states have towns named Smithville.[33] No record of this marriage has appeared and there is no preacher with the surname of Livingston on the Methodist rolls at either location. Ten years earlier, Colonel Jaquess had supported Louisa C. Williams with her sewing machine business; now he was helping Anna Marie Meixsel with her money problems. Whether she was or was not the colonel's wife, James Jaquess became Anna Marie Meixsel's ticket out of poverty. She gave every sign of believing that she had married the colonel and continued to call herself Mrs. Jaquess until her death.

Left: Photograph of Anna Marie Peregoy Meixsel taken in Washington, D.C., after her marriage to James F. Jaquess, which she said took place on June 27, 1878 (gift of Dr. Richard Meixsel). *Right:* Photograph of James F. Jaquess taken at the same location and time as Anna Marie's photograph (gift of Dr. Richard Meixsel).

If James and Anna Marie did marry in 1878, then he should have divorced Sarah Jane sometime earlier, although it was possible then (and sometimes even now) to have two wives residing in different locations. There is no record of this divorce in the court records at the two probable locations, Tunica County, Mississippi, and Ramsey County, Minnesota; but neither county has complete marriage and divorce records.[34] James Jaquess was already estranged from his wife before he met Anna Marie. The affair in Louisville had alienated Sarah Jane, who shared General Palmer's opinion that James Jaquess was not involved in the abortion but was undoubtedly the father of Louisa Williams' baby.[35] As one student at Illinois Conference Female College described her, "Mrs. Jaquess, born and bred a Quaker of Philadelphia, was the incarnation of propriety."[36]

The death in February 1878 of Colonel John Townley, owner of the Townley Estate, motivated Colonel Jaquess to travel to England to find out how he could prove that William T. Lawrence was the rightful Townley heir. John Townley, who had inherited the estate from his older brother Charles only eighteen months before, was the last male heir in the Townley line. Now the House of Lords would have to settle the question of who would receive the estate next.[37] Lord Norreys, the widower of John Townley's oldest daughter, had received his wife's expected share of the estate through her will. He initiated a friendly chancery suit to determine an equitable division of the Townley Estate among all family members.[38] It was now an opportune time for the colonel to travel from America to England. This change of residence also had the advantage of removing James F. Jaquess and Anna Marie from public comments and criticisms. Also, if they had indeed married a short time before, a voyage to England gave them an excellent honeymoon trip.

Jaquess had obtained power of attorney from William Townley Lawrence before he left for England so that he could legally represent the Lawrence interests and handle all the money from American investors. The first funds arrived at the bank in England on December 29, 1879, and from that date until October 18, 1893, when the account was closed, 33,746 BP, plus odd shillings and pennies, from American investors entered this account.[39] The value of this sum was $163,803 in 1879, about $3,538,582 today.[40] The funds were used to pay for any and all personal expenses of James and Anna Marie Jaquess as well as all future legal costs. Once the account was opened, the colonel set about searching for the evidence necessary to prove that W.T. Lawrence should receive the Townley land and fortune. Jaquess made some effort to research William's claim, but the Steward at Townley Hall reported that Jaquess visited him "several times" and "never would tell me what he wanted."[41] Jaquess later claimed that during his early years in England he had hired and then fired a legal firm from the North because they failed to keep his research confidential. But there is no evidence other than the colonel's word to confirm the existence of such an arrangement.

But the years spent in London between 1879 and 1885 were more a vacation abroad than a serious search for evidence. When he wrote early in 1880 to Judge William Thomas in Jacksonville, Jaquess was exuberant about his accomplishments since he arrived in England: "I have reached a point now in the line of progress, when I am assured by as good legal talent as in England in the British Empire, that my cause is a good one, proofs complete and success certain."[42] Periodically, Jaquess left England to report to American investors what progress he had made in finding evidence to support the claim of the American Townleys. In 1881 Anna Marie's sister Emma Peregoy visited her and James, and they all sailed back to New York together in June of the same year. "Mr. and Mrs. Jaquess" also traveled from England to New York together in January of 1883. There were other ocean crossings made by James and Anna Marie, separately or together, that did not appear in the *New York Times*.[43] When the colonel returned to the United States, he reported on any progress that he had made in gathering evidence of William Lawrence's heirship and sold additional bonds to an endless stream of willing investors.

Then two major events made it absolutely necessary for Jaquess to return to the state of New York. William Townley Lawrence, the presumed American heir, died in 1884; with no identifiable Townley heir, the colonel's fund-raising efforts were bound to suffer. Jaquess had to find another Lawrence to fill William's place, and Dow Hager Lawrence proved most willing to take over for his father. Of much greater concern, the House of Lords, after several years of deliberation, finally passed the Lawrence-Townley Act of 1885 determining the rightful heirs of Colonel John Townley. Written by Lord Norreys, this "Private Act" stated that the daughters of Colonel John Townley and his older brother Charles Townley were the true heirs to the Townley Estate. This act divided the inheritance among these seven women and Lord Norreys, who as the widower of one of the women named in the act, became heir to her share of the Townley inheritance.[44] He also became the resident of Townley Hall.

News of this decision soon arrived in America, but like most information about the Townley Estate, newspaper accounts could sometimes be more fantasy than fact. The basic assumption of these reports was that the heirs and heiresses were Americans. The (Oshkosh, Wisconsin) *Daily Northwesterner* announced that children of a Fond du Lac resident were "possible claimants for the fortune" because an act just passed by Parliament required that "all legal heirs" receive "their proper proportion of the money."[45] The Decatur (Illinois) *Republican* made similar assertions about residents of Minneapolis, Winona, St. Paul and Stillwater.[46] The *New York Times* claimed that although the Court of Queens' Bench had awarded the Townley Estate to American heirs, Colonel Jaquess had to bribe two members of the House of Lords to assure that Parliament passed an act "directing the payment of the amounts due into the United States Treasury."[47] Nothing that appeared in American newspapers was accurate except the assertion that Parliament had passed an act, of some sort or other, concerning the Townley Estate.

During the 1880s, while James Jaquess was dividing his time between America and England, two self-proclaimed genealogists, James Usher and Frank Alden Hill, capitalized on America's craze over the Townley Estate by warning their readers not to accept the word of anyone else. These men published two quite different books that claimed to provide the public with the real story. Usher, who published in 1833, informed his readers that "after years of continuous and assiduous labor under the most trying circumstances, I have satisfied myself that there is no fund now in the BANK of ENGLAND, or the COURT of CHANCERY."[48] But Americans ignored his warning that there was not a pot of gold awaiting them at the end of the Lawrence-Townley rainbow.

Then, five years later, the Rand-Avery Company published a book by Frank Alden Hill with a very lengthy title: *The Mystery Solved: Facts Relating to the "Lawrence-Townely," "Chase-Towneley," Marriage and Estate Question, with Genealogical Information Concerning the Families of Townley, Chase, Lawrence, Stephens, Stevens, and Other Families of America.* Unlike Usher's book, *The Mystery Solved* did not tell the public that there was no Townley fortune waiting in England but argued instead that an American, but not the candidate proposed by Jaquess, was the true heir of the estate and its accumulated income.[49] James F. Jaquess and George W. Chase may have "deceived the public" as Usher maintained, but they did so separately, not as a joint effort. No matter how often they were warned, the American public continued to invest in Lawrence-Townley bonds with the expectation that their investments would soon make them rich.

During their stay in London, Anna Marie gradually became more involved in what the colonel was doing with regard to the Lawrence-Townley claim. The bank account established by James F. Jaquess when he arrived in London became a joint account for the colonel and Anna Marie on August 23, 1882. Now each one could withdraw sums from the account. When passage of the Townley Estate Act of 1885 motivated the colonel to travel to America by himself, he left Anna Marie in charge of all Townley affairs in England. The British legal system differs greatly from the American system, and it is doubtful that either James or Anna Marie fully understood its workings. When a solicitor named Howell Thomas approached Mrs. Jaquess about representing the American heir to the Townley Estate, she hired him without checking into his background or reputation. Thomas told Anna Marie that he was familiar with the case because he had previously inquired about the Townley Estate for someone named Lewis. Although Jaquess later stated that he had been admitted to the bar in the United States and kept up to date in legal matters, he maintained that he had never actually practiced law. Whether or not this statement was accurate, only a British barrister could present evidence in a British equity court. Howell Thomas, as a solicitor, worked with the client in gathering evidence and then arranged for a barrister to present the case in court. As soon as she hired Thomas, Anna Marie immediately authorized payment of a check for 100 BP to him and another check for 20 BP to someone named S. Cade, who, according to Thomas, had evidence that would be valuable in winning Dow Lawrence's case. The Townley Estate Act of 1885 had persuaded Jaquess to announce that he had at last, after extensive research, found evidence to prove that a Lawrence was the heir to this estate. Of course, the Lawrence in question was Dow Hager Lawrence. At the colonel's request British solicitor Howell Thomas filed a "Statement of Claim" for Dow Lawrence on July 12, 1886.[50]

Two days later Jaquess signed a will that Thomas had drawn up for him suggesting that the colonel really did believe that the British courts were going to rule in favor of the American claimant. The colonel appointed his "dear wife Anna Marie Jaquess to be the Executor and Trustee" and gave one-half of all his "real and personal" property to her. He directed that the other half of his property be divided equally between his son, William Garretson Jaquess, and his daughter, Margaret Jaquess Castle, the wife of Henry A. Castle. He indicated that Margaret's inheritance was "for her sole and separate use," an advanced idea for 1886.[51] The Colonel may have bought some Lawrence-Townley bonds himself or, more likely, he expected that his American clients would award him a generous fee from the Townley millions. James F. Jaquess anticipated that there would be a rapid court decision in favor of Dow Lawrence. In reality the colonel was actually going to spend a lot of money and time in British courts for the next eight years. Maybe Jaquess would have known better if he had found time to read about the Jardyce case in Charles Dickens' *Bleak House*.

Chapter 10

Trials in London and Time in Pentonville Prison

Colonel Jaquess seemed certain that great wealth awaited him, Anna Marie and the many Americans who had financed his expensive lifestyle for the past fifteen years by buying Lawrence-Townley bonds. Jaquess gave his solicitor,[1] Howell Thomas, a genealogical chart tracing the Townley line from Sir Richard Townley to Dow Hager Lawrence's father, William Townley Lawrence, which he believed provided sufficient evidence that Dow was the true heir-at-law[2] to the Townley fortune. On July 12, 1886, Thomas delivered statements of claim to the High Court of Justice and to the solicitor of the Honorable Montague Charles Francis Bertie, called Lord Norreys, who was the widower of the eldest daughter of John Townley and, as the defendant in this case, represented not only himself but also all the daughters of Charles and John Townley.[3]

When the case came before the court in November, the solicitor for Lord Norreys argued that the claim of Dow Lawrence was "frivolous and vexatious" and "the action" should be "stayed or dismissed."[4] It soon became evident that Dow's claim, which depended entirely on a chart of ancestors, was also irrelevant because the statute of limitations[5] on the Townley Estate had expired many years before. To prevent immediate dismissal of Dow's case, Thomas received permission to amend the original claim. Already Colonel Jaquess was finding the British court system complicated, expensive and definitely frustrating.

There was only one argument that could persuade the court to consider Dow Lawrence's claim in spite of the statute of limitations. Dow had to prove that a Lawrence who preceded him on the genealogical chart did not know about his right to the Townley Estate. The new argument that

Thomas presented was that Dow did not know about his inheritance until a short time previously because his ancestor Lebbius Lawrence had been ignorant of his heirship because of "concealed fraud." Colonel Jaquess claimed that he had found a legal precedent for "concealed fraud" in the case of *Gibbs v. Guild* in J.P. Taylor's *Treatise on the Law of Evidence*. Cited in numerous cases in England and the United States, *Gibbs v. Guild* does discuss the defendant's concealment of fraud from the plaintiff. But the fraud in *Gibbs v. Guild* concerns "fraudulent misrepresentation by a promoter of a company whereby the plaintiff was induced to take shares in the company."[6] Ironically, this explanation of "concealed fraud" is exactly what Frank Alden Hill claimed Jaquess had been perpetrating in the United States for many years.[7]

While Howell Thomas spent nearly two years preparing an amended version of Dow's claim, the colonel remained confident of his future success. Still his usual jovial self, he sent "a cablegram of love and greeting" from London to the alumnae of Illinois Female College at the 1887 commencement.[8] The following year, Howell Thomas filed a new document stating that an Englishman named John Townley had committed fraud by preventing Dow from knowing his right to the Townley fortune. According to this argument, John Townley had failed to inform Dow's ancestor Lebbius Lawrence that his father, Jonathan the younger, had died in England after proving his claim to the estate and taking possession of the Townley inheritance. Instead John Townley had bribed the attorneys of Jonathan the younger, destroyed all evidence and seized the inheritance for himself. Because of these fraudulent actions, John Townley had wrongly possessed the Townley property until his own death and passed it on to his direct descendents. Meanwhile, Lebbius and the other Lawrences who followed him knew nothing of what had taken place.[9] When Dow Hager Lawrence finally learned of his rights to the Townley estate in 1886, he had supposedly instructed James Jaquess to secure a solicitor and instruct him to file his case. Obviously, Howell Thomas did not mention that Dow's ancestors had been selling Lawrence-Townley bonds for at least 30 years—strange behavior for a family that knew nothing about their right to the Townley estate.

The amended case also required inclusion of evidence to explain the claim of "concealed fraud" and why Thomas had not mentioned this essential information when he presented the original claim. His excuse was that Colonel Jaquess had previously concealed the existence of John Townley's fraud even from him, the colonel's own solicitor.[10] Jaquess' explanation for keeping Howell Thomas in the dark was the colonel's unpleasant experience with a law firm that he had hired when he first arrived in England. When he told these solicitors about John Townley's behavior and the probability of "concealed fraud," the firm had disclosed this information "to the persons then in possession of the Towneley Estates."[11] Jaquess never revealed the name of this law firm, possibly because he feared being sued for libel but more likely because such a law firm did not exist.

Mr. Justice Stirling, the judge who reviewed the evidence presented by Thomas and Jaquess, speculated about "whether the whole of the allegations in the Statement of Claims were fictitious or not."[12] He concluded that "an amendment of this kind" turns a claim "in its very nature and character shadowy" into a claim for which "now the utmost evidence which could be brought forward in the case is more shadowy still."[13] After questioning the truth of statements from Thomas and Jaquess, Justice Stirling ruled that the original claim could not be amended. The court dismissed the case on May 18 and ordered the plaintiff,[14] Dow Lawrence, to pay all court costs for both sides of the case.[15] Money to pay these expenses came from the bank account of James and Anna Marie Jaquess, which consisted entirely of money from Americans who had purchased the Lawrence-Townley bonds.

But Jaquess still refused to admit defeat and instructed Howell Thomas to take the case on to the court of appeal, where a panel of three justices heard oral arguments concerning the action in the lower court. All three judges voted to dismiss the case on June 15, 1888. Lord Justice Cotton, who wrote the joint opinion, stated that there was "no reasonable ground for making those allegations of fraud, and the conclusion which I draw is that they were made without any reasonable ground for making them."[16] He added, "The true way of looking at it is this, that this story, improbable as it is, relating a fraud alleged to have been committed in 1816, is made without any solid foundation in fact, and that the Plaintiff, or those acting for him, have no reasonable ground for making those statements."[17] Again the plaintiff, or actually the Americans misled by Jaquess, had to pay all the court costs. There was only one court higher than the court of appeal, the House of Lords. Bringing a case before the House of Lords in Britain was the same as bringing a case before the U.S. Supreme Court in America. Colonel Jaquess forged ahead.

Litigation in the British courts did not prevent Colonel and Mrs. Jaquess from continuing to make numerous trips to America. Now they tended to travel separately rather than together in order to take care of different kinds of business. A one-way trip by ocean liner from London or Liverpool to New York took only a few weeks. They owned a home at

1609 Diamond in Philadelphia, the city where Anna Marie was living when she met James. The occupation given for the colonel in the Philadelphia city directory was "lawyer."[18] But it is Anna Marie's name, rather than the colonel's, that appeared as homeowner in the index of the Philadelphia Deed Book of 1889.[19] James and Anna Marie sold their house in May of that year for $9000, the equivalent of about $200,000 today.[20] Although James and Anna Marie had considered returning to the United States permanently after winning Dow Lawrence's case, they now decided to sell their expensive Philadelphia home. They may have wanted to make London their permanent residence since they already rented or owned a house there[21] or planned to invest the money from sale of their Philadelphia house in other property in America. James and Anna Marie had shared a joint bank account at Brown, Shipley and Company in London since 1882. This bank cabled sums of money, sometimes quite large ones, to Mrs. Jaquess at a bank in Philadelphia.[22] Anna Marie was investing this money in buying and selling land in White County, Georgia, between 1887 and 1894 and she later lived in Clarkesville, Georgia, for several years.[23] When she died in Washington, D.C., in 1928, older Clarkesville residents remembered her name and her contributions to local society. An account of her death in a local newspaper reported: "Mrs. Jaquess and her daughter and granddaughter were very hospitable and did a great deal in forwarding the social life of the town."[24]

Colonel Jaquess made transatlantic voyages as casually as he had traveled by train or on horseback in the United States. An excellent example is his visit to the third reunion of the 73rd Illinois Regiment in 1889 on the anniversary of the regiment's first battle, at Perryville. According to the regimental history, Colonel Jaquess "made the trip of four thousand miles from London direct to Fairmont [Illinois], for the sole purpose of attending this reunion." He "remained in Fairmount twenty-four hours, and started on the return trip of four thousand miles to London, which city he reached in time for an imperative legal engagement on October 24."[25] Making a round-trip from England to America, very likely as a first class passenger, for a twenty-four-hour visit indicates that Colonel Jaquess was spending money without fear of its running out. He was returning to England to prepare for the final appeal of the Dow Lawrence case scheduled to begin in the House of Lords.

Although Jaquess hired two barristers to represent Dow Lawrence's case in the House of Lords, the final result was not what the colonel had promised to the Americans financing the case. Three judges — Lord Herschell, Lord Watson and Lord Macnaghten — heard the case and each one wrote his own opinion. All three lords agreed that the law concerning the statute of limitations required more than proving that there was "concealed fraud." This statute also required "that the fraud could not with reasonable diligence have been known or discovered."[26] They maintained that since Lebbius Lawrence must have known why his father made the trip to England, he "would ordinarily be led to make inquiries for the purpose of ascertaining what property his ancestor had died possessed of."[27] The lords agreed that Lebbius had not shown "reasonable diligence" by checking into what had taken place when his father failed to return home.

All three lords stated their reasons for agreeing with the decision made in the lower courts. Lord Herschell pointed out "when the heir-at-law claims through a pedigree, as Lawrence did, the best evidences of title are the certificates of births, deaths, and marriages."[28] The barristers representing Dow Lawrence had not provided such concrete evidence for the simple reason that there was none. Herschel also claimed that "it is impossible to conceive anything more shadowy or unsatisfactory than that gentleman's [Jaquess'] affidavit," and cited as an example the colonel's weak excuse for not telling Thomas about John Townley's concealment of Lebbius Lawrence's heirship.[29] Lord Watson summed up the court's overall opinion: "I have rarely seen a case in which fullness and candour of statement were more imperatively required than in the present; and I have met with no other case in which both were so studiously withheld."[30]

All three lords ruled unanimously that the decision of the lower courts should be upheld and, for the third and final time, Dow Lawrence's case was dismissed. Again the colonel had to pay the bill for both sides of the case with funds provided by the Americans who had purchased Lawrence-Townley bonds. When the House of Lords made its ruling on Dow Lawrence's claim on April 22, 1890, this case had been in and out of British courts for nearly four years.[31] This decision ended any possibility of retrying the case or appealing it to a higher court.

When the House of Lords ruled against Dow Lawrence because an argument based on "concealed fraud" did not apply to his case, they failed to mention what was certainly the best reason for rejecting his case. But very likely the British lords had no idea of what had been taking place in New York State for more than thirty years. Lebbius Lawrence's son, John Austin Lawrence, had sold Lawrence scrip as early as 1856 and his descendents had been selling Lawrence-Townley bonds ever since. In order to do this, they certainly could not have been victims of "concealed fraud." They may have had some idea that they might be the rightful heirs to Townley lands and riches or, more likely, they found out that selling bonds was an excellent way to make money by fooling others. The four years devoted by Jaquess to presenting Dow Lawrence's case and appealing the results had led to a dead end. The colonel's gravy train had derailed and now he had to decide what to do next.

Shortly after learning that the Lawrence-Townley Estate was lost forever, Jaquess headed back to the United States to present his side of the story to Americans who had purchased bonds from him. He convinced them that Howell Thomas was the real villain and that he should bring a suit against him to recover the money that Thomas had misappropriated. Because the bondholders believed the colonel's version of what happened in the British courts, he had their permission to use the funds remaining in his London bank account to pay for this litigation. And more important to Mr. and Mrs. Jaquess, they could continue to use money from the same account to fund their expensive lifestyle. Jaquess did such a good job of mollifying the investors that more funds continued to arrive from America for three years after the Dow Lawrence case had died forever in the House of Lords.[32]

Jaquess made still another trip to America for the 1890 reunion of the 73rd Illinois Infantry that took place in Springfield from October 8 to 10. The year before he had been able to stay only one day, but this time he was the keynote speaker for the event. His talk focused on the bloody battles of Chickamauga and Missionary Ridge and he claimed that there might have been fewer casualties at Chickamauga if he had been able to tell President Lincoln the vital information he had learned on his trip to the Confederacy in 1863. Although the shadow of fraud from the Lawrence fiasco hung over him, the colonel still remained a hero to the men of the 73rd.[33]

Although the court records of Dow Lawrence's claim from the Queen's Bench to the House of Lords do not prove that Thomas was a crook, they do show that he was not a competent solicitor. It should have been evident to any British lawyer that to win Dow Lawrence's case it was essential to find out whether the statute of limitations on the Townley Estate had expired and to insist that birth, marriage and death certificates be provided to support the colonel's genealogical chart. But then, James Jaquess, who claimed that he was admitted to the bar in America, should also have known these things. The real problem was that legitimate evidence in support of Dow's claim simply did not exist. Now the Colonel's plan was to use the British court system to shift the blame for the failure of Dow's claim from himself to Howell Thomas. The major reason for wanting to recover some of the funds that Jaquess had paid to Thomas was that James and Anna Marie were beginning to run out of money. When Jaquess had closed their joint account in the fall of 1893, it contained only 12 shillings and 7 pence.[34]

With permission from his American investors, Jaquess took his first step early in 1894 toward punishing Howell Thomas for the failure of Dow Lawrence's claim.[35] He hired a solicitor named Rolt[36] and instructed him to initiate an action against Thomas demanding that he account for all costs incurred in preparing cases for Jaquess on the pretense that he needed this information in order to determine proper taxation. The colonel did not realize that Thomas had already ceased being a solicitor two years before.[37] An officer of the chancery court, called a master, whose job was handling cases concerning money matters, ruled against Thomas and ordered him to give Jaquess an account of what the colonel had paid him and how he had spent this money. Thomas challenged the master's decision and his appeal appeared before the Queen's Bench on January 15, 1894.[38] Unlike Colonel and Mrs. Jaquess, Thomas had no money problems and hired three barristers to represent him. One was a Q.C. (Queen's Counsel), an honor bestowed on only a small number of barristers by the Crown.

The argument used by Mr. Willis, Q.C., to defend Thomas was that Jaquess was not a client of Thomas and therefore did not have a right to an accounting of money spent. Willis maintained that the relationship between Thomas and Jaquess was one of champerty, a legal arrangement in which one party finances a lawsuit in exchange for receiving part of the money awarded by the judge. After hearing the case, both Justice Mathew and Justice Collins rejected this argument. But Collins added that he still had grave doubts about Jaquess: "I could not take upon myself to say that Jaquess is fraudulent, but I am not certain that he is clear of fraud, and I should be sorry by my judgment to place any obstruction in the way of persons who may have any right against Jaquess." He added, "It must not be thought that this Court has absolved Jaquess from all suspicion of fraudulently combining with Thomas." The justices dismissed the appeal of Howell Thomas and ordered that all the trial records be sent to the Law Society.[39] But this decision did not end the litigation.

Thomas now appealed the decision at Queen's Bench to the Supreme Court of Judicature, Court of Appeal. These justices reviewed the arrangement between Thomas and Jaquess in great detail and came to the same decision as the previous courts. They ruled that Thomas and Jaquess were indeed solicitor and client and, for this reason, Thomas owed Jaquess an accounting of funds received and spent. They noted that selling bonds as a means of funding litigation was against the law in England although it was an accepted practice in the United States. However, this difference in laws did not affect their decision in favor of Jaquess. They stated that they would have disbarred Thomas if he had still been a member of the British bar.[40]

Once again the colonel did not escape criticism from the justices. They maintained that "there is much in Colonel Jaquess's conduct which, to say the least, looks like misleading his American friends and representing that he was spending much more money than he really was in prosecuting Lawrance's [sic] claim." The justices concluded: "There has been disclosed in this case such a tissue of fraud, uttering false documents, obtaining money under false pretences, conspiracy, perjury, and, perhaps, forgery that we are judicially bound to call the serious attention of the Public Prosecutor to the matter."[41] Sending all the evidence from this case to the public prosecutor led to the trial of Howell Thomas at Old Bailey.

Thomas was charged before Sir John Bridge at Bow Street on April 13, 1894, with obtaining 1,100 BP "by means of false pretenses." When Detective Inspector Froest had arrested him in Brighton the previous day, Thomas responded that he could answer all charges. Later he told the judge at Bow Street that his arrest was "a move on the part of Colonel Jaquess, who has been claiming the Townley estates for 15 years." He added, "It may have been unfortunate for me that I acted as his solicitor for five years."[42]

The trial of Howell Thomas began on June 25, 1894, at London's famous criminal court, Old Bailey. He "was indicted for unlawfully obtaining from James Frazier Jaquess certain valuable securities, with intent to defraud." Howell Thomas again had three barristers to present his defense, including one that was a Q.C. James Jaquess planned to make Howell Thomas the villain of the story and guarantee that he was the one sent to prison for perpetrating a fraud. This trial lasted several days, with Jaquess testifying most of the time. The barristers defending Thomas cross-examined Jaquess numerous times, probably in an effort to confuse him. If this was their intent, the lawyers were certainly successful. The colonel seemed as confused about happenings in his life before coming to London as he was about incidents involving Howell Thomas. For example, he contradicted an affidavit he gave under oath in May of 1888 by now crediting Thomas with thinking up the "concealed evidence" defense.[43] However, it might be argued that facts are generally easier to remember than fabrications. The confused behavior of James Jaquess is the topic of a brief publication entitled "Explanatory" that the anonymous author calls "a personal letter for private circulation" among the colonel's friends. The Minnesota Historical Society in St. Paul has the only extant copy of this document suggesting that the colonel's son-in-law, Henry A. Castle, a St. Paul resident, is very likely the author. This account argues that Colonel Jaquess had become an obsessed old man who no longer had the good judgment to know when to stop and "though visibly unbalanced on this subject, he was otherwise so intelligent that no measures could be taken to restrain him."[44]

Several credible witnesses for the prosecution provided evidence that destroyed the myth of the Townley fortune. For example, Sir A.K. Stephenson, solicitor for the Treasury, stated that there was no record of any action brought by John Lawrence the younger in 1814 that awarded the Townley estate to him and his descendents and that the Treasury held no wealth accumulated by the Townley Estate waiting for any heirs to claim. There was also testimony from George Story, agent and steward of the Townley Estate from 1864 to 1891 and, in 1894 still agent for the part of the estate that belonged to Lord Norreys. He indicated that there had been no legal action concerning the Townley Estate before the litigation brought by Howell Thomas representing Dow Lawrence.[45]

After listening to a week of testimony, the court ruled that Howell Thomas was guilty as charged and sentenced him to five years of penal servitude in the Wormwood Scrubs Prison. Constructed entirely by convict labor, this prison was completed in 1891, only a short time before the court sent Thomas there. Following this verdict, Judge Grantham added that there is "no doubt Colonel Jaquess had conspired with the prisoner to defraud the people in America, and that proceedings ought to be taken against him." Thomas had threatened Jaquess with this possibility in a letter written to the colonel in 1891, the year after the House of Lords had dismissed Dow Lawrence's claim. Jaquess chose to read this letter aloud during the trial of Howell Thomas at Old Bailey. The letter warned Jaquess that if he "went into the [witness] box" he "would not leave it as a prosecution would instantly follow."[46]

Howell Thomas' threat became a reality. Two days after the conviction of Thomas, Detective Sergeant John Nolan of Scotland Yard arrested James F. Jaquess and brought him to the Bow Street Court. The judge charged Jaquess with "conspiring with a solicitor named Howell Thomas to defraud persons in America." Nolan did not have a warrant for the colonel's arrest but had acted on orders from Inspector Frank Froest. The inspector, who had been present at the trial of Thomas and heard the colonel's testimony, wanted to make sure that Jaquess had no chance to slip away. The arrest warrant for Jaquess arrived the day after his arrest. When Jaquess made his first court appearance, the prosecutor asked that the prisoner be held for a week while his case was prepared. Officer Nolan stated that the colonel had 84 BP in his possession at the time of his arrest. The judge retained 50 BP in case this "was a portion of the money" the colonel "had received from America." He allowed the prisoner to retain the remaining 34 BP, the fee paid to Jaquess as a witness against Howell Thomas.[47]

On the day of the colonel's arrest, the *New York Times* announced that "the English lawyer" who represented American heirs to the Lawrence-Townley Estate had "been found guilty of fraud and forgery" and "sentenced to penal servitude for five years." As it had done many times before, the newspaper reminded the buyers of Lawrence-Townley bonds that they "could have saved their money if they had taken advantage of information which has been accessible to any intelligent American citizen during the last ten years."[48]

Howell Thomas had barely arrived at Wormwood Scrubs to begin his sentence when he was brought from prison by two warders and charged with conspiring with James F. Jaquess in deception and fraud.[49] Jaquess and Thomas were both held in custody while the prosecution sought witnesses in America to testify against Jaquess. Because New York residents refused to believe that Jaquess had fleeced them, an ad in the *New York Times* offering a free trip to London to testify brought no results.[50] Eventually, the prosecution found four men from Evansville, Indiana, who had purchased bonds in 1870, and paid the cost of sending all four to England.

Although Anna Marie Jaquess had testified briefly at the Howell Thomas trial, she left for the United States shortly thereafter. She arrived in Washington, D.C., sometime before July 21, when she sent a letter to the U.S. secretary of war on the letterhead of T.C. Dickson and Company, a real estate broker, in Washington, D.C., Anna Marie requested that the military record of Colonel Jaquess be sent to her in care of T.C. Dickson. Her stated reason for needing this record was "for defence [sic] of Colonel Jaquess" because "it has been represented that Colonel Jaquess never was in the Military Service of the United States."[51] There was a reply from the Record and Pension Office of the War Department a few days later indicating that her letter had been posted in the United States, probably in Washington, D.C., The reply included a brief account of Jaquess' military service "for use as evidence in his defense in a case now pending at London, England."[52] The reason that Anna Marie stated for needing this record is questionable. When Jaquess mentioned his military record at the beginning of his testimony at Thomas' trial, no one had questioned the truthfulness of his statement. Also, the newspaper accounts of the Howell

Thomas trial always called him "Colonel" Jaquess. Either Anna Marie was overreacting to the Colonel's arrest or she wanted this information for some other reason. Since she did not know Jaquess until the late 1870s, she had no firsthand knowledge of his military career and may have realized that this file might be of use to her at some future date. There is no evidence that Anna Marie returned to London or that she and James Jaquess ever saw one another again.

Jaquess, with or without Thomas as his associate, had tied up the British court system with a series of spurious cases since 1886. A man of the colonel's intelligence, education and background should have realized that this behavior had made him persona non grata in the British court system long before he ended up as the defendant in a criminal court. There is real doubt that a British court had any jurisdiction in a case involving an American citizen accused of perpetrating the crimes of deception and fraud against other American citizens in America. Justices presiding at the several trials of Howell Thomas had repeatedly called for Jaquess to be tried in England for these crimes while ignoring that the crimes were not against British citizens. It is possible that their dislike of Jaquess reflected a dislike for all Americans because of a conflict brewing between the United States and Great Britain over the boundary line between Venezuela and British Guiana. Although this dispute started as early as 1814, it had become a heated issue when gold was discovered in the disputed area. The two nations were moving toward war with one another and all things American were disliked in England.[53] Because he had not lost his fame in America, it was likely that he would not be tried and convicted in the United States. Not only did the British public prosecutor fail to find New York bond subscribers willing to travel free of charge to testify against Jaquess, but "nearly all the subscribers" stated "in an authentic declaration" that they were "perfectly satisfied, and pray for the release of Colonel Jaquess."[54] It appeared that if the British courts wanted Jaquess to be punished, they had to do it themselves.

When Howell Thomas appeared before Justice Henry Hawkins at Old Bailey on November 26, 1894, he pleaded guilty to the charge of "unlawfully conspiring, by false representations, to obtain large sums of money from persons unknown, with intent to defraud"[55] and was sentenced to twenty months of hard labor to be served concurrently with his previous sentence. He was relocated from Wormwood Scrubs to Pentonville Prison for the remainder of his time in custody.[56]

The court also charged James Frazier Jaquess, who would be 75 in eight days, with the same crime. Barrister Rolland, who was the only attorney defending him, entered a plea of not guilty. There were three barristers (C.F. Gill, Horace Avory and Guy Stephenson) prosecuting the case against Jaquess.[57] To show that Jaquess had tied up valuable court time with a series of frivolous cases, Philip Witham, solicitor for Lord Norreys, reviewed all the litigation brought by Howell Thomas in an effort to claim the Townley Estate for Dow Hagar Lawrence. Witham added that while Thomas was wasting court time, "he knew his client [Jaquess] had no case at all, and he had told him so."[58]

The witness selected to represent Americans who had been defrauded by James Jaquess was William Enoch French from Evansville, Indiana.[59] It seems odd that the prosecution would choose French, who had once been the partner of the colonel's brother Jonathan, as the best of the four Americans to testify, but the prosecution used him simply because they could find no one better than French to offer testimony.[60] The British were angry that an American had tried to use their courts to support his ridiculous scheme while the Americans fooled by Jaquess did not care at all. French testified that he had learned about the Lawrence-Townley bonds in 1871 when he met James and Jonathan Jaquess on a train traveling to Buffalo, New York, and that attorney Corydon Karr and James Jaquess had sold these bonds to him and fifteen or twenty other men from the Evansville area that summer. French explained that the colonel "spoke at length — he was a good talker." Karr did the paperwork, and Jonathan put the bonds in his safe.[61] French said little in his testimony that was damaging to the colonel. No doubt to the consternation of the prosecution, French stated that he "always found Jonathan Jaquess a perfectly honest

Sir Henry Hawkins and Jack, his dog. Hawkins presided over the trial of James F. Jaquess while mourning Jack's death (*The Reminiscences of Sir Henry Hawkins, Baron Brampton*, vol. 1, 1904).

and straightforward man, none better" and that James Frazier Jaquess had "fought for his country in the American War, and with credit too." French showed some bonds still in his possession and pointed out that "none of these bonds are signed by Colonel Jaquess or Jonathan Jaquess" but by Karr and "Jaziel Lawrance, and William F. Lawrance by power of attorney."[62] The colonel's attorney objected to French's testimony two different times in the course of the trial on the grounds that "the evidence of this witness" pertains "to matters occurring some fifteen years before ... any act of conspiracy alleged in the indictment." In spite of this seemingly legitimate objection, "Justice Hawkins ruled that the evidence was admissible."[63]

Although the trial of Howell Thomas had dragged on for many days, the colonel's trial lasted only five days. One piece of evidence not presented at earlier trials was a detailed account from the chief bookkeeper at Brown, Shipley and Company revealing how much money Americans had lost by purchasing Lawrence-Townley bonds.[64] The trial concluded with a public reading of the evidence given by Jaquess at the trial of Howell Thomas and some of the correspondence between Jaquess and Thomas.[65]

British justices have much greater leeway in expressing their opinions to a jury than that allowed to judges in the United States. They can comment on testimony and instruct the jury about what would be an appropriate verdict. With some assistance from Mr. Justice Hawkins, the jury discussed the case briefly and returned the verdict that Jaquess was guilty as charged. Hawkins sentenced Jaquess to 20 months of hard labor[66] and sent him to Pentonville Prison.[67]

James Jaquess had the bad luck of appearing before Mr. Justice Hawkins when the justice was certainly not in the best frame of mind. As Justice Hawkins recounted in *The Reminiscences of Sir Henry Hawkins, Baron Brampton*, earlier that year "some miscreant poisoned" his beloved dog Jack who "was taken very ill with symptoms of strychnine, and died in a few hours." Jack had slept in Sir Henry Hawkins' bedroom, traveled with him on the judicial circuit, and occasionally shared the bench with him. Hawkins wrote: "There is no abatement of my love for him, [or] hardly any of my sorrow."[68]

Following the jury's verdict, Justice Hawkins stated to everyone present that Jaquess "had been guilty of as vile a conspiracy as it was possible to imagine." When the colonel's attorney pointed out that "Jaquess was now penniless," Justice Hawkins replied, "If that were not so, and he had any of his ill-gotten gains left ... should certainly have imposed a heavy fine upon him."[69]

The Old Bailey Courthouse, London's central criminal court, 1673–1913 (© istock photo.com/Anthony Bagget).

James F. Jaquess had been a vigorous man of 51 when he first introduced investors to Lawrence-Townley bonds in his brother Jonathan's office in Evansville. Now the colonel had just turned 75, he was broke, and Anna Marie had left him. This sentence of hard labor did not mean that prisoners at Pentonville worked in chain gangs breaking up rocks as would have been the case in the United States. The hard labor of Pentonville prisoners involved such work as picking tarred rope or weaving at a loom in the confinement of their cells. Although Howell Thomas was also a prisoner at Pentonville, Jaquess would never have seen him, since prisoners were prevented from all personal contact. Pentonville Prison is famous for its system of solitary confinement, which included every prisoner and resulted in numerous cases of insanity and frequent suicide.[70]

Pentonville Prison was referred to as a "model prison" when it opened in 1842. It held 520 prisoners who were housed in one-man cells measuring 13 feet by 7 feet. The overall plan was circular so that a guard could observe all the cells on one level from a central location. Jeremy Bentham had proposed this design as a way to prevent prisoners from seeing or communicating with one another. Even when the convicts attended chapel every morning, they occupied chairs with high wooden sides so that they could not see each other. To ensure that there was total isolation at all times, Pentonville prisoners had to wear hoods whenever they left their cells. Originally, each cell had the modern conveniences of a water closet and a sink. Also, the cells were well ventilated and had small windows on the rear wall to provide light. But Pentonville had changed for the worse by the end of 1894 when Jaquess began his twenty-month sentence.[71]

Although the "separate system" guaranteed that they would never see each other, James F. Jaquess and Oscar Wilde served overlapping prison terms at Pentonville. The prison conditions that Wilde's biographer describes were the same ones that the colonel endured. Before being admitted to Pentonville, the convicted man had to relinquish all of his possessions, including every piece of clothing except his shirt. Then an officer carefully examined the prisoner and wrote a minute description of the man including color of eyes, hair and complexion and any distinguishing marks. Next the prisoner had to take a bath before dressing in full prison garb including loose shoes and a cap with a large bill.[72]

When the convict arrived at Pentonville, he received a thorough medical examination to determine whether he was fit enough to survive the first month's regime, which included exercising on a treadmill for six hours each day. He had to sleep on a bare board a few inches above the floor; it had sheets, a coverlet and two rugs but it did not have a mattress. Because

10. Trials in London and Time in Pentonville Prison

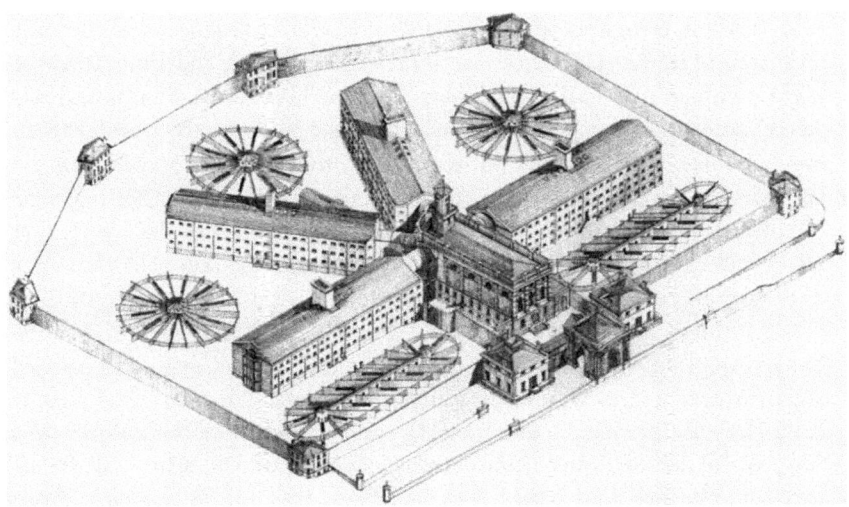

Drawing of Pentonville Prison, 1844. James F. Jaquess spent 11 months of his 20-month sentence here (http://boiteaoutils.blogspot.com/2010/04/forms-of-constraints-by-norman-johnston.html).

prisoners had learned to communicate with each other by banging on the water pipes, the overseers of the prison had long since removed the water closets, sinks and plumbing from the cells. Wilde, and very likely Jaquess, had to make do with a can that a warder emptied once a day. Breakfast was always cocoa and bread served at 7:30 A.M. The main meal was at noon. Depending on the day of the week, this meal included potatoes and bacon and beans, or potatoes and soup, or potatoes and cold Australian meat, or potatoes and brown suet pudding. The final meal of the day was tea at 5:30 P.M. Prisoners received each meal through a small door that a warder opened from the outside.[73]

After the first month the prisoner was able to exercise by walking outside. The convicts formed an Indian-style line. They were far enough apart not to communicate and so did not have to wear hoods. As had been the practice for more than fifty years, they worked in their cells at a trade such as tailoring, weaving or picking oakum. After three months of acceptable behavior, the convict might write and receive one letter and be visited for twenty minutes, but during the visit there was a metal screen between the prisoner and the visitor that prevented their seeing each other. Such visits could take place every three months thereafter. Oscar Wilde, who was forty years old, suffered greatly under this regime. Colonel Jaquess, who was nearly twice Wilde's age, could not have fared much better.[74]

Written as an apologia, "Explanatory" claims that Jaquess "became so absorbed in the [Lawrence] case and so enthusiastic in its pursuit, that it grew into an infatuation with him." When "his nearest friends and relatives" told him their "doubt of final success," he chose to consider them his "enemies." He was, the author claims, mentally unbalanced on the subject of securing the Townley fortune but normal in all other respects. "Explanatory" also gives a reasonably accurate account of the events that led to the colonel's imprisonment and interprets the colonel's character as that of an honorable man who was duped.[75]

Although Jaquess himself claimed that he had been admitted to the bar in America, "Explanatory" states that the colonel was "ignorant of legal procedures" as well as "infatuated and over trustful." The author calls Howell Thomas "a great rascal" and claims that the colonel was "duped and deluded" and "infatuated to the point of dementia." "Explanatory" maintained that James Frazier Jaquess was an old man unable to accept that he has wasted more than twenty years of his life pursuing something that did not exist, "but a swindler, never!"[76]

Immediately after his imprisonment, the colonel's friends, both in England and in America, began working to gain his release. They believed that he was innocent of the charge against him and the victim of an unscrupulous solicitor. Members of the American colony in London sent a petition to the Home Secretary asking that Jaquess be freed. They argued that a man of the colonel's advanced years would not survive imprisonment in Pentonville. The United States legation finally succeeded in winning his early release, but not until he had served about eleven months of his twenty-month sentence.[77] A free man once more, Colonel Jaquess had to try to create a new life for himself back in the United States.

Chapter 11

Return to America for His Last Years

James Jaquess returned from England to the United States shortly after his release from Pentonville Prison early in November 1895.[1] Thanks to the lobbying of his American friends, he had served only about 11 months of his 20-month sentence. Money was still his chief concern and he had neither the financial resources nor the good health to live alone after nearly a year in a Pentonville Prison cell. He knew that he would not be welcome in his son's home in Mississippi since Sarah Jane was already living there. Instead he decided to make St. Paul his home and moved in with his daughter, Margaret, and her husband, Henry Castle. His son-in-law insisted that the colonel apply for a veteran's pension as soon as possible to help pay for his living expenses.[2]

Following Castle's advice, Jaquess filled out an application for a Civil War pension at the office of the adjutant general of Minnesota on December 12, 1895, listing "old age, rupture and general debility" as reasons why he could not support himself. At the same time, Jaquess filed an application for an "Original Invalid Pension," which would provide a much more lucrative stipend. He based his claim for this disability pension on an injury that he had received at the Battle of Chickamauga more than thirty years ago. Shortly after he applied, the United States government awarded Jaquess a Civil War pension of $12 a month, stating the reason as senile debility, a 19th-century term for a physical or mental disability related to old age.[3] The more lucrative invalid pension required much additional information including physical examinations and supporting affidavits.

The myth that the Reverend James Jaquess converted Abraham Lincoln to Christianity was born shortly after the colonel became a resident of St. Paul. In 1896 his younger brother William moved to Minneapolis and rented one-half of a "double house" owned by the Hennepin Avenue Methodist Episcopal Church. The Reverend Edward L. Watson, who had recently come there from a congregation in Maryland, lived in the other half of the duplex, which served as the church's parsonage. Watson met James Jaquess when he visited his brother and heard from the colonel the story of his conversion of Lincoln when he had served the Methodist Episcopal Church in Springfield, Illinois.[4]

Watson published an article about this encounter in the *Methodist Christian Advocate* of November 11, 1909, one of many publications that appeared during that year in honor of the 100th anniversary of Lincoln's birth. There are several obvious mistakes in Watson's article; he misspells the colonel's last name as "Jacquess," he places the conversion in 1839 when Jaquess was 20 and still living on his father's farm, and he claims that the colonel was 80 or more years old when he met Lincoln. Jaquess would tell a different version of the same story at the 11th annual reunion of the 73rd Regiment in the fall of 1897, and Watson also includes this account of the conversion in his article.[5]

Sarah Jane Jaquess, the colonel's second wife, died on June 16, 1896, at almost 78 years of age. She and James had married more than 40 years earlier but had been divorced, or at least separated, for nearly half of that time. She was not buried in Mississippi near the home of their son William and his family, but in Maple Hill Cemetery in Helena, Arkansas. Her grave is in the family plot of Dr. George Jaquess, the younger brother of James, and the tombstone identifies her as "Sarah J. wife of J.F."[6] A logical explanation for burying her in Helena rather than in Mississippi is that she died while visiting there. Embalming of the dead was not widely practiced in rural areas of the United States until the beginning of the twentieth century. Although James would have been hard pressed to travel south in time for her funeral, he certainly knew about her death. Within a few months, the colonel moved from Minnesota to their son's house in Tunica, Mississippi. Now that Sarah Jane was no longer alive, Jaquess could visit William and old friends in the town where the he had lived for a few years after the Civil War without having to answer too many embarrassing questions.

Although "senile debility" prevented Jaquess from working for a living, it certainly did not keep him from taking long trips. The colonel traveled from Mississippi to Jacksonville, Illinois, to attend the semicentennial of the college where he had served as the first president. This event, held on the first two days of June, recognized the fiftieth anniversary of the school's receiving its charter in 1847. Three of the school's past presidents attended this celebration, but Jaquess was clearly the main attraction. He had kept in contact with Jacksonville friends and alumnae from his years at the college, even during his residence in London, and received a grand welcome on his return. Jaquess gave the address on Alumnae Day, was the guest of honor at a gathering in the home of an alumna, and encouraged the graduates that he remembered from his years as president to correspond with him.[7]

The subject of the colonel's address was women and their many important contributions to society, a talk that clearly demonstrated that his mind was still sharp and full of biblical and historical knowledge.[8] At the 50th anniversary of the college he still knew how to jolly "his girls," now ladies well past the age of 60. When questioned about what had happened to his black hair, he laughingly replied, "You go and attempt to control many hundred female tongues for fifteen years and your black head in all probability will give place to one that is white."[9] The time that Jaquess spent at the college's semicentennial celebration was the high point of the final months of his life. If the people of Jacksonville knew that Jaquess had served time in prison for defrauding American citizens, they certainly chose to ignore it.

Samuel W. Nichols, editor of the *Jacksonville Daily Journal*, wrote a sketch about Jaquess that appeared in the *Chicago Times-Herald* a few days after the colonel's highly successful visit at Illinois Female College. Jacksonville remembers Nichols as a local philanthropist nicknamed "Uncle Sammy" with a special interest in the welfare and education of children from poor families. Nichols established a fund, still existing today, to provide Christmas candy to poor school children and their younger brothers and sisters and personally financed many college educations. Important to the entire community was his gift of land and funds to establish a large park named for him southeast of the city.[10]

Nichols writes his brief biography of the colonel in the romanticized style of that day and creates a picture of Jaquess in the mold of the national martyr, Abraham Lincoln: "Jaquess was a barefooted boy in the very early days of this century. His parents dug a sparse living from the rocks and clods of Posey county. They could afford no luxury for the lad, and he shared in their struggle — killing prey for the table with his rifle and hewing wood for the market with his ax."[11] Although this account is full of factual errors, it pictures the James F. Jaquess that a great many people still firmly believed in: the man that Lincoln chose as his emissary to meet with Jefferson Davis had to be as fine a man as the president who sent him.

Jaquess made another long trip in September of that year, this time from Mississippi to Springfield, Illinois, to attend the eleventh annual reunion of the 73rd Illinois Infantry. He had last attended a regimental reunion in 1890 when he journeyed to Springfield from London to give the main address for the event. He was also the principal speaker at the 1897 gathering, but this was not his chief reason for being there. He had come to seek a vote of confidence from the regiment in support of his application for a disability pension.[12] Jaquess had kept this injury unknown to his regiment, and although the officers and men of the 73rd did pass a resolution, it mainly expressed their faith in the colonel's integrity.

The minutes of the 1897 reunion of his regiment contain the colonel's story of converting Abraham Lincoln that Watson would reprint in his 1909 article. Jaquess told this story during the part of the reunion devoted to reminiscences, a time usually restricted to memories of events from Civil War battles. Claiming that the mention of Lincoln's name had reminded him of a memorable incident, Jaquess talked about Lincoln coming to his congregation in Springfield on a Sunday morning in May and later visiting the Jaquess parsonage to discuss what he heard. The colonel concluded his tale with this assertion: "I have seen hundreds brought to Christ, and if ever a person was converted, Abraham Lincoln was converted that night in my house." The regimental publication includes no comments or questions about this account from veterans of the 73rd and the gathering moved on to an entirely different subject.[13]

Although Jaquess gave no date in his account of Lincoln's conversion, such an event had to have happened during the only year when he served the Methodist congregation in Springfield, November 1847 to October 1848. But May, the month given by Jaquess for this event, is not possible. Lincoln was absent from Springfield between October 28, 1847, and October 10, 1848, first visiting his wife's family and then serving in the U.S. Congress.[14] Because Lincoln was absent from Springfield for almost an entire year, he could not have heard James Jaquess preach on any Sunday in May 1848, the only May when Jaquess served the Springfield Methodist Church.

Whether Abraham Lincoln held Christian beliefs became a topic of interest, especially among ordained Protestant ministers, early in the 20th century, the time of the birth of fundamentalism. Although Lincoln often quoted the Bible and mentioned God in public and private statements, doubts about Lincoln's faith remained because he had never been converted or joined any church. Besides the Reverend Watson's article, biographies by Ervin Chapman and William E. Barton also address the issue of Lincoln's spiritual life. In *Latest Light on Lincoln* Chapman includes Jaquess among several preachers who influenced Lincoln and claims that "Dr. Jaquess' great courage and manifest sincerity won Mr. Lincoln's high esteem."[15] Chapman's two-volume work also includes a chapter entitled "The Jaquess-Gilmore Mission," which relies heavily on *Personal Recollection of Abraham Lincoln and the Civil War* by James R. Gilmore.[16] *The Soul of Abraham Lincoln,* written by William E. Barton, reprints Watson's article from the *Christian Advocate.* Although he admits that the colonel's story "must have had some element of truth," he states that "the present writer cannot say that he is convinced by the story."[17] Even as recently as the 1960s, Glenn I. Tucker, a successful author of popular history, proposed writing a Christmas book based around the conversion of Lincoln by James Jaquess,[18] but his publisher wisely ignored the idea.

Although it is obvious that the Reverend James F. Jaquess did not convert Abraham Lincoln, the question of why he told this story remains unanswered. It is interesting that Jaquess told this story two different times during the short period between his arrival from London and his death — first at his brother's home and then at his regiment's annual reunion. There is no indication that he ever mentioned this event at any other time in his life. The colonel, now a feeble and destitute man of 78, is reliving his life, not necessarily as it really happened but as he wishes it had taken place. Jaquess is reviewing and mentally rewriting his life, a process that gerontologists and geriatricians refer to as "life review."[19]

At the semicentennial in 1897 James Jaquess had become reacquainted with students he had known during his years in Jacksonville and began corresponding with some of them. He also became interested in the future of the school, soon to be renamed Illinois Woman's College, where he had begun his academic career in 1848. He wrote a letter from Clayton, Mississippi, on January 28, 1898, expressing his support of the college's hope of raising a half a million dollars and encouraging the alumnae "to help on with the great work before the Illinois Female College."[20] Jaquess certainly did not have any money of his own to contribute to this cause, but his support of the fund-raising plans of President Joseph R. Harker (1893– 1925) may have encouraged some of his former students to provide funds for Music Hall and Harker Hall, both erected in the subsequent ten years.

The disability claim filed by Jaquess shortly after his return from London rested on an injury that he had received at the Battle of Chickamauga on September 20, 1863. Although the colonel continued to receive the small Civil War pension of $12 a month, there had been no decision concerning a disability pension that would be much more lucrative. When it became evident that nothing was happening with regard to his claim, the colonel and his son journeyed from Mississippi to Memphis and simply appeared without an appointment at the office of the special examiner in April 1898. They claimed that they just happened to be in Memphis and decided to drop in. Since he could handle the colonel's "case at that time without prejudice to other cases," the special examiner allowed Jaquess to complete a detailed deposition.[21]

The colonel stated that during "a very disastrous charge" the enemy shot two horses from under him in a period of about five minutes. The first incident caused him to fall on the horn of his Mexican saddle and receive a double inguinal hernia. The fall of the second horse was "not so sudden" and "in the excitement [he] hardly realize[d] the extent or nature" of his injury. The reason the colonel gives for waiting 35 years before applying is "an inherited prejudice against personally drawing a pension." As he explains, "Both my grandfathers were Revolutionary soldiers and my father was a soldier in the war of 1812 and they never would and never did apply for a pension." Because of this family tradition, he had chosen not to apply for assistance until he was convinced that he was no longer able to earn a living.[22]

William Jaquess also filed a deposition in support of his father's claim. He stated that his father had told him of his injury at Chickamauga when they met in Chattanooga the month following the battle. William, 49 years old, identified himself as a merchant and planter from Clayton, Mississippi; he had been 13 when he was taken prisoner at Chickamauga. The special examiner then sent his recommendation to the commissioner of pensions on April 30, 1898, along with the depositions of the colonel and William and the resolution passed by the 73rd Illinois Infantry. He referred to the colonel as "a man of highest standing" and someone whose "word may be fully relied upon." The special examiner also stated that "full credit should be given" to William's testimony.[23]

The declarations of the colonel, William and the survivors of the 73rd were not sufficient, and the colonel's application ran aground for lack of supporting testimony. There was only one physician still living, Dr. George Pond of Adams County Illinois, surgeon of the 73rd Illinois, who was an "eyewitness to the incurrence of and nature of [Jaquess'] injury." The examiner recommended that, if this doctor "remembers the facts," the colonel's claim should definitely be approved. Although several members of the 73rd submitted depositions, they could only testify that two horses had been shot from under the colonel at Chickamauga. But they knew nothing about whether Jaquess had received a double inguinal hernia as a result. Jaquess also stated that he had mostly treated himself and sought little medical attention until 1865 when he got a suitable truss from his brother Dr. George D. Jaquess, but George had died in Helena two years earlier. The physician who examined Jaquess in connection with his pension application reported that the colonel certainly had a double inguinal hernia, but this doctor had no way of determining what had caused this condition or when it had taken place. The colonel's application remained in limbo.[24]

When the colonel visited the special examiner in Memphis, he also completed a deposition guaranteeing that Anna Marie Jaquess would never receive a widow's pension. The federal government began awarding pensions to indigent widows after 1890 and required that all soldiers receiving pensions complete a statement referred to as the "Marriage Circular." At this time a soldier's declaration about his marriage(s) was the only reliable means that the Pension Bureau had of verifying a widow's claim and preventing pension fraud. In his deposition Jaquess stated: "I have been twice married and only twice — both wives are dead and I have not since remarried." He identified his two wives as Mary Sciple and Sarah Jane Steel. The tone of "twice married and only twice" in the colonel's sworn statement suggests that he is trying to get even with Anna Marie for deserting him. As he had rewritten his life to include the conversion of Abraham Lincoln, James Jaquess was apparently changing the story of his life one more time to wipe out what he now considered his serious mistake of marrying Anna Marie or pretending that she was legally his wife.[25]

James and William Jaquess returned to Mississippi to wait for word from the federal government, but James Jaquess did not live long enough for a decision to be made. After a short rest, the colonel decided to travel to St. Paul by himself early in June in order to visit the Castle family while his son-in-law, now auditor for the Post Office Department in the Treasury Department, was in Washington, D.C., on business. The colonel probably thought that Henry Castle's absence provided a good opportunity to devote time exclusively to his daughter and grandchildren. He had been at his daughter's home for about a week when he died on June 17, 1898. Henry A. Castle was able to return to St. Paul in time for his father-in-law's funeral. The colonel was interred in Oakland Cemetery, a nonsectarian burial ground founded in 1853.[26]

Obituary notices appeared in several newspapers, but none of these accounts included the cause of the colonel's death. Neither was there more than a passing reference to the colonel's once famous trip with James Gilmore to meet with Jefferson Davis in Richmond. Neither the *St. Paul*

Globe nor the *St. Paul Pioneer Press* seemed to know much about James F. Jaquess other than that he was Captain Castle's father-in-law. The *St. Paul Globe* did mention that Jaquess was a member of "the famous peace commission appointed by President Lincoln" but stated that this "commission" had "three members" instead of the actual number of two.[27] A brief account of the colonel's death appeared in the *New York Times* on June 19,[28] and there was also a brief obituary of "Col. James F. Jaques [sic] of Quincy, Illinois," in the *Quincy Daily Journal* on the same day. It mentions "his son-in-law, Capt. Henry A. Castle of this city" as well as the colonel's commanding the 73rd and his appointment by Lincoln "to settle the differences between the North and South."[29]

A longer obituary appeared in the *Weekly Illinois Courier*, a Jacksonville newspaper, on June 22. The headline calls him "Col. Jacquess [sic]," while the article refers to him as "Col. James F. Jacques." He may have received more attention in Jacksonville because he had visited the community as recently as a year earlier. There are some factual errors such as placing St. Paul in Michigan and the colonel's birth in 1820. However, the article points out that Jaquess "was a friend of Lincoln and Yates and other prominent men of the anti-slavery party and was also one of the pioneers of Methodism and an intimate friend of Peter Cartwright."[30] In Jacksonville and especially at Illinois Female College, Jaquess was well known and still well loved. The account of his death in the college *Greetings* says this of Jaquess: "He had a notable war record, serving with 'distinction as colonel of Seventy-third Illinois Infantry, known as the 'Preachers Regiment.' The College will honor his memory, and counts his labors and influence and example one of its richest possessions."[31]

Because newspapers of that day did not consider obituaries the proper place to attack the good name and reputation of the deceased, none of these obituaries mentions that the colonel was found guilty of fraud and sentenced to prison in England. Jaquess' connection to the Lawrence-Townley Estate was certainly well known in the East where he sold bonds as a representative of the Lawrence family. Although people in Midwestern towns like Quincy had heard about the Lawrence-Townley fortune and read that four men from Evansville were going to London to testify against James Jaquess, none of this information had anything to do with them. Residents of Quincy had not bought Lawrence-Townley bonds nor did they know anyone who had purchased them. Besides, the Jaquess family had moved away from Illinois more than 30 years earlier, and Henry A. Castle, a Quincy boy who had made good, was the colonel's son-in-law.

One thing certain about James Jaquess is that he was no longer the wealthy man that he had expected to be but was a pauper who had no money to pay for his own funeral when he died. Using his knowledge of how the pension system worked, Castle sent a letter about this situation to the United States pension agent in Milwaukee shortly after the colonel's death. He explained that Jaquess "left no property" and, as his son-in-law, Castle was "responsible for the funeral expenses." He inquired whether "any pension money due for the fractional quarter can be collected and applied for that purpose."[32] It is unclear whether the government helped pay for the colonel's funeral or his son-in-law was stuck with the full bill.

Margaret Jaquess Castle, the daughter of James Jaquess and his first wife, Mary Sciple, died at her home in St. Paul on November 18, 1908, at the age of 65. She was the mother of 3 sons and 4 daughters and "enjoyed the distinction of being the daughter, the sister, the wife and the mother of a soldier." She was known for her work in "religious, patriotic and charitable" activities.[33]

Her husband, Henry Anson Castle, died a few days before his 75th birthday after a successful career as a "lawyer, journalist, politician and captain in the Civil War." His adopted state remembers him as the author of the three-volume work *Minnesota, Its Story and Biography*, published in 1915.[34] An obituary included in the annual publication of the 73rd Illinois states that Castle "was prominent in grand army circles, and in everything that was of interest to the old soldiers, and his council will be sadly missed."[35]

Dying at the age of 83 on December 11, 1932, William G. Jaquess had outlived both his older sister and her husband. He was a successful local politician, well-to-do landowner and popular musician in Tunica County, Mississippi.[36] The *New York Times* published a brief obituary of W.G. Jaquess two days following his death. It states that although he was "too young to enlist in the Civil War, he followed his father, Colonel Jaquess of Jacksonville, Ill., as drummer boy," but it identifies the regiment as the Thirty-seventh instead of the Seventy-third.[37]

When Anna Marie Jaquess made her final trip from London to the United States in 1894, she did not remain long in Washington, D.C., but returned to the residence she owned in Clarksville, Georgia, where both of her sons had been living. Although her younger son, Howard Frank Meixsel, had died the previous year, the older son, Caleb Peregoy Meixsel, remained in Clarksville for the rest of his life.[38] Later Anna Marie moved to Washington, D.C., permanently and became an active member of the Theosophical Society, an organization that practiced a belief based on a mystical insight into the divine. She claimed that Madame Helena Petrovna

Blavatsky, cofounder of the society, had told her in 1880 the name of the person who should become Blavatsky's rightful successor after her death.[39]

Anna Marie had spent the Lawrence-Townley money in her Philadelphia bank account and whatever profit she had made from buying and selling land in Georgia, and now she was as poor as she had been when James Jaquess met her for the first time. In the hope of receiving a monthly income, she filed for a widow's pension on April 25, 1908, less than a week after a new law concerning widows' pensions had gone into effect. She was 74 years old and indigent. To determine the validity of Anna Marie's application, the Pension Bureau checked the "Marriage Circular" that Jaquess had completed ten years earlier in Memphis. This document stated that he was "twice married and only twice" and named Mary Sciple and Sarah Jane Steel as his two wives, both deceased. Because of the information that the colonel had provided in 1898, Anna Marie would never receive a widow's pension. A government employee wrote an abbreviation on her application that looks like "cohab," probably meaning "cohabitation" rather than marriage.[40] Anna Marie's daughter, Emma Jones, admitted her to Eleonora Ruppert Home for the Aged and Indigent Residents of the District of Columbia on August 24, 1927. According to the home's records, Anna Marie died on January 19, 1928, at the age of 97, and was cremated at Lee's Establishment.[41] James Jaquess had gotten his revenge for her deserting him and had assured that Anna Marie would, like the colonel himself, die a pauper.

Although James F. Jaquess had served time in prison and died too poor to pay for his own funeral, the men of the 73rd Illinois Infantry continued to remember and admire him as their brave colonel. At the regimental reunion the October following his death, the men voted to establish a committee of three, with Captain Castle as chair, "to draft suitable resolutions to express the sentiments of the Association."[42] The regiment eventually decided to raise $350 to purchase a polished white marble tablet in the colonel's honor. The tablet was 4 feet by 6 feet in size with a bronze medallion portrait of Colonel Jaquess.[43] The Quincy English and German Seminary, where Jaquess had served as president before the Civil War, had become a Methodist orphanage called Chaddock Boys School and was located in the John Wood Octagonal House at 12th and State in Quincy. The tablet was unveiled there at a ceremony on June 23, 1905; the inscrip-

Opposite: Plaque honoring Colonel James F. Jaquess at Chaddock School for Boys, Quincy, Illinois (Minutes of Proceedings of the Nineteenth Annual Reunion of the Survivors Seventy-Third Regiment Illinois Volunteer Infantry, October 3, 1905, Abraham Lincoln Presidential Library).

11. Return to America for His Last Years

tion stated that Jaquess was "an eloquent speaker, a successful educator, a brave soldier [and a man] of the finest social qualities."[44]

The *Quincy Whig* published a lengthy article about the "impressive services" and recounted all aspects of the event. Officers and men from the 73rd Illinois Infantry and former students of Chaddock College (formerly Quincy English and German Seminary) formed ranks at 10th and State. Representatives from several military-related organizations, including the Grand Army of the Republic and the Daughters of the American Revolution, joined them and they all marched together for the two blocks to Chaddock Boys School "led by the Markee band."[45] Henry A. Castle gave a dedicatory speech praising Jaquess for his "ability, industry and sincerity." He mentioned some of the high points of the colonel's life but failed to mention the time that Jaquess spent as Lincoln's private agent; he also disguised the colonel's time in England as 15 years "spent in Europe in the prosecution of financial enterprises." He concluded by committing the Jaquess plaque "to the worthy hands of the conductors of this noble educational enterprise."[46]

Sixteen years later, St. Peter's Parish bought Octagonal House and used this building for a Roman Catholic grade school until it was demolished at the end of 1949. When St. Peter's moved into Octagonal House, Chaddock Boys School had relocated in a newly completed building that became part of a campus of buildings devoted to "residential treatment for children who have experienced severe abuse, neglect or other trauma in their early years."[47] The colonel's beautiful marble tablet may have been destroyed when Octagonal House was razed or it may have been moved to the new Chaddock campus. Whatever the case, the white marble plaque disappeared somewhere along the way and has never been found. The men of the 73rd Illinois kept their Colonel's memory alive for many years after the Civil War, but eventually all of them died and the Colonel's name was forgotten. Like the plaque honoring him, the knowledge of who Jaquess was and what he did during his life has disappeared over the years.

Epilogue

A Review of James F. Jaquess' Life

James Jaquess was a man of great self-confidence who marched to the beat of his own drum. Although only an army chaplain and not an officer, he traveled on his own to Pittsburg Landing to inform the Union forces of a Confederate attack planned for the following day. Grant told him to forget this silly idea and return to his regiment, but Jaquess paid no attention to the general and exhibited great bravery by removing wounded soldiers from the battlefield under fire. At the battle of Chickamauga, Jaquess ignored the painful injury he received when a Confederate soldier shot his horse from under him and continued leading the 73rd Infantry in this crucial battle. The same self-confidence persuaded Jaquess that he could win the Lawrence-Townley fortune in British courts for the Americans who had bought bonds from him and continue to live an expensive lifestyle with Anna Marie. Jaquess believed strongly in himself and his ability to come out on top.

Students who knew him as their college president in Jacksonville or Quincy overlooked anything that might change their admiration of him. Jaquess was the star of the semicentennial of the women's college in Jacksonville, and if his "girls" heard that Jaquess had served time in prison for defrauding American citizens, they refused to believe it. The men of the 73rd also remained loyal to their colonel and after his death honored him with a large white marble tablet containing a bronze medallion portrait of their hero. When the special examiner at the U.S. Army office in Memphis met the colonel for the first time in the spring of 1898, he described Jaquess as "a man of highest standing" whose "word may be fully relied upon." Jaquess still radiated the self-confidence, charisma and charm that had won the admiration of others throughout his life.

James Jaquess also exhibited a weakness for women. He loved the ladies and enjoyed romantic relationships with at least four different women during his lifetime. His first affair took place when he was in his third year at Indiana Asbury. This lady was a local girl named Mary Sciple, whom Jaquess married 16 days before their daughter, Margaret, arrived. Mary died 11 months later in Mount Carmel where Jaquess was teaching at the academy. Then in 1846 Jaquess married Sarah Jane Steel, who gave birth their son, William, in Jacksonville on October 26, 1849. She taught in both colleges where Jaquess was president and became a model of decorum for the female students. Louisa C. Williams, the third woman in the colonel's love life, died in Louisville in the summer of 1865 from the abortion of a baby that Jaquess had very likely fathered. The final lady in the colonel's life was a widow named Anna Marie Meixsel, whom he met on one of his trips East to sell Lawrence-Townley bonds. A will that Jaquess signed in England on July 14, 1886, identified Anna Marie as his wife and gave her one-half of the money that he expected to receive from the Townley fortune. Thirty years later, she claimed in the unsuccessful application that she submitted for a widow's pension that James had married her on June 27, 1878. But James had made certain that Anna Marie would never draw a widow's pension when he completed a "Marriage Circular" in 1898 stating he had been married twice and Anna Marie was not one of them. It is probable that these four women were not the only ladies in Jaquess' love life, but they are the ones about which evidence exists.

Jaquess spent all his money trying to save the college in Quincy and paying the costs of his trial in Louisville. After trying a variety of ways to restore his finances, he finally decided on selling Lawrence-Townley bonds in Evansville, Indiana, and in the state of New York. The colonel's unsuccessful attempt to prove the right of an American to inherit a fortune that did not exist finally led to his incarceration in Pentonville Prison in England. But his solitary confinement at Pentonville did not affect his mind as it did the minds of many of the other prisoners. Although he returned to America as a flat broke ex-convict, Jaquess still convinced a Methodist minister who lived next door to his brother that he had converted Lincoln when he served a congregation in Springfield. When he died in June of 1898 at his daughter's home in St. Paul, he remained a hero to those who had known him. The many events of his exciting life make entertaining reading while providing insight into many of the important events of the 19th century.

Chapter Notes

Chapter 1

1. "Posey" refers to Posey County in Southern Indiana.
This is reprinted as "Sketch of Dr. Jaquess" in *College Greetings,* March 8, 1898, MacMurray College Archives (hereafter Mac Arch.), Pfeiffer Library, MacMurray College, Jacksonville, IL.
Although James Frazier Jaquess' grandfather is always referred to as Jonathan Jaquess, he is actually Jonathan Jaquess, Jr. ("Genealogical Notes of the Families of Schnee and Jaquess," Typed Unnumbered Manuscript, Mt. Vernon, IN: General Thomas Posey Chapter DAR, 1980, Allen County Public Library, Ft. Wayne, IN).

2. Kathy Lindell, "If Walls Could Talk," typed unnumbered manuscript, March, 1986: includes excerpts from Asbury Cloud Jaquess, "A Short History of Three Communities," 1892; "An Account of the Coming of the Jonathan Jaquess Family to Indiana," n.d., Willard Library, Evansville, IN.

3. National Society of the Daughters of the American Revolution, *Lineage Book*, 23, 1898 (Washington, D.C.; Harrisburg, PA: 1907), 271.

4. Lindell.

5. Ibid.

6. Ann Eckert Brown, *American Wall Stenciling, 1790–1840* (Lebanon, NH: University Press of New England, 2003), 152. The Jonathan Jaquess house, 1825, is an example of the "Folk Group of Wall Stenciling"; the author also includes information about the Jaquess family.

7. William G. McLoughlin, *Revivals, Awakenings, and Reform: An Essay on Religion and Social Change in America, 1607–1977* (Chicago: University of Chicago Press, 1978), 132.

8. Ibid., 139.

9. Brown, 152.

10. McLoughlin, 137.

11. Brown, 152.

12. Lindell.

13. Frank Baker, *From Wesley to Asbury: Studies in Early American Methodism* (Durham, NC: Duke University Press, 1976), 16–17.

14. Ibid., 17.

15. Russell E. Richey, *Early American Methodism* (Bloomington Indiana University Press, 1991), 25, 53–54.

16. Jennifer St. John, *Posey County, Indiana, 1814–1989* (Paducah, KY: Turner Publications, 1989), 71.

17. Lindell.

18. Edward White, ed., *Evansville and Its Men of Mark* (Evansville, IN: Historical Publishing, 1873; repr., Evansville, IN: Whipporwil, 1985), 402–03.

19. *A Biographical Directory of the Indiana General Assembly*, comp. and ed. Rebecca A. Shepherd, Charles W. Calhoun, Elizabeth Shanahan-Shoemaker, and Alan F. January, 1 (1816–1899) (Indianapolis: Indiana Historic Bureau, 1980), 204.

20. Lindell.

21. Ibid.

22. Asbury C. Jaquess, "The Journals of Davy Crockett Commencing December 20th 1834," *Indiana Magazine of History* 102 (#1, March 2006), 8–24; Dawn E. Bakken, "A Young Hoosier's Adventure on the Mississippi River," *Indiana Magazine of History*, 102 (March 2006), 1–7.

23. Karl J. R. Arndt, *A Documentary History of the Indiana Decade of the Harmony Society, 1814–1824*, vol.1, 1814–1819; vol. 2, 1820–1824 (Indianapolis: Indiana Historical Society, 1978), 1: George Wall to Jonathan Jaquess, February 28, 1819, p. 658; Jonathan Jaquess to George Rapp, March 5, 1819, p. 663.

24. Carroll D. Cox and Gloria M. Cox, *New Harmony, Indiana Newspaper Gleanings* (Owensboro, KY: Cook-McDowell, 1980), 407.

25. St. John, 81.

26. Special Collections, Transylvania University Library, Lexington, KY.

27. William Warren Sweet, *Indiana Asbury-DePauw University, 1837–1937; A Hundred Years of Higher Education in the Middle West* (New York: Abbingdon Press, 1937), 48.

28. Johnson Brigham, *James Harlan, Iowa Biographical Series* (Iowa City: State Historical Society of Iowa, 1913), 18.

29. Brigham, 16.

30. George B. Manhart, *DePauw Through the Years* (Greencastle: DePauw University, 1962), 1:21, 38.

31. Brigham, 24.

32. 1840 Census, Putnam County Indiana.

33. Minnetta L. Wright, ed., *Marriage Records of Putnam County Indiana*, comp. Washburn Chapter DAR, 1940, from Putnam County Court House, vol. July 1822 to May 1843 (Greencastle, Indiana, June 1940), 114.

34. *List of Appointments of Methodist Episcopal Ministers in Indiana, 1800–1900*, 1: 167, Greencastle, Indiana: Archives and Special Collections, DePauw University, 1998.

35. Henry A. Castle and Drew W. Castle, "Castle-Jaquess Families" (genealogical charts begun by Henry A. Castle and completed by his grandson Drew) (Joliet, IL, 1970); typewritten manuscript, Abraham Lincoln Presidential Library (ALPL).

36. Jaquess, *Mount Carmel Register*, November 19, 1896.

37. Historical Cemetery records from Mount Carmel Illinois Public Library. Since James F. Jaquess' first wife was buried in a Mt. Carmel Cemetery on March 22, 1844, the Jaquess family must already have moved there (obituary of Margaret Jaquess Castle included in the publication of the Twenty-Third Annual Reunion, Seventy-Third Regiment Illinois Volunteer Infantry, 20–21; ALPL, contained in Castle-Jaquess Families folder).

38. *Mount Carmel Register*, October 2, 1844.

39. Obituary, Gilbert Cook Turner, *Mount Carmel Register*, April 12, 1894.

40. *Enrolled Acts of the General Assembly* (R.S., 103–030), photocopies of handwritten originals located in the Illinois State Archives, Springfield, IL.

41. *Mount Carmel Register*, October 2, 1844.

42. Brigham, 25, 34.

43. Testimony of Jaquess at trial of Howell Thomas, http://www.oldbaileyonline.org/static/Proceedings.jsp.

44. *150 Years of Methodism in Shawneetown, Illinois*, 5, Methodist Archives, McKendree College, Lebanon, IL.

45. John H. Wigger, *American Saint: Francis Asbury and the Methodists* (New York: Oxford University Press, 2009), 8–9; *Taking Heaven by Storm: Methodism and the Rise of Popular Christianity in America* (Urbana: University of Illinois Press, 1998), 43.

46. *The Book of Discipline of the United Methodist Church* (Nashville: United Methodist Publishing House, 2004).

47. Terminology used in Methodist Episcopal Churches is indicated by quotations. *History of the Methodist Episcopal Church in Southern Illinois from the Formation of the First Class in 1793 to the Year 1903* (MECSIL), comp. Thomas H. Herdman, Conference Historian of Southern Illinois Conference, 1: 335.

48. James Leaton, *Methodism in Illinois* (Illinois Conference Historical Society, 1889), 3: 185 (typed from original handwritten unpublished manuscript, Great Rivers Methodist Archives).

49. *150 Years of Methodism in Shawneetown, Illinois*, 5; Methodist Archives, McKendree College, Lebanon, Illinois.

50. MECSIL, 1: 344; *Illinois Conference Minutes, Methodist Church, 1836–1847*, Conference of 1845, typed from handwritten manuscript, 13 (IL Conf.), Great Rivers Methodist Archives.

51. *Illinois Statewide Marriage Index, 1763–1900*. http://www.cyberdriveillinois.com/departments/archives/marriage.html.

52. Typewritten unpublished manuscript, Robinson Public Library District, Robinson, IL.

53. Robert Bray, *Peter Cartwright, Legen-*

dary Frontier Preacher (Urbana: University of Illinois Press, 2005), 212.

54. Henry B. Rankin, *Personal Recollections of Abraham Lincoln* (New York: Knickerbocker, 1916), 318–19.

55. *History of Menard and Mason Counties, Illinois* (Chicago: Baskin, 1879), 725.

56. *The Lincoln Log: A Daily Chronology of the Life of Abraham Lincoln, which Includes, Corrects and Adds to* Lincoln Dayby-Day: A Chronology, http://www.thelincolnlog.org/view.

57. Joseph R. Harker, "History of MacMurray College," manuscript, 142, Mac Arch.

58. IL Conf., 9.

59. Lincoln to Rosecrans May 28, 1863, Abraham Lincoln Papers at the Library of Congress, transcribed and annotated by the Lincoln Studies Center, Knox College, Galesburg, Illinois.

60. Robert P. Howard, *Illinois: A History of the Prairie State* (Grand Rapids: William Eerdmans, 1972), 132.

61. J. Gordon Melton, *Log Cabins to Steeples* (Nashville: Commission on Archives and History of the Northern, Central, and Southern Illinois Conferences, 1974), 21.

62. Howard, 63–64.

63. *The Northwest Ordinance, 1787: A Bicentennial Handbook,* ed. Robert M. Taylor, Jr. (Indianapolis: Indiana Historical Society, 1987), 73.

64. Peter S. Onuf, *Statehood and Union: A History of the Northwest Ordinance* (Bloomington: Indiana University Press, 1987), 87.

65. Howard, 129.

66. Michael Burlingame, *Abraham Lincoln: A Life,* vol. 1 (Baltimore: Johns Hopkins University Press, 2008), 380.

67. Melton, 99.

68. Bray, 220.

69. MECSIL, 363, 365.

70. IL Conf., 9.

71. Mary Watters, *The First Hundred Years of MacMurray College* (Jacksonville, IL: MacMurray College for Women, 1947), 42.

72. Bray, 200.

73. *Autobiography of Peter Cartwright: 53 Years as a Pioneer Preacher,* Centennial edition, introduction by Charles B. Wallis (Nashville: Abington Press, 1956), 296.

74. Leaton, 238–39.

75. IL Conf., Belleville, 1848, 5.

76. Watters, 42–44.

Chapter 2

1. Don Harrison Doyle, *The Social Order of a Frontier Community: Jacksonville, Illinois, 1825–70* (Urbana: University of Illinois Press, 1978), 19–20, 261.

2. Robert P. Howard, *Illinois: A History of the Prairie State* (Grand Rapids, MI: William B. Eerdmans, 1972), 209–10.

3. Doyle, 30.

4. Frank J. Heinl, "Jacksonville and Morgan County: An Historical Review," *Journal of the Illinois State Historical Society* 18, (#1 April 1925), 7 (hereafter *JISHS*). This special publication honored the 100th anniversary of Jacksonville's founding.

5. Doyle, 53; Elizabeth Duncan Putnam, *The Life and Services of Joseph Duncan, Governor of Illinois, 1834–1838* (reprinted from *Transactions* of the Illinois State Historical Society, Springfield, 1921), 160.

6. Turner to Siebert, March 6, 1896, #39, Wilbur Siebert Collection, Ohio Historical Society, 159–60.

7. #40, Wilbur Siebert Collection, Ohio Historical Society.

8. Charles M. Eames, *Historic Morgan and Classic Jacksonville* (Jacksonville: Daily Journal Steam Job Printing Office, 1885), 143–44.

9. Doyle, 69.

10. Minnie Wait Cleary, "History of the Illinois School for the Deaf," *Journal of the Illinois State Historical Society* 35 (#4, 1942): 368–77; Bill Stark, "Illinois School for the Deaf: The Pioneer Institution," *Illinois Advance* 108 (#7, April 1975): n.p.

11. Carl E. Black, MD, "Origin of Our State Charitable Institutions," *JISHS* 18 (#1, April 1925): 183–84.

12. Charles E. Frank, *Pioneer's Progress: Illinois College, 1829–1979* (Carbondale: Southern Illinois University Press, 1979), 36.

13. Doyle, 70.

14. Black, 187–88.

15. Ibid., 191.

16. Doyle, 72.

17. Walter B. Hendrickson, *From Shelter to Self-Reliance: A History of the Illinois Braille and Sight Saving School* (Jacksonville: Illinois Braille and Sight Saving School, 1972), 16.

18. *JISHS* 18 (#1, April 1925): 161–62. From 1893 to 1925, Harker was president of the college where Jaquess served as the first president.

19. Frank, 31.

20. Letter from Jas. H. Dickens to James Leaton, written ca. 1878–80, typed from original handwritten copy, 3 unnumbered pages, Great Rivers Methodist Archives (hereafter GRM Arch.), Pfeiffer Library, MacMurray College.
21. McKendree College Catalog, 1879, lists honorary degrees previously awarded, including the Rev. Peter Cartwright, DD, in 1845, McKendree College Archives Lebanon, IL.
22. Dickens to Leaton.
23. Jeanette Hadden, *Ebenezer* (Jacksonville: Morgan County Historical Society, 1998), 6.
24. Mary Watters, *The First Hundred Years of MacMurray College* (Jacksonville: MacMurray College for Women, 1947), 1, 23, 13–14, 42; *Illinois Conference Female Academy, Illinois Conference Female College, Record of Trustees' Meetings Beginning October 10, 1846, Ending May 19, 1858,* bound photocopy of original handwritten document, MacMurray College Archives, MacMurray College, Jacksonville, IL, Oct. 10, 1846, 3–7, and Jan. 16, 1847, 8.
25. Dickens to Leaton.
26. Joseph R. Harker, "History of MacMurray College," typewritten manuscript, Mac Arch., 161. Harker served as president from 1893 to 1925.
27. Clarence P. McClelland, "The Education of Females in Early Illinois," *JISHS* 36 (#4, December 1943): 396, 399–400. McClelland followed Harker and served until 1952.
28. Eames, 155, 199.
29. D. Duane Cummins, *The Disciples Colleges: A History* (St. Louis: CBP, 1987), 49; Nathaniel S. Haynes, *History of the Disciples of Christ in Illinois, 1819–1914,* (Cincinnati: Standard, 1915), 60–62; Vernon R.Q. Fernandes, *Passavant Area Hospital: 125 Years of Caring* (Jacksonville, IL: Passavant Area Hospital, 1999), 180.
30. McClelland, 399.
31. Harker, 145–48.
32. http://www.rootsweb.ancestry.com/~ilmaga/census-morg50/censindx.htm.
33. Watters, 18–19, 39.
34. Doyle, 41.
35. Jo Anne Beard, *The Legacy of Historic Jacksonville: Its Homes and Buildings,* (Jacksonville, IL: City of Jacksonville Historic Preservation Commission, 1986), 54.
36. *Minutes of Illinois Conference of Methodist Episcopal Church,* September 1849, Quincy, GRM Arch., 4.
37. *Catalog of Illinois Conference Female Academy for 1851,* Mac Arch., 9, 12.
38. Watters, 71, 77, 78.
39. Ibid., 66.
40. Harker, 161.
41. Watters, 50–52.
42. Ibid., 48, 81.
43. Ibid., 43, 66.
44. Ibid., 62.
45. *College Greetings,* June 1898, "College Life in the 50s," 3, Mac. Arch.
46. Watters, 67.
47. Records of Trustees' Minutes, April 26, 1855, Mac. Arch.
48. Watters, 61.
49. Trustees' Minutes, October 12, 1852.
50. Watters, 77.
51. Trustees' Minutes, July 19, 1852; Watters, 124–28.
52. Harker, 181–82, 192.
53. Watters, 110–14; Dickens to Leaton.
54. *Illinois Journal,* July 15, 1854.
55. Helen Wilmans, *A Search for Freedom* (Sea Breeze, FL: Freedom, 1898), 221. Chapter 12 of this autobiography deals with her life at Illinois Conference Female College (215–32).
56. Dickens to Leaton.
57. Eames, 138.
58. Dickens to Leaton.
59. Watters, 109.
60. Beryl Satter, *Each Mind a Kingdom: American Women, Sexual Purity, and the New Thought Movement, 1875–1920* (Berkeley: University of California Press, 1999), 152, 155.
61. Wilmans, 224–25.
62. *College Greetings,* November 1897, 8.
63. *Illinois Daily Journal,* July 28, 1854.
64. Dickens to Leaton.
65. Annual Minutes of the Illinois Conference of the Methodist Episcopal Church for 1852, Great Rivers Methodist Archives (GRM Arch.), Pfeiffer Library, MacMurray College, 30.
66. *Quincy Daily Whig* (hereafter *QDW*), December 28, 1853 (newspapers digitized by the Quincy Public Library), http://archive.quincylibrary.org/Default/Skins/QPL/Client.asp?skin=QPL&enter=true&AppName=2.
67. Paul Farthing and Chester Farthing, *Philo History: Chronicles and Biographies of the Philosophian Literary Society of McKendree College* (Lebanon, IL: Published for the Society, 1911), 66–67.
68. James Leaton, handwritten document, Paris Circuit and Station Folder,

GRM Arch., Pfeiffer Library, MacMurray College.
    69. Document entitled "Paris Male and Female Seminary," GRM Arch.

Chapter 3

1. Pamphlet published by City of Quincy, Vertical File, Abraham Lincoln Presidential Library (ALPL), n.p. Now called Washington Square or Park.
2. Carl and Shirley Landrum, *Images of America: Quincy, Illinois* (Charleston, SC: Arcadia, 1999), n.p.
3. *The History of Adams County Illinois* (Cleveland, Ohio: Bell & Howard, 1964), 262. Reprint of original publication (Chicago: Murray, Williamson & Phelps, 1879), 262; Pamphlet published by City of Quincy, n.p.
4. Pamphlet published by City of Quincy, n.p.
5. Robert P. Howard, *Illinois: A History of the Prairie State* (Grand Rapids, MI: William B. Eerdmans, 1972), 86
6. Theodore L. Carlson, *The Illinois Military Tract: A Study of Land Opportunities, Utilization and Tenure* (Urbana: University of Illinois Press, 1951), 51.
7. Ibid., 89.
8. Rodney O. Davis and Douglas L. Wilson, *The Lincoln-Douglas Debates* (Urbana: Knox College Lincoln Studies Center and University of Illinois Press, 2008), 212.
9. Allen C. Guelzo, *Lincoln and Douglas: The Debates that Defined America* (New York: Simon & Schuster, 2008), 242–43.
10. Davis and Wilson, 212.
11. *Mormon Historical Studies* 2 (#1, Spring 2001): 105.
12. *Reminiscences of Quincy, Illinois, Containing Historical Events, Anecdotes, Matters Concerning Old Settlers and Old Times, etc.* (Quincy: D. Wilcox & Sons, 1883), 153.
13. Robert Bruce Flanders, *Nauvoo: Kingdom on the Mississippi* (Urbana: University of Illinois Press, 1965), 12–13.
14. Owen W. Muelder, *The Underground Railroad in Western Illinois* (Jefferson, NC: McFarland, 2008), 13.
15. Ibid., 35.
16. Ibid., 13.
17. Asbury, 65–66.
18. Muelder, 36–39.
19. Asbury, 71–72; Muelder, 37–38.
20. Muelder, 38.
21. Carl A. Landrum, "Colleges in Quincy" (Sketch 42) *Historical Sketches of Quincy, Illinois* (Quincy: Historical Sketches of Quincy and Adams County, revised ed., 1986), 193–96.
22. W.T. Beadles (president the board of trustees), "History of Chaddock College and the Deaconess Boys' School," *Illinois Methodist Journal* (June 27, 1901): 2; W.A. Fifer, Secretary of the Quincy, Illinois, Chamber of Commerce, to Mr. L.E. Lackland of Sycamore, Illinois, November 5, 1941, Illinois Wesleyan University Archives, Ames Library, Bloomington, IL. Additional information about the fire was provided by the archivist.
23. Beadles, 2.
24. *QDW,* December 28, 1853, newspapers digitized by the Quincy Public Library, http://archive.quincylibrary.org/Default/Skins/QPL/Client.asp?skin=QPL&enter=true&AppName=2.
25. Beadles, 2.
26. Ibid.
27. *QDW,* August 14, 1356.
28. Ibid., September 6, 1856.
29. Beadles, 2.
30. Illinois Conference Minutes, Quincy, 1856, 14–15.
31. Ibid., Springfield, 1854, 20.
32. *QDW,* August 14, 1856. Identical advertisements appeared in numerous issues of Quincy newspapers.
33. Genealogy of the children of I.N. Jaquess and Jane Tilton, Mount Carmel Public Library.
34. *QDW,* August 14, 1856.
35. Catalog page, GRM Arch.
36. *QDW,* November 24, 1855.
37. *Quincy Daily Republican* (hereafter *QDR*), June 29, 1861.
38. Michael K. Brinkman, *Quincy, Illinois: Immigrants from Münsterland, Westphalia, Germany* (Westminster, MD: Heritage Books, 2010), I, 100.
39. Ibid., 123.
40. Ibid., 101.
41. *QDW,* August 14, 1856.
42. Ibid.
43. Beadles, 2.
44. *QDW,* August 12, 1859.
45. Two other societies were the Platonium and Calliopean. Two similar literary societies were founded while Jaquess was president of Illinois Conference Female College: Belle Lettres in 1851 and Phi Nu in 1852 (Watters, 102–03).
46. *Commencement Programs and Exhibition Programs of Literary Societies of*

Quincy College, Abraham Lincoln Presidential Library, Springfield, IL.

47. Minutes of the trustees of Quincy English and German Seminary as quoted or summarized in Marquis D. Hornbeck, *A General Statement of the Financial History and Present Condition of Chaddock College, Presented May 1889* (Quincy: Skinner, 1889), 10–17, GRM Arch. The original records no longer exist.

48. Ibid.

49. *Portrait and Biographical Album of Morgan and Scott Counties, Illinois* (Chicago: Chapman Brothers, 1889), 303.

50. Patrick H. Redmond, *History of Quincy and Its Men of Mark* (Quincy: Heirs & Russell, 1869), 31–32.

51. Hornbeck, 10–17; Chancery Records A-8, April 9, 1861 to November 22, 1862, Adams County, Adams County Clerk's Office, 576–79.

52. David Costigan, dissertation submitted in partial fulfillment of the requirements for the degree of doctor of arts, Department of History, Illinois State University, 1994, 21.

53. *Quincy Whig Republican* (hereafter *QWR*), June 29, 1861.

54. Hornbeck, 10–17.

55. *QDW,* July 16, 1862.

56. Hornbeck, 10–17.

57. Ibid.

58. *QDW,* July 16, 1862, June 25 and August 8, 1863.

59. Hornbeck, 10–17.

60. Archives of Truman State University, Kirksville, Missouri, http://library.truman.edu/manuscripts/C3-CWC%20Archives.asp.

61. Ibid.

62. Chancery Records A-8, April 9, 1861 to November 22, 1862, Adams County, Adams County Clerk's Office, 576–79.

63. *Daily Whig Republican,* March 23, 1859. Loan was dated January 16, 1858.

64. *Reminiscences,* 104.

65. Norman L. Freeman (counselor at law), *Reports of Cases at Law and in Chancery, Argued and Determined in the Supreme Court of Illinois* (Chicago: E.B. Myers & Chandler, Law, 1866), vol. 33: 262–73.

66. 1860 census.

Chapter 4

1. http://www.cyberdriveillinois.com/departments/archives/datcivil.html.

2. 1853 Catalog, Illinois Conference Female Academy, MacMurray College Archives (Mac Arch.), Pfeiffer Library, MacMurray College; Rebecca Cavanaugh, the wife of Thomas H. Cavanaugh, Sr., is listed in the "Official Class Leaders Minutes from Jacksonville Station 1850–1865" (now Centenary United Methodist).

3. Charles M. Eames, *Historic Morgan and Classic Jacksonville* (Jacksonville: Daily Journal Steam Job Printing Office, 1885), 127 (Eames misspells the name as Kavenaugh); *Historical Encyclopedia of Illinois,* ed. Newton Bateman and Paul Selby; *History of Morgan County,* ed. William. T. Short (Chicago: Munsell, 1906), 715.

4. Cavanaugh to Yates, April 24, 1861, Archives, Abraham Lincoln Presidential Library (hereafter Arch. ALPL).

5. This house was listed on the National Register of Historic Places in 1980. Philip H. Decker, *A Window on the Past* (Jacksonville, IL: Production Press for the Morgan County Historical Society, 1990), 27.

6. William H. Leckie and Shirley A. Leckie, *Unlikely Warriors: General Benjamin H. Grierson and His Family* (Norman: University of Oklahoma Press, 1984), 30–46.

7. Ibid., 47–48.

8. Ibid., 54–56.

9. Roy P. Basler, ed., *The Collected Works of Abraham Lincoln* (New Brunswick, NJ: Rutgers University Press, 1953), 2: 469n, 3: 521n, http://www.heritech.com/soil/genealogy/camden/cambat.htm.

10. http://www.cyberdriveillinois.com/departments/archives/datcivil.html.

11. (Brig. Gen. Benjamin H. Grierson, "Lights and Shadows of Life" (autobiography) 1892 (hereafter "L&S"), typescript, Arch. ALPL, 142. Grierson's autobiography has survived as a typed manuscript; spelling mistakes may be typographical errors.

12. Cavanaugh to Grant, January 4, 1862; Cavanaugh to Grant, January 7, 1862; Grant to Cavanaugh, January 8, 1862, in *The Papers of Ulysses S. Grant,* 4: January 8–March 31, 1862, ed. John Y. Simon; asst. ed. Roger D. Bridges (Carbondale: Southern Illinois University Press, 1972): 13–14.

13. It is interesting to note that Governor Yates, as well as the Cavanaugh family, belonged to this church. Likewise the obituary of Thomas H. Cavanaugh, Jr., in the *Topeka Journal,* September 1, 1909, states that he was a teetotaler. It seems probable that his father held the same persuasion.

14. Letter from Chaplain Isaac Newton Jaquess, November 13, 1889, in W.H. Newlin, D.F. Lawler, and J.W. Sherrick, *A History of the Seventy-third Regiment of Illinois Infantry Volunteers* (Springfield: Regimental Reunion Association of Survivors of the 73rd Infantry, 1890), 680.
15. David S. Heidler and Jeanne T. Heidler, eds., *Encyclopedia of the American Civil War: A Political, Social and Military History* (Santa Barbara, CA: ABC-CLIO, 2000), 1910–11.
16. *New York Times* (hereafter *NYT*), December 20, 1863.
17. "L&S," 125.
18. Cavanaugh to Yates, February 7, 1862, Illinois Archives (hereafter IL Arch.), Springfield, IL.
19. "L&S," 125.
20. Fry to Fuller, January 26, 1862, IL Arch.
21. Yates to Scott, January 18, 1862; Scott to Yates, January 19, 1862, *War of the Rebellion*, Series 3, 1 (Washington Government Printing Office, 1899): 803.
22. Cavanaugh to Yates, January 28, 1862, IL Arch.
23. Grant to Kelton, January 28, 1862; Halleck to Grant, January 30, 1862, *Papers of Ulysses S. Grant*, 4: 101–02
24. "L&S," 137.
25. Ibid., 145.
26. Thirty-seventh Congress, Sess. I, Ch. 9, 1861, pp. 270–71, *A Century of Lawmaking for a New Nation: U.S. Congressional Documents and Debates, 1774–1875*, http://memory.loc.gov/ammem/amlaw/lawhome.html.
27. Cavanaugh to Yates, February 7, 1862, IL Arch.
28. Second Petition calling for Cavanaugh's resignation, Arch. ALPL.
29. Olney to Yates, February 14, 1862, IL Arch.
30. Olney to Yates, March 8, 1862, Arch. ALPL.
31. Cavanaugh to Halleck, March 23, 1862; Cavanaugh to Kelton, April 5, 1862, both in Cavanaugh's Military File (hereafter CMF), National Archives and Records Administration (hereafter NARA); "L&S," 159.
32. "Sixth Illinois Cavalry," in *Illinois Adjutant General's Report: Regimental and Unit Histories Containing Reports for the Years 1861–1866*, http://www.cyberdriveillinois.com/departments/archives/reghist.pdf.

33. Captain T.J. Bryant, surviving pages from "War Reminiscences: History of Company D, 14th Illinois Infantry," Great Rivers Methodist Archives (GRM Arch.), Pfeiffer Library, MacMurray College.
34. Wiley Sword, *Shiloh: Bloody April* (New York: William Morrow, 1974), 115–16.
35. Bryant, n.p.
36. Bryant, n.p.; Sword, 137.
37. Thomas J. Bryant, *Who Is Responsible for the Advance of Army of the Tennessee Toward Corinth?* ca. 1885, Arch. ALPL, 18–19.
38. Yates to Lincoln, January 30, 1864, NARA, RG 94, M1064, #101.
39. Sword, 430.
40. *QDW*, April 10, 1862; *NYT*, April 11, 1862; *QDW*, April 11, 1862; *QWR*, April 14, 1862; *NYT*, April 21, 1862; *Quincy Daily Herald*, April 19, 1862.
41. Jaquess MF, NARA
42. Kentucky's Historical Society, "Confederate Governor George W. Johnson" (1811–1862), http://www.lrc.ky.gov/record/Moments09RS/web/Lincoln%20moments%2017.pdf.
43. Sword, 399.
44. Ibid., 431.
45. Ed Porter Thompson, *History of the Orphan Brigade* (Louisville KY: Lewis N. Thompson, 1898), 520.
46. Sword, 431.
47. *NYT*, April 11, 1862; *QDW*, April 10, 11, and 25, 1862; *QWR*, April 19, 20 and May 17, 1862; E.L. Kimball, 'Richard Yates," *JISHS* 23 (April 1930–31): 44.
48. Olney to Grierson, April 9, 1862, Arch. ALPL.
49. Olney to Fuller, April 12, 1862, IL Arch.
50. http://memory.loc.gov/ammem/amlaw/lawhome.html.
51. Olney to Fuller, April 12, 1862, IL Arch.
52. "L&S," 163.
53. Leckie, 102.
54. John Olney MF, NARA.
55. Olney to Yates, July 14, 1862, IL Arch.
56. Olney to Yates, January 1864 and February 1, 1864, Arch. ALPL; Yates Letterbook, October 7, 1863, to January 8, 1864, pp. 428–29, Archives of Lilly Library, Wabash College, Crawfordsville, IN.
57. Cavanaugh to Yates, June 2, 1862, Arch. ALPL.
58. Loomis to Stanton, March 4, 1863, IL Arch.

Chapter 5

1. Victor Hicken, *Illinois in the Civil War*, 2nd ed. (Urbana: University of Illinois Press, 1991), 3.
2. Identified in this chapter as "the regimental history"; authored by W.H. Newlin, D.F. Lawler, and J.W. Sherrick (Springfield: Regimental Reunion Association of Survivors of the 73rd Infantry, 1890), 645 (hereafter RH); Kenneth A. Hafendorfer, *Perryville, Battle for Kentucky* (Owensboro, KY: McDowell, 1981), 80.
3. RH., 21.
4. Ibid., 70.
5. Hicken, 7; Paul Farthing and Chester Farthing, *Philo History; Chronicles and Biographies of the Philosophian Literary Society of McKendree College* (Lebanon, IL: Published for the Society, 1911), 66–67.
6. B.R. Maryniak, "Yankee Preacher Regiments," *Civil War* 3 (#6): 32–33.
7. RH, 25, 54.
8. RH, 645–46.
9. Illinois Civil War database, http://www.cyberdriveillinois.com/departments/archives/datcivil.html.
10. RH, 92–93.
11. Kenneth W. Noe, *Perryville: This Grand Havoc of Battle* (Lexington: University Press of Kentucky, 2001), 94.
12. James Lee McDonough, *War in Kentucky from Shiloh to Perryville* (Knoxville, TN: University of Tennessee Press, 1994), 224.
13. Ibid., 111.
14. Noe, 139.
15. McDonough, 235.
16. Ibid., 287.
17. Steven E. Woodworth, *Decision in the Heartland: The Civil War in the West* (Westport, CT: Praeger, 2008), 37.
18. Noe, 326.
19. RH, 98–100.
20. Ibid.; Noe, 281.
21. Hicken, *Illinois in the Civil War*, 105.
22. Edna J. Shank Hunter, *One Flag, One County, and Thirteen Greenbacks a Month* (San Diego, CA: Hunter Publications, 1980), 42.
23. RH, 674.
24. Noe, 341–42.
25. Ibid., 395, fns. 59, 60, 399, fn. 51. An account of the Buell Commission can be found in *Operations of the Army Under Buell from June 10th to October 30th and the Buell Commission* (New York: D. Van Nostrand, 1884).
26. http://memory.loc.gov/ammem/amlaw/lawhome.html.
27. RH,113.
28. Letter from Wayne C. Temple, Archivist, State Records Section, Illinois Secretary of State to Lester Swift, May 18, 1967.
29. Jaquess to unnamed person, December 17, 1862, Jaquess Military File (hereafter JMF), NARA.
30. Jaquess to unnamed General, December 17, 1862, JMF, NARA.
31. Yates to Stanton, December 24, 1862, IL Arch., Springfield; Yates to Lincoln, December 24, 1862, NARA, Record Group (RG), 94.
32. Jaquess to Trumbull, December 24, 1862, IL Arch.
33. Lincoln's request to the Secretary of War is in the president's handwriting and is dated January 2, 1863; it appears on the back of Yates' letter to Lincoln located at NARA. There is also a copy of the Yates to Lincoln letter at IL Arch. See also Lester L. Swift, "Tribulations of the Rev. Col. Jaquess and the Preacher Regiment: A New Lincoln Note Discovered," *Lincoln Herald* 69 (Winter 1967): 165–77.
34. United States War Department, *The War of the Rebellion: A Compilation of the Official Records of the Union and Confederate Armies*, (hereafter OR), Series 1, Vol. 20, Part I: 176, 215. http://digital.library.cornell.edu/m/moawar/waro.html.
35. RH, 115.
36. James Lee McDonough, *Stones River: Bloody Winter in Tennessee* (Knoxville: University of Tennessee Press, 1980), 235.
37. Ibid., 83.
38. RH, 126.
39. Ibid., 134.
40. Peter Cozzens, *No Better Place to Die* (Urbana: University of Illinois Press, 1991).
41. RH, 133.
42. Henry A. Castle, "Sheridan with the Army of the Cumberland," in *Minutes of Proceedings of the Twentieth Annual Reunion of the Survivors Seventy-Third Regiment Illinois Volunteer Infantry*, October 6, 1906, 16, ALPL.
43. RH, 143.
44. Ibid., 674.
45. OR, Series 1, Vol. 20 (Part 1): 215.
46. The Jaquess Military File states whether he is present or absent and cites the orders granting him absence with leave. It contains a letter—Jaquess to Colonel Goddard, April 29, 1863—requesting a leave of 48 hours to transfer $12,000 be-

longing to members of the 73rd to a Springfield bank so that checks can be sent to their friends at home by letter. Other reasons for his absence are not documented.

47. RH, 72.
48. Ibid., 202–03.
49. *Minutes of Proceedings of the Third Annual Reunion of the Survivors Seventy-Third Regiment Illinois Volunteer Infantry*, October 8–10, 1890, 39, ALPL.
50. Cozzens, 55–59.
51. "Report of Col. Bernard Laiboldt, Second Missouri Infantry, Commander of the Second Brigade," OR, Series 1, Vol. 30 (Part III): 589–91.
52. Ibid.
53. *Minutes of Proceedings of the Fourteenth Annual Reunion of the Survivors Seventy-Third Regiment Illinois Volunteer Infantry*, September 27, 1900, 13, ALPL.
54. RH, 236.
55. *Minutes of Proceedings of the Eighteenth Annual Reunion of the Survivors Seventy-Third Regiment Illinois Volunteer Infantry*, October 4, 1904, 16, ALPL. There are two men with the surname Jack in the 73rd and the speaker is identified only as "Comrade Jack."
56. RH, 674.
57. Jaquess to Yates, November 10, 1863, NARA, RG 94.
58. Willie G. Jaquess Military File, NARA.
59. William G. Jaquess, "Narrative of Chickamauga and Chattanooga," in "Proceedings of the Southwestern Indiana Historical Society," in *Indiana History Bulletin* 6 (extra #3, August 1929): 27.
60. Ibid., 30.
61. Ibid., 24–29.
62. Ibid.; General Bragg wrote to General Rosecrans on September 28, 1863, about this prisoner exchange (see OR, Series 2, Vol. 6: 326).
63. "The Boy of Chickamauga" can be downloaded in portable document format at http://www.edinborough.com/Learn/CivilWarLife/Social%20Images/Chicka-munga.pdf.
64. These matters are discussed in greater detail in subsequent chapters.
65. OR, Series 1, Vol. 30, Part I: 84.
66. J.F. Jaquess Military File.
67. *Lincoln Herald* 72 (Summer 1970): 58.
68. Ibid.
69. Steven E. Woodworth, *Six Armies in Tennessee: The Chickamauga and Chattanooga Campaigns* (Lincoln: University of Nebraska Press, Bison Edition, 1999), 201.
70. RH, 271.
71. *Minutes 73rd*, October 8–10, 1890, 13.
72. Ibid., 15.
73. RH, 173.
74. W. Jaquess, 35.
75. RH, 273.
76. OR, Series 1, Vol. 31, Pt. 2: 201.
77. RH, 674.
78. Ibid., 518.
79. OR, Series 1, Vol. 38, Pt. 1, 91; Vol. 45, Pt. 2, 456; Vol. 38, Pt. 1, 316.
80. OR, Series 1, Vol. 45, Pt. 1: 248.
81. RH, 674.
82. Ibid., 518.
83. *Report of the Adjutant General of the State of Illinois, Containing Reports for the Years 1861–66, Revised by Brigadier General J.W. Vance, Adjutant General* (Springfield: H. W. Rokker, State Printer and Binder, ca. 1886), 578.
84. Thomas to Lincoln, November 26, 1863, NARA, RG 94, M1064, Roll #101.
85. Yates to Lincoln, December 10, 1863, NARA, RG 94, M1064, Roll #101; this comment may have been added to Thomas' letter before Yates forwarded it to the president.
86. Yates to Lincoln, January 30, 1864, NARA, RG 94, M1064, Roll #101.

Chapter 6

Note: An earlier version of this chapter by Patricia Bauer Burnette was published as "Jaquess and the Lincoln Connection," JISHS 101 (#3–4, Fall/Winter 2008): 272–84.

1. F. Lauriston Bullard, "Abraham Lincoln and George Ashmun," *The New England Quarterly* 19 (#2, June 1946): 197–200; Stephen F. Knott, *Secret and Sanctioned: Covert Operations and the American Presidency* (New York: Oxford University Press, 1996), 145.
2. Knott, 147–48.
3. John J. Carter, *Covert Action as a Tool of Presidential Foreign Policy from the Bay of Pigs to Iran-contra* (Lewiston, NY: Edwin Mellen, 2006), 123–24.
4. *Totten v. United States*, 92 U.S. 105 (1875).
5. Gavin Mortimer, *Double Death: The True Story of Pryce Lewis, the Civil War's Most Daring Spy* (New York: Walker, 2010),

passim, but especially pp. 142–45; 184–85; 204–07; 219–23; 228–29.

6. *The American Church History Series* 11; Gross Alexander et al., *A History of the Methodist Church, South, the United Presbyterian Church, the Cumberland Presbyterian Church and the Presbyterian Church, South, in the United States* (New York: Christian Literature, 1894), 15–43.

7. Robert Bray, *Peter Cartwright. Legendary Frontier Preacher* (Urbana: University of Illinois Press, 2005), 216.

8. American Church History, History of MECS, 15–43.

9. Unless cited otherwise, all correspondence in the remainder of this chapter comes from the Abraham Lincoln Papers at the Library of Congress, http://lcweb2.loc.gov/ammem/alhtml/malhome.html. Jaquess to Garfield, May 19, 1863.

10. Ibid.

11. William S. Rosecrans to Abraham Lincoln, both messages on May 21, 1863.

12. Abraham Lincoln to William S. Rosecrans, May 21, 1863, in Roy E. Basler, et al., eds., *The Collected Works of Abraham Lincoln* (New Brunswick, NJ, 1953–55), 6:225.

13. James F. Jaquess to Abraham Lincoln, May 23, 1863.

14. James R. Gilmore to Abraham Lincoln, May 27, 1863.

15. James R. Gilmore (Edmund Kirke), *Down in Tennessee* (New York: Carleton, 1864), 229–32.

16. Abraham Lincoln to William S. Rosecrans, May 28, 1863.

17. James F. Jaquess to General Rosecrans, June 4, 1863, in Jaquess Military Record, National Archives and Records Administration (NARA).

18. Robert C. Schenck to Abraham Lincoln, July 13, 1863.

19. Knott, *Secret and Sanctioned*, 146–47.

20. James F. Jaquess to Abraham Lincoln, July 22, 1863.

21. James R. Gilmore (Edmund Kirke), *Personal Recollections of Abraham Lincoln and the Civil War* (London: J. MacQueen, 1898), 165.

22. John Nicolay and John Hay, *Abraham Lincoln: A History* (New York: Century, Co., 1890), 9:204, 205; John C. Waugh, *Reelecting Lincoln: The Battle for the 1864 Presidency* (New York: Crown Publishers, 1997), 254–55. The latter shares the opinion of Nicolay and Hay and calls Jaquess "another visionary bent on bringing peace" and a man whose "illusions were so strong, and earnest that others half believed them."

23. Jaquess to Gilmore, November 4, 1863, Archives of the Lincoln Library and Museum, Harrogate, TN, reproduced in Lester L. Swift, "Col. Jaquess' First Peace Mission," *Filson Club Quarterly* 41 (January 1967): 32–33.

24. *Address of Colonel James F. Jaquess, Minutes of Proceedings of the Third Annual Reunion of the Survivors Seventy-Third Regiment Illinois Volunteer Infantry*, October 8–10, 1890, 12, ALPL.

25. Knott, *Secret and Sanctioned*, 147.

26. Report of the Committee on Military Affairs, Ordered to be printed June 14, 1870, Library of Congress: *A Century of Lawmaking for a New Nation: U.S. Congressional Documents and Debates, 1774–1875*, http://memory.loc.gov/ammem/amlaw/lawhome.html.

27. Ervin Chapman, *Latest Light on Lincoln* (New York: Fleming H. Revell, 1917), 1: 95.

28. The articles "Our Visit to Richmond," *Atlantic Monthly* (September 1864): 372–83; "Our Last Day in Dixie," *Atlantic Monthly* (December 3, 1864): 715–26; and "A Suppressed Chapter of History," *Atlantic Monthly* (April 1887): 435–48 are available at http://cdl.library.cornell.edu; *Down in Tennessee* and *Personal Recollections of Abraham Lincoln and the Civil War* (Boston: L.C. Page, 1898).

29. Lincoln to Greeley, August 22, 1862.

30. Greeley to Lincoln, July 7, 1864.

31. James M. McPherson, "Presidential Address: No Peace Without Victory, 1861–1865," *American Historical Review* 109 (#1, February 2004): 1–2.

32. Nicolay and Hay, *Abraham Lincoln*, 9:209. They may have been misled because Gilmore used General Garfield to deliver his letter dated June 15, 1864, to Lincoln because "not even a Private Sect'y should see it" (see "Our Visit to Richmond," 373).

33. Gilmore to Thomas, May 24, 1864, IL Arch., containing a copy of Lincoln's note drafted May 18, 1864.

34. James F. Jaquess to James R. Gilmore, June 10, 1864, Gilmore Papers Ms 37, Johns Hopkins University.

35. James R. Gilmore to Abraham Lincoln, June 15, 1864.

36. James F. Jaquess to Brigadier General Whipple, June 28, 1864, IL Arch.

37. Jaquess to James R. Gilmore, telegram June 30, 1864, Gilmore Papers Ms 37.

38. Lincoln to Grant, July 6, 1864, Basler, 7:429.
39. United States War Department, *The War of the Rebellion: A Compilation of the Official Records of the Union and Confederate Armies* (OR), Navy, II, 3: 1190–94 (OR), http://cdl.library.cornell.edu/moa/browse.monographs/waro.html.
40. Grant to Lee, July 8, 1864, *The Papers of Ulysses S. Grant*, ed. John Y. Simon (Carbondale: Southern Illinois University Press, 1984), 11:190.
41. Ro. Ould to officer commanding the U.S. forces at Deep Bottom, VA, July 12, 1864, Gilmore Papers Ms 37; unless otherwise indicated, the account of the 1864 trip relies on "Our Visit to Richmond." A letter from Gilmore to Lincoln on August 3, 1864, indicates that the president reviewed the manuscript of this article before its publication.
42. The Confederate account in OR, Navy, II, 3: 1193–94; Jefferson Davis, *The Rise and Fall of the Confederate Government* (New York: D. Appleton, 1881), 610–11.
43. Robert S. Harper, *Lincoln and the Press* (New York: McGraw-Hill, 1951), 313.
44. *New York Times* (hereafter *NYT*), July 21 and 24, 1864.
45. Gilmore to Lincoln, July 21, 1864.
46. Jaquess to Gilmore, July 21, 1864, Gilmore Papers.
47. *NYT*, July 21, 1864.
48. *NYT*, July 24, 1864.
49. Lincoln Log: A Daily Chronology of the Life of Abraham Lincoln (hereafter Linc. Log), http://www.papersofabrahamlincoln.org/.
50. *Union Congressional Committee* (1 broadside), and *Rebel Terms of Peace* (6 pp.) (Washington: L. Towers, 1864), ALPL.
51. Ibid.
52. W.H. Newlin, D.F. Lawler, and J.W. Sherrick, *A History of the Seventy-third Regiment of Illinois Infantry Volunteers* (Springfield: Regimental Reunion Association of Survivors of the 73rd Infantry, 1890 (hereafter RH)), 518, 555.
53. The Muster Roll from April-May 1864 shows Jaquess as "Absent with Leave SFO No. 161 HdQrs. D.C., June 3, 1864. On June 28, 1864, Jaquess writes Brigadier General Whipple for an extension of the "thirty (30), days leave of absence" provided under SFO No. 150 "to perform a Special Service." General Thomas orders that the colonel's leave "be extended indefinitely." This letter is in IL Arch., but there is no SFO No. 150 in the Muster Roll. Instead, "SO No. 248 War Department," granted by Thomas, extends Jaquess' leave indefinitely (Jaquess MF, NARA).
54. This information is also found in the Regimental History.
55. "Report of the Proceedings of the Committee on Military Affairs of the United States Senate," ordered to be printed June 14, 1870, Library of Congress, in *A Century of Lawmaking for a New Nation: U.S. Congressional Documents and Debates, 1774–1875*, http://memory.loc.gov. All statements credited to Colonel Jaquess come from this report.
The colonel's testimony before this committee received newspaper coverage. For example, there were lengthy articles in the *New York Herald* on June 21 and 22, 1870, and a long article in his hometown paper, the *Quincy Daily Whig*, on June 27, 1870. Jaquess showed the Military Affairs Committee a note from Lincoln dated May 18, 1864, that stated "Colonel James F. Jaquess, of the Seventy-third Illinois volunteers, is hereby given leave of absence until further notice." This is the same note quoted by Gilmore in his letter to General Thomas on May 24, 1864.
56. Frank H. Severance, "The Peace Conference at Niagara Falls in 1864: An Episode of the Civil War," Cornell Library, New York Historical Literature, http://historicallibrary.cornell.edu. In answer to a question from Senator Howell about his trips to Niagara, Jaquess provided the only exact date in the printed report of the hearing: "I made my report to him [Lincoln] in reference to my first visit to Niagara Falls, I think, on the morning of the 18th July, 1864." The date is, of course, incorrect since Jaquess and Gilmore returned from their interview with Jefferson Davis on the evening of July 18.
57. Abraham Lincoln to Abram Wakeman, July 25, 1864.
58. Abraham Lincoln, Memorandum, August 23, 1864.
59. *NYT*, October 12 and 17, 1864.
60. Lincoln's proclamation on October 20, 1864, established the day for Thanksgiving as the last Thursday of November.
61. (New York and Washington: Neale, 1906, reprinted by Time-Life, 1981), 277. It was nicknamed Greek fire, a liquid fire used by the Byzantine Empire that could not be put out with water.
62. Nat Brandt, *The Man Who Tried to*

Burn New York (New York: Syracuse University Press, 1986), 77.
63. Clint Johnson, *"A Vast and Fiendish Plot": The Confederate Attack on New York* (New York: Citadel Press, Kensington, 2010), 217–18.
64. Linc. Log.
65. Henry A. Castle and Drew W. Castle, "Castle-Jaquess Families," genealogical charts begun by Henry A. Castle and completed by his grandson Drew, Joliet, IL, 1970, typewritten manuscript, Abraham Lincoln Presidential Library; *QWR*, April 22, 1865.
66. *A Century of Lawmaking for a New Nation: U.S. Congressional Documents and Debates, 1774–1875.*

Chapter 7

1. E. Merton Coulter, *The Confederate States of America, 1861–1865*, vol. 7, *History of the South* (Baton Rouge: Louisiana State University Press and the Littlefield Fund for Southern History of the University of Texas, 1950), 560–61.
2. Henry A. Castle and Drew W. Castle, "Castle-Jaquess Families," genealogical charts begun by Henry A. Castle and completed by his grandson Drew, Joliet, IL, 1970, typewritten manuscript, Abraham Lincoln Presidential Library (hereafter ALPL); *QWR*, April 22, 1865.
3. W.H. Newlin, D.F. Lawler, and J.W. Sherrick, *A History of the Seventy-third Regiment of Illinois Infantry Volunteers* (Springfield: Regimental Reunion Association of Survivors of the 73rd Infantry, 1890), 518.
4. Jaquess to Fisk, June 27, 1865, National Archives and Records Administration (hereafter NARA), Microfilm (M), 999, Newberry Library.
5. "Today in History, January 9," American Memory, Library of Congress, http://memory.loc.gov/ammem/today/jan09.html.
6. Jaquess to Fisk, June 27, 1865, NARA, M 999.
7. Fisk to Col. D.C. Jaquess, August 15 [1865], NARA, M 999, as transcribed and printed in Richard D. Sears, *Camp Nelson, Kentucky: A Civil War History* (Lexington: University Press of Kentucky, 2002), 239–40.
8. In Richard O. Curry, ed., *Radicalism, Racism and Party Realignment: The Border States During Reconstruction* (Baltimore: Johns Hopkins University Press, 1969), 126.

9. Fisk to Jaquess, August 15, 1865, Sears, 239–40.
10. Ibid.
11. Sears, *Camp Nelson*, ixx–lxiv. Sears barely mentions Jaquess in his "Historical Introduction" but does include his letters in the body of the text.
12. Ibid.
13. Ibid.
14. Jaquess to Fisk, telegram, August 23, 1865, and Jaquess to Fisk, letter, August 23, 1865, M 999.
15. Cochrane to Jaquess, August 24, 1865, Sears, 244.
16. Obituary of John G. Fee, *New York Times*, January 5, 1900; Sears, *Camp Nelson*, xliii–xlv. Excellent information on John G. Fee is found in William W. Freehling, *The Road to Disunion*, vol. 2, *Secessionists Triumphant, 1854–1861* (New York: Oxford University, 2007).
17. Jaquess to Fisk, August 29, 1865, M 999.
18. Wheeler to Whipple, August 31, 1865, in Sears, *Camp Nelson*, 246–47.
19. Eric Foner, *Reconstruction: America's Unfinished Revolution, 1863–1877* (New York: Harper & Row, 1988), 37.
20. Wheeler to Whipple, August 31, 1865.
21. Fee to Fisk, September 4 and 5, 1865, in Sears, *Camp Nelson*, 249–51.
22. Jaquess to Fisk, September 9, 1865, Microfilm 999, National Archives and Record Service, consulted at the Newberry Library, Chicago.
23. Colton to Whipple, September 10, 1865, in Sears, *Camp Nelson*, 253–54.
24. Fee to Strieby, September 15, 1865, in Sears, *Camp Nelson*, 254–56.
25. Edward P. Smith to Strieby, October 4, 1865, in Sears, *Camp Nelson*, 269–71.
26. "Notable Kentucky African American Database," University of Kentucky Libraries, http://www.uky.edu/Libraries/NKAA/record.php?note_id=425k.
27. Linda B. Selleck, *Gentle Invaders: Quaker Women Educators and Racial Issues During the Civil War and Reconstruction* (Richmond, IN: Friends United Press, 1980), 47.
28. Ibid., 94.
29. Ibid., 48.
30. Ibid., 126.
31. "Southland College," Encyclopedia of Arkansas History and Culture, http://www.encyclopediaofarkansas.net/encyclopedia/entry-detail.aspx?entryID=361.

32. Jaquess to Fisk, September 9, 1865, M 999.
33. Jaquess to Fisk, September 11, 1865, M 999.
34. *Louisville Daily Journal* (hereafter *LDJ*), September 23, 1865; *Louisville Democrat* (hereafter *LD*), September 23, 1865.
35. James C. Mohr, *Abortion in America: The Origins and Evolution of National Policy* (New York: Oxford University Press, 1978), 46–47.
36. Ibid., 47.
37. Ibid., 147–48.
38. Ibid., 226.
39. Ibid., 229.
40. Palmer to Yates, telegram, September 23, 1865, Jaquess MF.
41. Thomas to Palmer, September 30, 1865, Palmer Papers, Archives, Abraham Lincoln Presidential Library (hereafter ALPL).
42. Palmer to his wife, September 26, 1865, Palmer Papers, ALPL.
43. Fee to Strieby, September 26, 1864, in Sears, *Camp Nelson*, 259–60.
44. E. Merton Coulter, *The Civil War and Readjustment in Kentucky* (Gloucester, MA: Peter Smith, 1966), 254–55.
45. *Quincy Daily Herald,* December 2, 1865.
46. Fisk to Palmer, telegram, and Palmer to Fisk, telegram, September 28, 1865, MF.
47. Jaquess to Fisk, September 30, 1865, M 999.
48. Ibid.
49. *LD,* October 6 and 8, 1865.
50. *LDJ,* October 7, 1865.
51. *LD,* October 8, 1865.
52. *LDJ,* October 14, 1865.
53. *LD,* December 9, 1865
54. *LDJ,* January 12, 1866.
55. *LDJ,* May 10, 1866. There are no criminal indexes from Jefferson County, Kentucky, for the 1860s, so the original case record does not exist. However, the major decisions of the case are recorded in the Criminal Order Book of 1866, Education Cabinet, Kentucky Department for Libraries and Archives. This document was used whenever possible to verify the accuracy of the newspaper accounts.
56. *LDJ,* May 11, 1866.
57. *Daily Courier* (hereafter *DC*), May 11, 1866.
58. Ibid.
59. *DC,* May 16, 1866.
60. Ibid.
61. *DC,* May 17, 1866.

62. Reprint of article from *DC*, May 21, 1866, in *Quincy Daily Herald*, May 30, 1866.
63. *DC,* May 16. 1866; *LDJ,* May 16, 1866.
64. Fisk to Barrett, September 28, 1865, in Sears, *Camp Nelson,* 262–63.
65. Farwell to Fisk, March 14, 1866, in Sears, *Camp Nelson,* 328.
66. See Sears, lvii–lx, and 274–328 for the full account of closing the camp.
67. *QWR,* April 1, 1865.
68. *Quincy Daily Herald,* June 2, 1866.
69. Debby Applegate, *The Most Famous Man in America: The Biography of Henry Ward Beecher* (New York: Doubleday, 2006).
70. Ibid., 439.
71. Ibid., 441.
72. Ibid., 449.
73. Ibid., 451.
74. Jaquess to Fisk, June 27, 1865.
75. Jaquess to Fisk, September 30, 1865, NARA, M 999.
76. Palmer to his wife, September 26, 1865, Palmer Papers, ALPL.
77. *Mt. Carmel (IL) Democrat,* May 31, 1866.
78. *Danville (IL) Commercial,* May, 1866.
79. *[Illinois] Conference Minutes,* Methodist Church, Conference of 1866, p. 32, Great Rivers Methodist Archives, Pfeiffer Library, MacMurray College.

Chapter 8

1. *Louisville Democrat* (hereafter *LD*), October 8, 1865.
2. *Quincy Daily Herald* (hereafter *QDH*), May 30, 1866.
3. *LD,* October 8, 1865.
4. *Biographical and Historical Memoirs of Eastern Arkansas* (Chicago: Goodspeed, 1890), 778; Edward C. Kirkland, "James Frazier Jaquess," in *Dictionary of American Biography,* ed. Allen Johnson and Dumas Malone (New York: Charles Scribner's Sons, 1960 reprint), 5: 615–16, states that Jaquess "cultivated cotton, first in Arkansas and later in northern Mississippi."
5. *Minutes of the Illinois Conference of the Methodist Episcopal Church, 1866, 1867, 1868,* Great Rivers Methodist Archives (hereafter GRM Arch.), Pfeiffer Library, MacMurray College.
6. *QWR,* April 1, 1865.
7. *QDW,* April 13, 1865.
8. Obituary of Margaret Jaquess Castle," *Minutes of Proceedings of the Twenty-Third Annual Reunion of the Survivors Sev-*

enty-Third Regiment Illinois Volunteer Infantry, 1909, 20–21, Abraham Lincoln Presidential Library (ALPL).

9. *QWR*, August 27, 1864; *Quincy Daily Herald*, February 22, 1865, *QWR*, July 8, 1865.

10. Quotes from the *Quincy Daily Whig*, February 15, 1865.

11. Marquis D. Hornbeck, *A General Statement of the Financial History and Present Condition of Chaddock College, Presented May 1889* (Quincy: Skinner, 1889), 17–18, GRM Arch.

12. *Biographical and Historical Memoirs of Mississippi, Embracing an Authentic and Comprehensive Account of the Chief Events in the History and a Record of the Lives of the Most Worthy Families and Individuals* (Chicago: Goodspeed, 1891), 1, Pt. 1, 1016.

13. Tunica County Deed Book F, 1860–1879, pp. 690–91, Mississippi Department of Archives and History, Jackson, MS (hereafter MDAH).

14. *Memoirs of Mississippi*, 1016.

15. John W. Dulaney, Jr., *Tunica County Scraps of History* (Xlibris, 2006), 25.

16. *Memoirs of Mississippi*, 1016.

17. *New York Times*, December 14, 1932.

18. Tunica County Deed Book F, 687–90.

19. Source Materials for Mississippi History, Tunica County, unbound, MDAH.

20. Dulaney, *Scraps of History*, 25.

21. Source Materials, MDAH.

22. Dulaney, *Scraps of History*, 25–26.

23. Thomas A. DeBlack, *With Fire and Sword: Arkansas, 1861–1874* (Fayetteville: University of Arkansas Press, 2003), 87.

24. Ibid., 153.

25. Randy Finley, *From Slavery to Uncertain Freedom: The Freedmen's Bureau in Arkansas, 1865–1869* (Fayetteville: University of Arkansas Press, 1996), 18.

26. Ibid., 73.

27. Ibid., 82.

28. Ibid., 158.

29. Carl H. Moneyhon, *The Impact of the Civil War and Reconstruction on Arkansas: Persistence in the Midst of Ruin* (Fayetteville: University of Arkansas Press, 2002), 242; *New York Times*, February 20. 1867; Reprint from *Arkansas Republican*, May 1, 1867, in *New York Times*, May 10, 1867.

30. Moneyhon, *Impact*, 246.

31. *Quincy Daily Herald*, December 19, 1867.

32. Moneyhon, *Impact*, 247.

33. Ibid., 250.

34. Ibid., 249.

35. Ibid., 250.

36. Arkansas Reconstruction Telegram Collection, Ark. Arch., provides accounts of the numerous violent incidents.

37. *Biographical Memoirs of Eastern Arkansas* (Chicago: The Goodspeed Publishing Company, 1890), 778.

38. Special Collections, Transylvania University Library, Lexington, KY; "George D. Jaquess," Nineteenth Century Indiana Physicians Created by Special Collections Department, Ruth Lilly Medical Library, Indiana University School of Medicine, http://www.medlib.iupui.edu/body.cfm?id=140

39. *Helena Clarion*, March 24, 1869, gives a list of property taxes (Arkansas History Commission and State Archives, Little Rock).

40. Dunbar Rowland, *History of Mississippi, the Heart of the South* (Chicago: S.J. Clarke, 1925), 840–41; *Inventory of the County Archives of Mississippi, No. 72, Tunica County*, prepared by the Mississippi Historical Records Survey, Service Division, Work Projects Administration, Jackson, MS, Survey, 1942, Newberry Library, 15–24.

41. Inventory of Tunica County Archives, 15–24.

42. Dulaney, Jr., *Scraps of History*, 43–44.

43. James Wilford Garner, *Reconstruction in Mississippi* (Gloucester, MA: Peter Smith, 1969), 171–76.

44. Ibid., 175.

45. Ibid., 176.

46. Tunica County Deed Record, Book F, 1860–1870, pp. 560–62, MDAH.

47. Testimony of William Enoch French, James F. Jaquess Trial, Old Bailey, November 19, 1894, http://www.oldbaileyonline.org/.

48. *Biographical Directory of the Indiana General Assembly*, vol. 1, *1816–1899* (Indianapolis: Select Committee on the Centennial History of the Indiana General Assembly, 1980), 204.

49. Tunica County Deed Record, Book F, 1860–1870, pp. 560–62.

50. *Reports of Cases Argued and Decided in the Supreme Court of the United States by United States Supreme Court*, ed. Stephen Keyes Williams, Edwin Burritt Smith, Ernest Hitchcock (Lawyers Co-operative, 1885), 91–93; Deed Record Book F, 690–91.

51. Tunica County Deed Record, Book F, 1860–1870, pp. 560–62.

52. Testimony of James F. Jaquess, Howell Thomas Trial, Old Bailey, June 25, 1894, http://www.oldbaileyonline.org/.
53. Col. J.F. Jaquess to Hon. Senator Yates and to Hon. James Harlan, both dated March 8, 1869, Richard Yates Papers, Box 27, Archives, Abraham Lincoln Presidential Library, Springfield, IL (Arch. ALPL).
54. Senate Executive Journal, Executive Mansion, June 29, 1870 and December 17, 1870, http://memory.loc.gov.
55. Documents from headquarters, 4th Military District, MDAH.
56. Dulaney, *Scraps of History,* 25.
57. Mississippi Memoirs 1016.
58. Dulaney, *Scraps of History,* 25.
59. Deed Record Book F, 687–90.
60. Ibid., 690–91.
61. James is in District 1 and William is in District 3.
62. *Minutes of the Illinois Conference of the Methodist Episcopal Church.*
63. Report of the Committee on Military Affairs, Ordered to be printed June 14, 1870, Library of Congress, *A Century of Lawmaking for a New Nation: U.S. Congressional Documents and Debates, 1774–1875,* http://memory.loc.gov.
64. Documents concerning reimbursement for horses, Record Group 94, National Archives and Records Administration, Washington, D.C.
65. http://www.uspto.gov I am indebted to Dr. Martha Steffens, a Jaquess descendent, for information about the patent.
66. Definitions of these terms come from Matthews Simpson's *Cyclopedia of Methodism* (Philadelphia: Everts and Stewart, 1878), 842–3, and Lauretta Schiller, Archivist, GRM Arch. The actions are recorded in "Minutes for the Illinois Conference of the Methodist Church, 1856–1874," GRM Arch.

Chapter 9

1. James M. Cox, *Mark Twain: The Fate of Humor* (Princeton, NJ: Princeton University Press, 1966), 129. Quotation is Mark Twain's.
2. *The Autobiography of Mark Twain, Including Chapters Now Published for the First Time,* ed. Charles Neider (New York: Harper, 1959), 19. See also Arlin Turner, "James Lampton, Mark Twain's Model for Colonel Sellers," *Modern Language Notes* 70 (#8, Dec. 1955): 15–17, and Edward H. Weatherly, "Beau Tibbs and Colonel Sellers," *Modern Language Notes* 59 (#5, May 1944): 310–13.
3. Patrick Polden, "Stranger Than Fiction?: The Jennens Inheritance in Fact and Fiction," part 2, "The Business of Fortune Hunting," *Common Law World Review* 32 (#4, 2003): 342.
4. Patrick Polden, "Stranger than Fiction? The Jennens Inheritance in Fact and Fiction," part 1, "The Jennens Fortune in the Courts," *Common Law World Review* 32 (#3, 2003): 212.
5. Ibid. 217.
6. Ibid. 225.
7. Ibid. 235.
8. Ibid. 247.
9. Polden, Part 2, 34.
10. Ibid. 363.
11. The *New York Times* warned Americans about estates in England on November 10, 1879; April 16, 1881; December 22, 1885; January 11, 1886; October 18, 1886; March 6, 1887; May 23, 1887; January 31, 1888; February 21, 1890; January 19, 1894; January 15, 1895; January 27, 1895; July 30, 1895; November 8, 1895; January 24, 1897; September 7, 1902, and possibly other dates as well. Stories from the *Times* were often reprinted in newspapers in other towns and states.
12. *New York Times* (hereafter *NYT*), November 10, 1879.
13. Ibid., May 23, 1887.
14. The American spelling of Townley is used throughout.
15. *Quincy Daily Herald,* December 2, 1865.
16. Testimony of William Enoch French, Records from First Session of Old Court, 1894–95, recorded 11/26–30/94, 60. Identified as CRIM 10/85, National Archives, United Kingdom.
17. Ibid.
18. Ibid.
19. http://chnm.gmu.edu/lostmuseum/lm/328/.
20. Herman Melville, *The Confidence-Man: His Masquerade,* ed. Harrison Hayford, Hershel Parker, G. Thomas Tanselle, historical note by Watson Branch (Evanston: Northwestern University Press, 1984).
21. James Usher and Frank Alden Hill discuss this claim.
22. This version of the Townley and Lawrence marriage is the one that Jaquess presents in court. There are several other versions.

23. James Usher, *History of the Lawrence-Townley and Chase-Townley Estates of England, with Copious Historical and Genealogical Notes of the Lawrence-Chase and Townely Families and Much Other Valuable Information* (New York: 1883), 49.

24. Unless otherwise identified, Lawrence-Townley bonds and certificates come from the collection of Sherry Jones, whose ancestors purchased them.

25. Jasiel is sometimes spelled Jaziel.

26. Bonds issued in 1879 have signatures for both Jasiel and William, but both names appear to have been written by the same person, very likely Jasiel. There is no longer any indication of Corydon Karr's involvement. The handwriting of Jaquess, which is easily identified, does not appear on any bonds in the Jones collection.

27. "Lawrence Townley" Estate of England and Heirship of William Townley Lawrence of Troy, N.Y., Collections of the New York Public Library.

28. *NYT*, January 27, 1895.

29. Much of the information about Anna Marie Peregoy Meixsel comes from Richard B. Meixsel's unpublished article, "Preacher, Soldier, Bigamist, Thief?: The Strange Career of Colonel James F. Jaquess," and other family information provided by Dr. Meixsel.

30. 1870 census.

31. Card file of about 17,000 names, Church Family Daily Journal, Mss. No. V: B-71 and Mss. No. III: B-11), Western Reserve Historical Society, as provided by Jerry V. Grant, Shaker Museum and Library, Old Chatham, NY.

32. Ibid.

33. Application of Anna Marie Jaquess for a widow's pension after the death of James Jaquess, National Archives and Records Administration.

34. Chancery Records, Tunica County, 1868–1894, Mississippi Department of History and Archives, Jackson, MS.; Ramsey County Civil Case Files, Minnesota Historical Library, St. Paul.

35. Palmer to his wife, September 26, 1865, Palmer Papers, Archives, Abraham Lincoln Presidential Library.

36. "Reminiscences of Elvira Hamilton Adams," ed. Caroline Adams Griffin, Alice Griffin Andrews and Douglas Q. Adams, MacMurray College Archives.

37. *Dictionary of National Biography*, ed. Sir Leslie Stephen and Sir Sidney Lee, Oxford, 1921–22 reprint), 19.1025 (DAB); L.G. Pine, *The New Extinct Peerage 1884–1971, Containing Extinct, Abeyant, Dormant and Suspended Peerages with Genealogies and Arms* (London: Heraldry Today, 1972), 175.

38. Usher, *History of ... Estates*, 59.

39. Affidavit of Colonel Jaquess, sworn 15th May 1888, item No. 16, Parliamentary Archives, House of Lords Record Office, *Lawrence v. Lord Norreys* Case, Main Papers, HL/PO/JO/10/9/1264, CRIM 10/85, 64. These papers (referred to as the "Book"), include full accounts of the original case and the appeal of this decision at the Court of Appeal.

40. http://www.measuringworth.com/exchange/.

41. Usher, 68.

42. *Jacksonville Daily Journal*, March 4, 1880.

43. *NYT*, June 26, 1881, and January 13, 1883.

44. Usher, *History of ... Estates*, 59.

45. *Oshkosh (WI) Daily Northwesterner*, September 11, 1865.

46. *Decatur (IL) Daily Republican*, October 20, 1885.

47. *NYT*, March 19, 1885.

48. Usher, *History of ... Estates*, 52.

49. Frank Alden Hill, *The Mystery Solved: "Lawrence-Townley," "Chase-Townley," Marriage and Estate Questions* (Boston: Rand Avery, 1888), 37, 63.

50. CRIM 10/85, 64, *Jaquess v. Thomas*, Supreme Court Judicature, Court of Appeal, March 17, 1894; affidavit of Jaquess, 15th May 1888, *Jaquess v. Thomas*, before Justice Matthew and Justice Collins, Queen's Bench, January 11, 12, 15, 1894.

51. Wills and Administrations, Historical Society of Pennsylvania, Philadelphia. James and Anna Marie owned a home in Philadelphia and very likely took the will there.

Chapter 10

1. A British solicitor is a lawyer who performs the same functions of an attorney in America except representing a client in court. In England this function is handled by another British lawyer called a barrister.

2. Parliamentary Archives, House of Lords Record Office, *Lawrence v. Lord Norreys* Case, Main Papers, HL/PO/JO/10/9/1264, 8. The 120 page document (hereinafter called the "Book"), includes full ac-

counts of all actions up to and including the House of Lords.
3. Ibid., 7, 9.
4. Ibid., 11.
5. "Statute of limitations" is a statute defining the period within which legal action may be taken.
6. Joseph Chitty and J.M. Lely, *A Treatise of the Law of Contracts* (London: Sweet & Maxwell, 1896), 685.
7. Frank Alden Hill, *The Mystery Solved: "Lawrence-Townley," "Chase-Townley," Marriage and Estate Questions* (Boston: Rand Avery, 1888), 37, 63.
8. *Jacksonville (IL) Daily Journal*, June 2, 1887.
9. "Book," No. 15, Affidavit of Mr. Howell Thomas, sworn 15th May 1888, 35–38.
10. Ibid.
11. Ibid., No. 16, Affidavit of Colonel Jaquess, sworn 15 May 1888, 39.
12. Ibid., No. 17, Judgment of Mr. Justice Stirling, dated 18 May 1888, 45.
13. Ibid., 46.
14. The plaintiff is a person who initiates a lawsuit by bringing a complaint to a court of law; the person who brings evidence against this complaint is the defendant.
15. "Book," No. 18, 48–49.
16. Ibid., No. 20, Judgment of the Court of Appeal, 15 June 1888, 53.
17. Ibid., 55.
18. Philadelphia City Directory of 1889, Archives of Historical Society of Pennsylvania (hereafter Arch. Hist. Soc. PA), 1300 Locust Street, Philadelphia, PA, 908.
19. This information listed in July 1888, Arch. Hist. Soc. PA.
20. "Real Estate Transfers," J.F. Jaquess to C. Stern, *Philadelphia Inquirer*, May 9, 1889.
21. James Jaquess stated that he was residing at 26 Denbigh Place, Pimlico, SW, and previously had lived at Woburn Place, Russell Square (Trial of Howell Thomas for Deception, June 15, 1894, 769–94, in original document), http://www.oldbaileyonline.org/static/Proceedings.jsp.
22." CRIM 10/85," National Archives, Kew, Richmond, Surrey, 64
23. Information provided by Dr. Richard Meixsel.
24. *Tri-County Advertiser* (Clarksville, GA), January 19, 1928.
25. W.H. Newlin, D.F. Lawler, and J.W. Sherrick, *A History of the Seventy-third Regiment of Illinois Infantry Volunteers* (Springfield: Regimental Reunion Association of Survivors of the 73rd Infantry, 1890), 557.
26. House of Lords, Tuesday, 22nd April 1890, Lawrance, Appellant, and Lord Norreys and Other Respondents, Judgment, 5.
27. Ibid., 11.
28. Ibid., 17.
29. Ibid., 19.
30. Ibid., 27.
31. Ibid., 30.
32. "CRIM 10/85," 64.
33. *Address to the 73rd Regiment, Illinois Volunteer Infantry, by Colonel James F. Jaquess, at a Reunion Held in Springfield, Illinois, October 8th–10th, 1890*, Abraham Lincoln Presidential Library, 12.
34. "CRIM 10/85," 64.
35. *The Times* (London), January 11 and 12, 1894, refer to filing of this case.
36. Only the solicitor's surname is given.
37. *The Times* (London), April 19, 1894.
38. Ibid., January 15, 1894.
39. Ibid., January 15, 1894.
40. Ibid., March 17, 1894.
41. Ibid.
42. Ibid., April 14, 1894.
43. Trial of Howell Thomas, http://www.oldbaileyonline.org/browse.jsp?id=def1-579-18940625&div=t18940625-579#highlight.
44. *"Explanatory"* (1894), Minnesota Historical Society Library, St Paul, MN.
45. Trial of Howell Thomas, http://www.oldbaileyonline.org/browse.jsp?id=def1-579-18940625&div=t18940625-579#highlight.
46. Ibid.
47. *The Times* (London), July 4, 1894.
48. *New York Times (NYT)*, July 4, 1894.
49. *The Times* (London), July 18, 1894.
50. CRIM 10/85, 63.
51. Mrs. Anna M. Jaquess to Hon. Daniel Lamont, July 17, 1894, National Archives and Records Administration (hereafter NARA), Record Group (RG), 94.
52. Record and Pension Office of the War Department to Mrs. Anna M. Jaquess, July 25, 1894, NARA, RG 94.
53. George Brown Tindall and David E. Shi, *America: A Narrative History*, 5th ed., 2 (New York: W.W. Norton, 1999), 1042; Richard B. Morris, ed., *Encyclopedia of American History* (New York: Harper, 1953), 286.
54. CRIM 10/85, 57.
55. CRIM 10/85, 56, 57.
56. CRIM 9/40, "Calendar of Prisoners for the Session Commencing on Monday,

19th of November, 1894"(London: Harrison and Sons, n.d.), National Archives, 8.
57. CRIM 10/85, 57.
58. Ibid., 58.
59. "William E. French," *Evansville and Its Men of Mark* (Evansville, IN: Historical Publishing, 1873, reprint Whipporwill, 1985), 416–18.
60. CRIM 10/85, 57, 63
61. Ibid., 61.
62. Ibid., 63.
63. Ibid., 60.
64. Ibid., 64–65.
65. Ibid., 67–69.
66. Ibid., 69.
67. CRIM 9/40.
68. Justin Hawkins, *The Reminiscences of Sir Henry Hawkins, Baron Brampton*, ed. Richard Harris, K.C. (London: Edward Arnold, 1904), 1, 238.
69. *London Daily Telegraph*, December 1, 1894.
70. Pentonville Prison, http://www.victorianweb.org/periodicals/iln/11.html.
71. Lee Jackson and Eric Nathan, *Victorian London* (London: New Holland, 2004), 60. Norval Morris and David J. Rothman, eds., *The Oxford History of the Prison* (New York: Oxford University, 1995), picture of Pentonville prisoners in their hoods, 102; http//:www.victorianlondon.org.
72. Richard Ellmann, *Oscar Wilde* (New York: Alfred A. Knopf, 1988), 479–80.
73. Ibid.
74. Ibid.
75. "Explanatory."
76. Ibid.
77. *NYT*, November 7, 1895.

Chapter 11

1. *New York Times*, November 8, 1895.
2. As an attorney in Quincy, Castle specialized in filing claims for Union soldiers (see *Quincy Whig Republican*, April 1, 1865).
3. James F. Jaquess, Pension File, National Archives and Records Administration (NARA).
4. Watson's article is included in the appendix of William Eleazar Barton, *The Soul of Abraham Lincoln* (New York: George H. Doran, 1920, reprinted Urbana: University of Illinois Press, 2005).
5. Ibid.
6. L.L. Turner, *Phillips County Arkansas Cemeteries* (Brinkley, AK: L.L. Turner and F.M. Turner, 1991), 2, 95.
7. *College Greetings*, July 1897, MacMurray College Archives (Mac Arch.), Pfeiffer Library, MacMurray College.
8. Ibid.
9. Ibid., November 1897.
10. Obituary of S.W. Nichols, *Jacksonville (IL) Courier*, October 24, 1927.
11. "Sketch of Dr. Jaquess," reprinted in *College Greetings*, March 8, 1898, Mac Arch. Published originally in *Chicago Times-Herald*, June 17, 1897.
12. *Minutes of Proceedings of the Eleventh Annual Reunion, Survivors Seventy-Third Regiment, Illinois Infantry Volunteers*, September 28 and 29, 1897 (Springfield, IL: 1897), Abraham Lincoln Presidential Library.
13. Ibid.
14. Lincoln Log, http://www.thelincolnlog.org/view.
15. Ervin Chapman, *Latest Light on Lincoln* (New York: Fleming H. Revell, 1917), 1: 39.
16. Ibid., 83–140.
17. Barton, *The Soul of Abraham Lincoln*, Appendix III, 309–13.
18. "Conversion of Abraham Lincoln" and Lester L. Swift Letters, June 28; July 7, 29; Dec. 2, 21, 1963, in Papers of Glenn I. Tucker, Archives and Special Collections, DePauw University, Greencastle, IN.
19. Robert N. Butler, "The Life Review: An Interpretation of Reminiscence in the Aged" in (chapter 14) *Philosophical Foundations of Gerontology*, ed. Patrick L. McKee (New York: Human Sciences Press, 1982).
20. *Greetings*, February 1898, Mac Arch.
21. Pension File, NARA, including a letter from the Special Examiner, Memphis, TN, April 30, 1898.
22. Ibid.
23. Ibid.
24. Ibid.
25. Ibid.
26. http://oaklandcemeterymn.com/tours.html.
27. *St. Paul Globe*, June 18, 1898; *St. Paul Pioneer Press*, June 18. 1898.
28. *New York Times*, June 19, 1898.
29. *Quincy Daily Journal*, June 18, 1898.
30. *Weekly (Jacksonville) Illinois Courier*, June 22, 1898.
31. *Greetings*, June 1898.
32. Pension File, NARA.
33. "Obituary of Margaret Jaquess Castle," *Minutes of Proceedings of the Twenty-*

Third Annual Reunion of the Survivors Seventy-Third Regiment Illinois Volunteer Infantry, 1909, Abraham Lincoln Presidential Library (ALPL).

34. "Henry Anson Castle," http://discovery.mnhs.org/MN150/index.php?title=Henry_Anson_Castle.

35. *Minutes of Proceedings of the Thirtieth Annual Reunion of the Survivors of the Seventy-Third Reg't. Illinois Volunteer Infantry*, 1916, ALPL.

36. *Biographical and Historical Memoirs of Mississippi, Embracing an Authentic and Comprehensive Account of the Chief Events in the History and a Record of the Lives of the Most Worthy families and Individuals* (Chicago: Goodspeed, 1891), 1, Pt. 1, p. 1016.

37. *New York Times*, December 13. 1932.

38. Information provided by Dr. Richard Meixsel.

39. *New York Times*, October 1, 1909.

40. Deposition from April 1898 with his statement about "twice married and only twice," Anna Marie's application, Pension File, NARA.

41. Her record at the Eleonora Ruppert Home comes from the Kiplinger Research Library, Historical Society of Washington, D.C.

42. *Minutes of Proceedings of the 73rd Infantry*, October 20 and 21, 1898.

43. Ibid., October 4, 1904.

44. Ibid., October 3, 1905, includes a picture of the tablet, 18.

45. *Quincy Whig*, June 25, 1905.

46. Ibid.

47. http://www.chaddock.org/home/about-chaddock.

Bibliography

Primary Sources

ARCHIVES

Abraham Lincoln Presidential Library (ALPL), Springfield, IL, formerly Illinois State Historical Library: Pamphlet published by City of Quincy, Vertical File. Commencement Programs and Exhibition Programs of Literary Societies of Quincy College; Benjamin H. Grierson Papers: *Lights and Shadows of Life.* Typed autobiography; John M. Palmer Papers; Richard Yates Papers (Box 27)

Adams County, Quincy, IL, Clerk's Office: Chancery Records A-8, April 9, 1861 to November 22, 1862.

Allen County Public Library, Fort Wayne, IN: "Genealogical Notes of the Families of Schnee and Jaquess." Typed Unnumbered Manuscript. Mt. Vernon, IN: General Thomas Posey Chapter DAR.

Arkansas History Commission and State Archives Little Rock, AR: Arkansas Reconstruction Telegram Collection; *Helena (AR) Clarion*, March 24, 1869.

DePauw University Archives and Special Collections, Greencastle, IN: Papers of Glenn I. Tucker.

Great Britain, Parliamentary Archives, House of Lords Record Office: *Lawrence v. Lord Norreys* Case. Main Papers. HL/PO/JO/10/9/1264.

Great Rivers Archives of United Methodist Church at MacMurray College. Pfeiffer Library, Jacksonville, IL: Bryant, Captain Thomas J. Surviving pages from "War Reminiscences: History of Company D, 14th Illinois Infantry"; Dickens, James H. To James Leaton, ca. 1878–80. Typed from handwritten copy, 3 unnumbered pages; Leaton, James. *Methodism in Illinois.* Illinois Conference Historical Society, 1889: 3. Typed from original handwritten unpublished manuscript; *Illinois Conference Minutes, Methodist Church, 1836–1847, Conference of 1845.* Typed from handwritten manuscript; *Minutes of the Illinois Conference of the Methodist Episcopal Church, 1866–1874; Minutes of Illinois Conference of Methodist Episcopal Church* (September 1849, Quincy; Springfield, 1854; Quincy, 1856).

Historical Society of Pennsylvania: Wills and Administrations; Philadelphia Grantee Index, July 14, 1888.

Illinois State Archives: *Enrolled Acts of the General Assembly*, R.S. 103–030. Photocopies of handwritten originals; Papers of the Sixth Illinois Cavalry; Papers of Governor Richard Yates.

Illinois Wesleyan University Archives, Ames Library, Bloomington, IL: Fifer, W.A., Secretary of the Quincy, IL, Chamber of Commerce. To Mr. L.E. Lackland of Sycamore, IL, November 5, 1941.

Johns Hopkins University: James R. Gilmore Papers.

Kentucky Department for Libraries and Archives: Criminal Order Book of 1866, Education Cabinet.

Library of Congress: Abraham Lincoln Papers. Transcribed and annotated by the Lincoln Studies Center, Knox College, Galesburg, Illinois.

Lincoln Memorial University: Archives of the Lincoln Library and Museum, Harrogate, TN (Jaquess to Gilmore, November 4, 1863).

MacMurray College Archives, Pfeiffer Library, Jacksonville, IL: James R. Harker. "History of MacMurray College." Typewritten manuscript; *Illinois Conference Female Academy, Illinois Conference Female College, Record of Trustees' Meetings Beginning October 10, 1845, Ending May 19, 1858*. Bound photocopy of original handwritten document; Catalogs of Illinois Conference Female Academy for 1851 and 1853; Adams, Elvira Hamilton. *Reminiscences of Elvira Hamilton Adams*. Edited by Caroline Adams Griffin, Alice Griffin Andrews and Douglas Q. Adams.

McKendree College, Lebanon, IL, Methodist Archives: *150 Years of Methodism in Shawneetown, Illinois* 5; McKendree College Catalog, 1879.

Minnesota Historical Library, St. Paul, MN: Ramsey County Civil Case File; "Explanatory" (1894 and 1898).

Mississippi Department of Archives and History, Jackson, MS: Tunica County Deed Record, Book F, 1860–1870; Source Materials for Mississippi History, Tunica County (unbound); Inventory of the County Archives of Mississippi, No. 72, Tunica County; Documents from Headquarters 4th Military District; Chancery Records, Tunica County, 1868–1894.

Mount Carmel Illinois Public Library: Historical Cemetery Records: Genealogy of the Children of I.N. Jaquess and Jane Tilton.

National Archives (formerly Public Record Office), United Kingdom: CRIM 10/85; CRIM 9/40.

National Archives and Record Service: Colonel Thomas Cavanaugh Military File; Col. James F. Jaquess Military File; Willie G. Jaquess Military File Lt. Col. John Olney Military File; Record Group 94, M1064, Roll #101; Microfilm (M) 999, consulted at Newberry Library; Application of Anna Marie Jaquess for Widow's Pension; James F. Jaquess Pension File.

New York Public Library: Collections: "Lawrence Townley" Estate of England and Heirship of William Townley Lawrence of Troy, NY.

New York State Library, Albany, NY: "Lawrence Scrip."

Ohio Historical Society: Wilbur Siebert Collection.

Robinson, IL, Public Library District: Williams, Joy Steel. "My Ancestry." Typewritten manuscript.

Shaker Museum and Library, Old Chatham, NY.

Transylvania University Library, Lexington, KY: Special Collections.

Virginia Polytechnic Institute Library, Blacksburg, VA: Guy di Carlo, Jr., Civil War Research Papers, Special Collections and Archives.

Wabash College, Lilly Library, Archives: Winfred A. Haribson Papers relating to Richard Yates. Now in ALPL.

Western Reserve Historical Society, Cleveland, OH: Card files of about 17,000 names, Church Family Daily Journal; Mss. No. V: B-71 and Mss. No. III: B-11.

Willard Library, Evansville, IN: Lindell, Kathy. "If Walls Could Talk." Typed Unnumbered Manuscript, March 1986. Includes excerpts from Jaquess, Asbury Cloud. *A Short History of Three Communities* (1892), and "An Account of the Coming of the Jonathan Jaquess Family to Indiana," n.d.

PRINTED PRIMARY SOURCES

Arndt, Karl R.J. *A Documentary History of the Indiana Decade of the Harmony Society, 1814–1824*, vol. 1, *1814–1819*; vol. 2, *1820–1824*. Indianapolis: Indiana Historical Society, 1978.

Bryant, Thomas J. *Who Is Responsible for the Advance of Army of the Tennessee Toward Corinth?* Circa 1885. ALPL.

Cartwright, Peter. *Autobiography of Peter Cartwright: 53 Years as a Pioneer Preacher*. Centennial edition, with an introduction by Charles B. Wallis. Nashville, TN: Abington Press, 1956.

Freeman, Norman L. *Reports of Cases at Law and in Chancery, Argued and Determined in the Supreme Court of Illinois*. Vol. 33. Chicago: E.B. Myers & Chandler, 1866.

Grant, Ulysses S. *The Papers of Ulysses S. Grant*. Vol. 4, January 8-March 31, 1862. Edited by John Y. Simon; assistant editor, Roger D. Bridges. Carbondale: Southern Illinois University Press, 1972.

Grierson, Benjamin H. *A Just and Righteous Cause: Benjamin H. Grierson's Civil War Memoir*. Edited by Bruce J. Dinges and Shirley A. Leckie. Carbondale: Southern Illinois University Press, 2008.

Hawkins, Sir Henry. *The Reminiscences of Sir Henry Hawkins, Baron Brampton*. Edited by Richard Harris, K.C. 2 vols. London: Edward Arnold 1904.

Lawrence-Townley Bonds and Certificates purchased by the ancestors of Sherry Jones.
Lincoln, Abraham. *The Collected Works of Abraham Lincoln.* Edited by Roy P. Basler, et al. 9 volumes and index. New Brunswick, NJ: Rutgers University Press, 1953. *First Supplement, 1832–1865.* Edited by Roy P. Basler, 1974. *Second Supplement, 1848–1865.* Edited by Roy P. Basler and Christian O. Basler, 1990.
Philadelphia City Directory of 1889.
Report of the Adjutant General of the State of Illinois: Containing Reports for the Years 1861–66. Revised by Brigadier General J.W. Vance, Adjutant General. Springfield: H.W. Rokker, ca. 1886.
Reports of Cases Argued and Decided in the Supreme Court of the United States by United States Supreme Court. Stephen Keyes Williams, Edwin Burritt Smith, Ernest Hitchcock, Lawyers Co-operative, 1885.
Sears, Richard D. *Camp Nelson, Kentucky: A Civil War History.* Lexington: University Press of Kentucky, 2002.
Union Congressional Committee (broadside), and *Rebel Terms of Peace* (6 pp.). Washington, DC: L. Towers, 1864 (Abraham Lincoln Presidential Library).
United States Census Bureau. 1840 Census, Putnam County, Indiana.1850 Census. 1860 Census. 1870 Census. 1880 Census.
United States War Department. *War of the Rebellion: Official Records of the Union and Confederate Armies.* Edited by Robert N. Scott, et al. 70 vols. Washington, DC: GPO, 1880–1901.
War of the Rebellion. Series 3: 1. Washington, DC: Government Printing Office, 1899.

Secondary Sources

Books

Alexander, Gross, et al. *A History of the Methodist Church, South, the United Presbyterian Church, the Cumberland Presbyterian Church and the Presbyterian Church, South, in the United States.* Vol. 11 in *The American Church History Series.* New York: Christian Literature, 1894.
American National Biography. Edited by John A. Garraty and Mark C. Carnes. 24 vols. New York: Oxford University Press, 1999.
Applegate, Debby. *The Most Famous Man in America: The Biography of Henry Ward Beecher.* New York: Doubleday, 2006
Asbury, Henry. *Reminiscences of Quincy, Illinois, Containing Historical Events, Anecdotes, Matters Concerning Old Settlers and Old Time, etc.* Quincy: D. Wilcox, 1882.
Baker, Frank. *From Wesley to Asbury: Studies in Early American Methodism.* Durham, NC: Duke University Press, 1976.
Barton, William Eleazar. *The Soul of Abraham Lincoln.* New York: George H. Doran, 1920. Reprinted Urbana: University of Illinois Press, 2005.
Beard, Jo Anne. *The Legacy of Historic Jacksonville: Its Homes and Buildings.* Jacksonville, IL: City of Jacksonville Historic Preservation Commission, 1986.
A Biographical Directory of the Indiana General Assembly. Compiled and edited by Rebecca A. Shepherd, Charles W. Calhoun, Elizabeth Shanahan-Shoemaker, and Alan F. January, 1 (1816–1899). Indianapolis: Indiana Historic Bureau, 1980.
Biographical and Historical Memoirs of Eastern Arkansas. Chicago: Goodspeed, 1890.
Biographical and Historical Memoirs of Mississippi, Embracing an Authentic and Comprehensive Account of the Chief Events in the History and a Record of the Lives of the Most Worthy Families and Individuals. Chicago: Goodspeed, 1891.
The Book of Discipline of the United Methodist Church. Nashville: United Methodist Publishing House, 2004.
Brandt, Nat. *The Man Who Tried to Burn New York.* New York: Syracuse University Press, 1986.
Bray, Robert. *Peter Cartwright, Legendary Frontier Preacher.* Urbana: University of Illinois Press, 2005.
Brigham, Johnson. *James Harlan.* Iowa Biographical Series. Iowa City: State Historical Society of Iowa, 1913.
Brinkman, Michael K. *Quincy, Illinois, Immigrants from Munsterland Westphalia Germany.* 2 vols. Westminster, MD: Heritage Books, 2010.
Brown, Ann Eckert. *American Wall Stenciling, 1790–1840.* Lebanon, NH: University Press of New England, 2003.
Burlingame, Michael. *Abraham Lincoln: A Life.* 2 volumes. Baltimore: Johns Hopkins University Press, 2008.
Butler, Robert N. "The Life Review: An Interpretation of Reminiscence in the Aged." Chapter 14 in *Philosophical Foun-*

dations of Gerontology. Edited by Patrick L. McKee. New York: Human Sciences Press, 1982.

Carlson, Theodore L. *The Illinois Military Tract: A Study of Land Opportunities, Utilization and Tenure*. Urbana: University of Illinois Press, 1951.

Carter, John J. *Covert Action as a Tool of Presidential Foreign Policy, from the Bay of Pigs to Iran-contra*. Lewiston, NY: Edwin Mellen, 2006.

Castle, Drew W., and Henry A. Castle. "Castle-Jaquess Families." Genealogical charts begun by Henry A. Castle and completed by his grandson Drew. Joliet, IL: 1970 (ALPL).

Chapman, Ervin. *Latest Light on Lincoln*. 2 vols. New York: Fleming H. Revell, 1917.

Chitty, Joseph, J.M. Lely. *A Treatise of the Law of Contracts*. London: Sweet & Maxwell, 1896.

Costigan, David. "A City in Wartime: Quincy, Illinois and the Civil War." Doctor of Arts diss., Illinois State University, Bloomington, IL, 1994.

Coulter, E. Merton. *The Civil War and Readjustment in Kentucky*. Gloucester, MA: Peter Smith, 1966 (repr.).

———. *The Confederate States of America 1861–1865*. Vol. 7, *History of the South*. Baton Rouge: Louisiana State University Press and the Littlefield Fund for Southern History of the University of Texas, 1950.

Cox, Carroll D., and Gloria M. Cox. *New Harmony, Indiana, Newspaper Gleanings*. Owensboro, KY: Cook-McDowell, 1980.

Cozzens, Peter. *No Better Place to Die: The Battle of Stones River*. Urbana: University of Illinois Press, 1991.

Cummins, D. Duane. *The Disciples Colleges: A History*. St. Louis: CBP 1987.

Davis, Jefferson. *The Rise and Fall of the Confederate Government*. New York: D. Appleton, 1881.

Davis, Rodney O., and Douglas L. Wilson, eds. *The Lincoln-Douglas Debates*. Urbana: Knox College Lincoln Studies Center and the University of Illinois Press, 2008.

DeBlack, Thomas A. *With Fire and Sword: Arkansas, 1861–1874*. Fayetteville: University of Arkansas Press, 2003.

Decker, Philip H. *A Window on the Past: Residences of Jacksonville, Illinois, Their History and Design, 1833–1925*. Jacksonville: Production Press for Morgan County Historical Society, 1990.

Doyle, Don Harrison. *The Social Order of a Frontier Community: Jacksonville, Illinois, 1825–70*. Urbana: University of Illinois Press, 1978.

Dulaney, John W., Jr. *Tunica County Scraps of History*. Xlibris, 2006.

Eames, Charles M. *Historic Morgan and Classic Jacksonville*. Jacksonville, IL: Printed at the *Daily Journal*, 1885.

Ellmann, Richard. *Oscar Wilde*. New York: Alfred A. Knopf, 1988.

Farthing, Paul, and Chester Farthing. *Philo History: Chronicles and Biographies of the Philosophian Literary Society of McKendree College*. Lebanon, IL: Published For the Society, 1911.

Fernandes, Vernon R.Q. *Passavant Area Hospital: 125 Years of Caring*. Jacksonville, IL: Passavant Memorial Area Hospital, 1999.

Finley, Randy. *From Slavery to Uncertain Freedom: The Freedmen's Bureau in Arkansas, 1865–1869*. Fayetteville: University of Arkansas Press, 1996.

Flanders, Robert Bruce. *Nauvoo: Kingdom on the Mississippi*. Urbana: University of Illinois Press, 1965.

Foner, Eric. *Reconstruction: America's Unfinished Revolution, 1861–1877*. New York: Harper & Row, 1988.

Frank, Charles E. *Pioneer's Progress: Illinois College, 1829–1979*. Carbondale: Southern Illinois University Press, 1979.

Freehling, William W. *The Road to Disunion*. Vol. 2, *Secessionists Triumphant, 1854–1861*. New York: Oxford University Press, 2007.

Garner, James Wilford. *Reconstruction in Mississippi*. Gloucester, MA: Peter Smith, 1969 (repr.).

Gilmore, James R. (aka Edmund Kirke). *Down in Tennessee*. New York: Carleton, 1864.

———. *Personal Recollections of Abraham Lincoln and the Civil War*. London: J. MacQueen, 1898.

Guelzo, Allen C. *Lincoln and Douglas: The Debate That Defined America*. New York: Simon & Schuster, 2008.

Hadden, Jeanette. *Ebenezer*. Jacksonville, IL: Morgan County Historical Society, 1998.

Hafendorfer, Kenneth A. *Perryville: Battle for Kentucky*. Owensboro, KY: McDowell, 1991.

Haynes, Nathaniel S. *History of the Disciples*

of Christ in Illinois, 1819–1914. Cincinnati: Standard, 1915.

Headley, John W. Confederate Operations in Canada and New York. New York and Washington: Neale, 1906 (reprinted by Time-Life, 1981).

Heidler, David S., and Jeanne T. Heidler, eds. Encyclopedia of the American Civil War: A Political, Social and Military History. Santa Barbara, CA: ABC-Clio, 2000.

Hendrickson, Walter B. From Shelter to Self-Reliance: A History of the Illinois Braille and Sight Saving School. Jacksonville: Illinois Braille and Sight Saving School, 1972.

Hicken, Victor. Illinois in the Civil War. 2nd ed. Urbana: University of Illinois Press. 1991.

Hill, Frank Alden. The Mystery Solved: "Lawrence-Townley," "Chase-Townley," Marriage and Estate Questions. Boston: Rand Avery, 1888.

Historical Encyclopedia of Illinois, Newton Bateman and Paul Selby, eds., and History of Morgan County, William T. Short, ed. Chicago: Munsell, 1906.

The History of Adams County Illinois. Cleveland, OH: Bell & Howell, 1964. Reprint of Chicago: Murray, Williamson & Phelps, 1879.

History of Menard and Mason Counties, Illinois. Chicago: Baskin, 1879.

History of the Methodist Episcopal Church in Southern Illinois from the Formation of the First Class in 1793 to the Year 1903. Compiled by Thomas H. Herdman, Conference Historian of Southern Illinois Conference. MEC-S IL.

Hornbeck, Marquis D. A General Statement of the Financial History and Present Conditions of Chaddock College, Presented May 1889. Quincy: Skinner, 1889.

Horner, Harlan Hoyt. Lincoln and Greeley. Urbana: University of Illinois Press, 1953.

Howard, Robert P. Illinois: A History of the Prairie State. Grand Rapids, MI: William Eerdmans, 1972.

Hunter, Edna J. Shank. One Flag, One Country, and Thirteen Greenbacks a Month. San Diego, CA: Hunter, 1980.

Jackson, Lee, and Eric Nathan. Victorian London. London: New Holland, 2004.

Johnson, Clint. "A Vast and Fiendish Plot": The Confederate Attack on New York City. New York: Kensington, 2010.

Knott, Stephen F. Secret and Sanctioned: Covert Operations and the American Presidency. New York: Oxford University Press, 1996.

Landrum, Carl, and Shirley Landrum. Images of America: Quincy, Illinois. Charleston, SC: Arcadia, 1999.

Landrum, Carl A. "Colleges in Quincy." Sketch 42. In Historical Sketches of Quincy, Illinois. Revised ed. Quincy: Historical Society of Quincy and Adams County, 1986.

Leckie, William H., and Shirley A. Leckie. Unlikely Warriors: General Benjamin H. Grierson and His Family. Norman: University of Oklahoma Press, 1984.

List of Appointments of Methodist Episcopal Ministers in Indiana, 1800–1900. Greencastle, IN: Archives and Special Collections, DePauw University, 1998.

McDonough, James Lee. Stones River: Bloody Winter in Tennessee. Knoxville: University of Tennessee Press, 1980.

_____. War in Kentucky from Shiloh to Perryville. Knoxville: University of Tennessee Press, 1994.

McLoughlin, William G. Revivals, Awakenings, and Reform: An Essay on Religion and Social Change in America, 1607–1977. Chicago: University of Chicago Press, 1978.

Manhart, George B. DePauw Through the Years. Greencastle, IN: DePauw University Press, 1962.

Marriage Records of Putnam County Indiana. Compiled by Washburn Chapter DAR 1940, from the Putnam County Courthouse. Vol. July 1822 to May 1843. Edited by Minnetta L. Wright. Greencastle, IN: June 1940.

Melton, J. Gordon. Log Cabins to Steeples. Nashville: Commission on Archives and History of the Northern, Central, and Southern Illinois Conferences, 1974.

Minutes of Proceedings of the Eighteenth Annual Reunion of the Survivors Seventy-Third Regiment Illinois Volunteer Infantry. October 4, 1904. Pittsfield, IL: Printed at the Pike County Times, 1904 (ALPL).

Minutes of Proceedings of the Eleventh Annual Reunion, Survivors Seventy-Third Regiment Illinois Volunteer Infantry. September 28 and 29, 1897. Pekin, IL: Daily Post Print, IL (ALPL).

Minutes of Proceedings of the Fourteenth Annual Reunion of the Survivors Seventy-Third Regiment Illinois Infantry Volunteers. September 27, 1900. Green Valley, IL: Banner Print, 1900 (ALPL).

Minutes of Proceedings of the Nineteenth Annual Reunion of the Survivors Seventy-Third Regiment Illinois Volunteer Infantry. October 3, 1905. ALPL.

Minutes of Proceedings of the Seventeenth Annual Reunion, Survivors Seventy-Third Regiment Illinois Volunteer Infantry. September 29, 1903. ALPL.

Minutes of Proceedings of the Third Annual Reunion of the Survivors Seventy-Third Regiment Illinois Volunteer Infantry. October 8–10, 1890. ALPL.

Minutes of the Proceedings of the Thirtieth Annual Reunion of the Survivors of the Seventy-Third Reg't Illinois Volunteer Infantry. Springfield: Sept. 15, 1916. ALPL.

Minutes of Proceedings of the Twelfth Annual Reunion, Survivors Seventy-Third Regiment Illinois Volunteer Infantry. October 20–21, 1898. Springfield: Edw. W. Sholty (ALPL).

Minutes of Proceedings of the Twentieth Annual Reunion of the Survivors Seventy-Third Regiment Illinois Volunteer Infantry. October 6, 1906. ALPL. See Henry A. Castle, "Sheridan with the Army of the Cumberland."

Minutes of the Proceedings of the Twenty-Ninth Annual Reunion of the Survivors Seventy-Third Reg't Illinois Volunteer Infantry. Springfield: September 21, 1915. ALPL.

Minutes of Proceedings of the Twenty-Third Annual Reunion of the Survivors Seventy-Third Regiment Illinois Volunteer Infantry, 1909. ALPL.

Mohr, James C. *Abortion in America: The Origins and Evolution of National Policy, 1800–1900.* New York: Oxford University Press, 1978.

Moneyhon, Carl H. *The Impact of the Civil War and Reconstruction on Arkansas: Persistence in the Midst of Ruin.* Fayetteville: University of Arkansas Press, 2002.

Morris, Norval, and David J. Rothman, eds. *The Oxford History of Prisons.* New York: Oxford University Press, 1995.

Morris, Richard B., ed. *Encyclopedia of American History.* New York: Harper, 1953.

Mortimer, Gavin. *Double Death: The True Story of Pryce Lewis, the Civil War's Most Daring Spy.* New York: Walker, 2010.

Muelder Owen W. *The Underground Railroad in Western Illinois,* Jefferson, NC: McFarland, 2008.

National Society of the Daughters of the American Revolution. *Lineage Book* 23 (1898). Washington, DC, Harrisburg, PA: 1907.

Newlin, W.H., D.F. Lawler, and J.W. Sherrick. *A History of the Seventy-third Regiment of Illinois Infantry Volunteers.* Springfield: Regimental Reunion Association of Survivors of the 73rd Infantry, 1890. Reprinted Salem, MA: Higginson Book, 1998.

Nicolay, John G., and John Milton Hay. *Abraham Lincoln: A History.* 10 vols. New York: Century, 1890.

Noe, Kenneth W. *Perryville: This Grand Havoc of Battle.* Lexington: University Press of Kentucky, 2001

Onuf, Peter S. *Statehood and Union: A History of the Northwest Ordinance.* Bloomington: Indiana University Press, 1987.

Operations of the Army Under Buell from June 10th to October 30th and the Buell Commission. New York: D. Van Nostrand, 1884.

Pine, L.G. *The New Extinct Peerages, 1884–1971, Containing Extinct, Abeyant, Dormant and Suspended Peerages with Genealogies and Arms.* London: Heraldry Today, 1972.

Portrait and Biographical Album of Morgan and Scott Counties, Illinois. Chicago: Chapman, 1889.

Putnam, Elizabeth Duncan. *The Life and Services of Joseph Duncan, Governor of Illinois, 1834–1838.* Reprinted from *Transactions of the ISHS,* Springfield: 1921.

Rankin, Henry B. *Personal Recollections of Abraham Lincoln.* New York: Knickerbocker, 1916.

Redmond, Patrick H. *History of Quincy and Its Men of Mark.* Quincy: Heirs & Russell, 1869.

Richey, Russell E. *Early American Methodism.* Bloomington: Indiana University Press, 1991.

Rowland, Dunbar. *History of Mississippi, the Heart of the South.* Chicago: S.J. Clarke, 1925.

Satter, Beryl. *Each Mind a Kingdom: American Women, Sexual Purity, and the New Thought Movement, 1875–1920.* Berkeley: University of California Press, 1999.

Selleck, Linda B. *Gentle Invaders: Quaker Women Educators and Racial Issues During the Civil War and Reconstruction.* Richmond, IN: Friends United, 1995.

Simpson, Matthews. *Cyclopedia of Methodism.* Philadelphia: Everts and Stewart, 1878.

South Eastern Reporter. 2nd series. St. Paul, MN: West, 1897.

St. John, Jennifer. *Posey County, Indiana, 1814–1989.* Paducah, KY: Turner, 1989.

Stephen, Sir Leslie, and Sir Sidney Lee, eds. *Dictionary of National Biography.* Vol. 19. Oxford: Oxford University Press, 1921–22.

Sweet, William Warren. *Indiana Asbury-DePauw University, 1837–1937: A Hundred Years of Higher Education in the Middle West.* New York: Abbingdon Press, 1937.

Sword, Wiley. *Shiloh: Bloody April.* New York: William Morrow, 1974.

Taylor, Robert M., Jr., ed. *The Northwest Ordinance 1787: A Bicentennial Handbook.* Indianapolis: Indiana Historical Society, 1987.

Tindall, George Brown, and David E. Shi. *America: A Narrative History.* 5th ed. Vol. 2. New York: W.W. Norton, 1999.

Turner, L.L. *Phillips County Arkansas Cemeteries.* Brinkley, AR: L.L. Turner and F.M. Turner, 1991.

Usher, James. *History of the Lawrence-Townley and Chase-Townley Estates of England: with Copious Historical and Genealogical Notes of the Lawrence-Chase, and Townley Families and Much Other Valuable Information.* New York: s.n.,1883.

Watters, Mary. *The First Hundred Years of MacMurray College.* Jacksonville, IL: MacMurray College for Women, 1947.

Waugh, John C. *Reelecting Lincoln: The Battle for the 1864 Presidency.* New York: Crown, 1997.

Webb, Ross. "Kentucky: 'Pariah Among the Elect.'" In *Radicalism, Racism and Party Realignment: The Border States During Reconstruction.* Edited by Richard O. Curry. Baltimore: Johns Hopkins University Press, 1969.

White, Edward, ed. *Evansville and Its Men of Mark.* Evansville, IN: Historical, 1873. Reprinted Evansville, IN: Whipporwill, 1985.

Wigger, John. *American Saint: Francis Asbury and the Methodists.* New York: Oxford University Press, 2009.

_____. *Taking Heaven by Storm: Methodism and the Rise of Popular Christianity in America.* Urbana: University of Illinois Press, 2001, Originally published by Oxford University Press in 1998.

Wilmans, Helen. *A Search for Freedom.* Sea Breeze, FL: Freedom, 1898.

Woodworth, Steven E. *Decision in the Heartland: The Civil War in the West.* Westport, CT: Praeger, 2008..

_____. *Six Armies in Tennessee: The Chickamauga and Chattanooga Campaigns.* Bison edition. Lincoln: University of Nebraska Press, 1999.

ARTICLES

Bakken, Dawn E. "A Young Hoosier's Adventure on the Mississippi River." *Indiana Magazine of History* 102 (#1, March 2006): 1–7.

Beadles, W.T. "History of Chaddock College and the Deaconess Boys' School." *Illinois Methodist Journal* (June 27, 1901).

Bennett, Richard E. "'Quincy: The Home of Our Adoption': A Study of the Mormons in Quincy, Illinois, 1838–40." *Mormon Historical Studies* 2 (#1, Spring 2001).

Black, Carl E. "Origins of Our State Charitable Institution." *Journal of the Illinois State Historical Society* 18 (#1, April 1925): 175–94.

Bullard, F. Lauriston. "Abraham Lincoln and George Ashmun." *New England Quarterly* 19 (#2, June 1946): 197–200.

Burnette, Patricia Bauer. "Jaquess and the Lincoln Connection." Lincoln Bicentennial Issue, 1809–2009. *Journal of the Illinois State Historical Society* 101 (#3–4, Fall/Winter 2008): 272–84.

Butler, Robert N. "The Life Review: An Interpretation of Reminiscence in the Aged." In *Philosophical Foundations of Gerontology.* Edited by Patrick L. McKee. New York: Human Sciences Press, 1982.

Gilmore, James R. "Our Last Day in Dixie." *Atlantic Monthly* (December 3, 1864): 715–26.

_____. "Our Visit to Richmond." *Atlantic Monthly* (September 1864): 372–83.

_____. "A Suppressed Chapter of History." *Atlantic Monthly* (April 1887): 435–48.

Harker, Joseph R. "A Century of Educational Progress in the Illinois Conference, 1824–1924." *Journal of the Illinois State Historical Society* 18 (#1, April 1925): 159–74.

Heinl, Frank J. "Jacksonville and Morgan County: An Historical Review." *Journal of the Illinois State Historical Society* 18 (#1 April 1925): 5–38.

Jaquess, Asbury C. "The Journal of the *Davy Crockett* Commencing December 20th, 1834." *Indiana Magazine of History* 102 (#1, March 2006): 8–24.

"James F. Jaquess." In *Who Was Who in*

America: Historical Volume, 1607–1896. Chicago: Marquis-Who's Who, 1963.

Jaquess, William G. "Narrative of Chickamauga and Chattanooga." *Proceeding of the Southwestern Indiana Historical Society.* In *Indiana History Bulletin* 6 (extra # 3, August 1929): 21–36.

Kimball, E.L. "Richard Yates." *Journal of the Illinois States Historical Society* 23 (April 1930–31): 1–83,

Kirkland, Edward C. "James Frazier Jaquess." In *Dictionary of American Biography.* Edited by Allen Johnson and Dumas Malone. New York: Charles Scribner's Sons, 1960.

McClelland, Clarence P. "The Education of Females in Early Illinois." *Journal of the Illinois State Historical Society* 36 (#4, December 1943): 378–407.

———. "An Illinois Colonel's Visit to Jeff Davis in 1864: His Contribution to Lincoln's Re-election." *Journal of the Illinois State Historical Society* 55 (#1, March 1962): 31–44.

McPherson. James M. "Presidential Address: No Peace Without Victory, 1861–1865." *American Historical Review* 109 (#1, February 2004): 1–18.

Maryniak, B.R. "Yankee Preacher Regiments." *Civil War* 3 (#6, Nov.-Dec. 1987): 32–34.

Meixsel, Richard B. "Preacher, Soldier, Bigamist, Thief?: The Strange Career of Colonel James F. Jaquess." Unpublished article, 17 pp.

Polden, Patrick. "Stranger Than Fiction?: The Jennens Inheritance in Fact and Fiction." Part 1, "The Jennens Fortune in the Courts." *Common Law World Review* 32 (#3, 2003): 211–47.

———. "Stranger Than Fiction?: The Jennens Inheritance in Fact and Fiction." Part 2, "The Business of Fortune Hunting." *Common Law World Review* 32 (#4, 2003): 338–57.

Stark, Bill. "Illinois School for the Deaf: The Pioneer State Institution." *Illinois Advance* 108 (#7, April 1975): n.p.

Swift, Lester L. "Col. Jaquess' First Peace Mission." *Filson Club Quarterly* 41 (January 1967): 26–34.

———. "The Preacher Regiment in Chickamauga and Missionary Ridge." *Lincoln Herald* 72 (#2, Summer 1970): 51–60.

———. "Tribulations of the Rev. Col. Jaquess and the Preacher Regiment: A New Lincoln Note Discovered." *Lincoln Herald* 69 (Winter 1967): 165–77.

NEWSPAPERS

Danville (IL) Commercial. May 1866.
Decatur (IL) Daily Republican, October 20, 1885.
Decatur (IL) Weekly Republican, January 3, 1895.
Hornellsville (NY) Weekly Times, December 7, 1888.
Jacksonville (IL) Courier, October 24, 1927.
Jacksonville Illinois Daily Journal, July 28, 1854.
Jacksonville Illinois Journal, July 15, 1854.
London Daily Telegraph, December 1, 1894.
Louisville Daily Courier, May 11, 16, 17, 21, 1866.
Louisville Daily Journal, September 23, 1867; October 7, 9, 14, 1865; January 12, 1866; May 10, 1866; May 11, 1866; May 16, 1866.
Louisville Democrat, September 23, 1865; October 6, 8, 1865; December 9, 1865.
MacMurray College. *College Greetings.* November 1897; February 1898; March 8, 1898; June 1898; *Jubilee Greetings,* January 1897; July 1897.
Mount Carmel Register, October 2, 1844; April 12, 1894; November 19, 1896.
Mt. Carmel (IL) Democrat, May 31, 1866.
New York Herald, June 21, 22, 1870.
New York Times, April 11, 21, 1862; December 20, 1863; July 21, 24, 1864; January 5, 1900; December 14, 1932; February 20, 1867; May 10, 1867; June 26, 1881; January 13, 1883; March 19, 1885. June 6, 1890; October 1, 1939; November 8, 1895; June 19, 1898; December 13, 1932.
Oshkosh (WI) Daily Northwesterner, September 11, 1885.
Philadelphia Inquirer, May 9, 1889.
Quincy (IL) Daily Journal, June 18, 1898; June 24, 1905; April 30. 1885; March 26, 1886; May 18, 1891; July 25, 1894; January 25, 1895; June 18, 1898.
Quincy (IL) Daily Whig, digitized by the Quincy Public Library (see Web sites). December 28, 1853; November 24, 1855; August 14, 1856; September 6, 1856; March 23, 1859; August 12, 1859; June 29, 1861; April 10, 11, 25, 1862; July 16, 1862; June 25 and August 8, 1863; June 27, 1870; April 13, 1865; February 15, 1865.
Quincy (IL) Herald, April 19, 1862; February 22, 1865; December 2, 1865; May 30, 1866; June 2, 1866; December 19, 1867.
Quincy (IL) Whig Republican, March 23, 1859; June 29, 1861; April 14, 19, 20 and May 17, 1852; August 2, 27, 1864, April 1, 22, 1865; July 8, 1865.

Quincy (IL) Whig, June 29, 1905.
St. Paul (MN) Globe, June 18, 1898.
St. Paul (MN) Pioneer Press, June 18, 1898.
The Times (London, England), March 2, 6, 8, 17, 1894; April 14, 17, 18, 19, 24, 1894; May 8, 23, 1894; June 29 and 30, 1894; July 4, 18, 1894; August 1, 1894; September 12, 1894; October 4 and 10, 1894; November 1, 1894.
Topeka (KS) Journal, September 1, 1909.
Tri-County Advertiser, January 19, 1928.
Weekly (Jacksonville) Illinois Courier, June 22, 1898.

Web Sites

Abraham Lincoln Papers at the Library of Congress. http://lcweb2.loc.gov/ammem/alhtml/malhome.html.
"The Boy of Chickamauga" can be downloaded as a pdf: www.edinborough.com/Learn/Civil_War_Life/.../Chickamauga.pdf.
Census Records. http://www.rootsweb.ancestry.com/~ilmaga/census-morg50/censindx.htm.
A Century of Lawmaking for a New Nation: U.S. Congressional Documents and Debates, 1774–1875. http://memory.loc.gov/ammem/amlaw/lawhome.html.
"George D. Jaquess." Nineteenth Century Indiana Physicians Created by Special Collections Department, Ruth Lilly Medical Library, Indiana University School of Medicine. http://www.medlib.iupui.edu/body.cfm?id=140.
Illinois Civil War Muster and Descriptive Rolls Database, Illinois State Archives. http://www.cyberdriveillinois.com/departments/archives/datcivil.html.
Illinois Statewide Marriage Index, 1763–1900. http://www.cyberdriveillinois.com/departments/archives/marriage.html.
James R. Gilmore (aka Edmund Kirke) writings are available at http://cdl.library.cornell.edu.
James Jaquess Patent. http://www.uspto.gov.
John Olney in William R. Carr. "The Battle of Camden: The Only Civil War Action Fought in Johnson County, Illinois." Heritage.com (Heritage Technologies). http://www.heritech.com/soil/genealogy/cambat.him.
Kentucky Historical Society. "Confederate Governor George W. Johnson (1811–1862). http://www.lrc.ky.gov/record/Moments09RS/web/Lincoln%20moments%2017.pdf.
The Lincoln Log: A Daily Chronology of the Life of Abraham Lincoln Which Includes, Corrects and Adds to Lincoln Day-by-Day: A Chronology. http://www.thelincolnlog.org/view.
Pentonville Prison. http://www.victorianweb.org/periodicals/iln/11.html.
Quincy Newspapers. http://archive.quincylibrary.org/Default/Skins/QPL/Client.asp?skin=QPL&enter=true&AppName=2.
Senate Executive Journal, Executive Mansion, June 29, 1870 and Dec. 17, 1870. http://memory.loc.gov.
Severance, Frank H. "The Peace Conference at Niagara Falls in 1864: An Episode of the Civil War." Cornell Library New York Historical Literature. http://historicallibrary.cornell.edu.
"Sixth Illinois Cavalry" in Illinois Adjutant General's Report, Regimental and Unit Histories, Containing Reports for the Years 1861–1866. http://www.cyberdriveillinois.com/departments/archives/reghist.pdf.
Testimony of James Jaquess at trial of Howell Thomas. http://www.oldbaileyonline.org/static/Proceedings.jsp.
Testimony of William Enoch French, James J. Jaquess Trial, Old Bailey, November 19, 1894. http://www.oldbaileyonline.org/.
"Today in History, January 9." American Memory. Library of Congress. http://memory.loc.gov/ammem/today/jan09.html.
War of the Rebellion: Official Records (OR). http://www.digital.library.cornell.edu/m/moawar/waro.html.

Index

Numbers in ***bold italic*** indicate pages with photographs

abortion 101
Adams, John Quincy 36
Akers, Peter 25–26, 34
Allen Pinkerton Detective Agency 80
Andrew, John A. (governor of Massachusetts) 92–93
Asbury 12–13, 15
Ashmun, George 79

Bacon, Joseph 24
Beecher, Edward 22
Beecher, Henry Ward 108
Benjamin, Judah 5, 87
Berean College 26–27
Black Hawk (steamer) 59
Blavatsky, Madame Helena Petrovna 161–62
Bragg, Gen. Braxton 65–66, 70, 72, 84
Bray, Robert 17, 81
Brown, Shipley and Company 139
Browning, Orville H. 23
Bryant, Thomas J. 58
Buchanan, James 90–91
Buell, Gen. Don Carlos 53, 64–65
Buell Commission 66–67
Burnside, Maj. Gen. Ambrose E. 97
Burroughs, Wilson 63, 77, 90

Camp Butler 95
Camp Nelson 96–100, 102–3, 107
Cane Ridge, Kentucky 8, 9
Cartwright, Peter 9, 16, 19, 25, 160
Castle, Henry A. 43, 64, ***69***, 93, 95, 108, 112, 152–53, 161–62
Castle, Margaret Jaquess 13, 135, 153, 161
Cavanaugh, Thomas 34, 49–53, 55, 55–57, 60–61
Chaddock College 40, 162–64

Chancery Case, Illinois 47
Chase, George W. 125, 134
Chickamauga, Battle of 70–74
Clay, Clement C. 90

Davidson, James I. 63, 70, 76, 96, 109–10
Davis, Brig. Gen. Jefferson Columbus 77
Davis, Pres. Jefferson 5–6, 85, 87–88
Davy Crockett Boat 11
Dickens, Charles 122
Dickens, James W. 25–26, 31–34
Dix, Dorothea 23–24
Dockins, Rebecca 104–6
Douglas, Stephen A. 37
Doyle, Don Harrison 24
Duncan, Joseph 37

Eames, Charles M. 22
East Charge Church (Centenary, United Methodist Church, Jacksonville) 19, 61
Eels, Dr. Richard 39
"Explanatory" Document 143–44, 152

Fee, Rev. John G. 97–99, 102
Fisk, Gen. Clinton B. 95–96, 103
Freedman's Bureau 95–96, 100
Fremont, John C. 51
French, William Enoch 117, 148
Froest, Det. Inspector Frank 144
Fry, Capt. James B. 53
Fuller, Gen. Richard 53

Garfield, James A. 81
Germans 42, 46
Gilmore, James R. 5–6, 73, 82–89

Grant, Ulysses S. 51–54, 57–58, 87, 118
Greek Fire 93
Greeley, Horace 85, 90, 93
Grierson, Benjamin 49–57, 60–61

Halleck, Gen. Henry 54, 56–57
Harker, Joseph R. 24, 157
Harlan, James 12–13, 15, 89, 94, 119
Hawkins, Justice Henry 146, *147*, 148
Hay, John 83
Headley, John W. 92–93
Helena, Arkansas 111
Hicken, Victor 66
Hill, Frank Alden 134
Hirons, Samuel C. 11
Hood, Conf. Gen. John Bell 91
Hornbeck, Marquis D. 46
Howard, O.O. 100
Howard, Robert P. 18
Hurlburt, Surg. Maj. 72

Illinois College 21–22
Illinois Conference Female Academy 20, 25–28, *29*, 30–34
Illinois Conference of the Methodist Episcopal Church 110, 120
Illinois Constitution Convention of 1848 18
Illinois Female College 157
Illinois School for the Deaf 23
Illinois School for the Visually Impaired 24
Illinois State Hospital for the Insane 23–24
Illinois Woman's College 157
Indiana Asbury (later DePauw) 12–13, 15

Jacksonville, Illinois 21–35
Jacksonville Female Academy 25, 27
Jaquess, Anna Marie Peregoy Meixsel 130, *131*, 132–35, 138–39, 145, 159, 161–62
Jaquess, Asbury Cloud 10–11
Jaquess Brothers 117
Jaquess, Garrison 9
Jaquess, George D. 12, 115, 117
Jaquess, George F. 12
Jaquess, Isaac Newton 13–14, 42, 109
Jaquess, James Frazier *131*
Jaquess, John Wesley 10, 11
Jaquess, Jonathan 7–11
Jaquess, Jonathan S. 117, 124
Jaquess, Margaret 13–14, 28, 41, 104, 135
Jaquess, Rachel 28, 73
Jaquess, Sarah Jane Steel 16–17, 19–20, 25, 27–28, 30, 41, 112, 154
Jaquess, Thomas Coke 117
Jaquess, William 154
Jaquess, William "Willie" Garrison 28, 41, 72–73, 76, 95, *112*, 113, 135, 161
Jasper, Thomas 44–46
Javins, Charles 87
Jennens Estate 122–23
Johnson, George W. (Kentucky) 59
Johnston, Judge George W. 104–5, 107, 109
Johnston, Conf. Gen. Albert Sidney 57

Karr, Corydon 124–25, 127
King, J.O. 23
Kirke, Edmund (pen name for Gilmore) 73
Koy, Esther E. 7, 13

Ladies Education Society 24–25
Laiboldt, Col. Bernard 69, 71
Lawrence, Dow Hager 133, 135, 137, 140
Lawrence, Jasiel 124, 127, 129
Lawrence, Lebbius 127
Lawrence, William 124, 127, 129, 132
Lawrence-Townley Estate Certificate *128*, *129*
Leaton, Rev. James 35
Lewis, Pryce 80
Lincoln, Abraham 17–18, 67–68, 79–81, 86, 89, 93–94, 101, 155–57
Lloyd, William 80
Lockwood, Samuel D. 27
Louisville Newspaper 101–7
Lovejoy, Elijah 22

McClelland, George B. 80
McIntyre, Lt. Col. William 73
McKendree College 15, 19
M.E.C., South 57, 80–81
Meixsel, Anna Marie Peregoy *see* Jaquess, Anna Marie Peregoy Meixsel
Melville, Herman 125
Methodism 9–10, 15–20
Methodist Episcopal Church 110, 120
Milburn, Nicholas 27
Milburn, Rev. William Henry 27
military pension 153, 156, 158–59
Missionary Ridge, Battle of 74, *75*, 76
Mitchell, Belle 98–100
Moore, Jesse H. 34–35, 40, 63–64
Mormons 38
Motherspaw, Thomas W. 63, 77, 90
Mount Carmel, Illinois 14–16
Mount Carmel Academy 14–15
Mueller, Owen 38

Nelson, Dr. David 38
Niagara Peace Conference 90–91
Nichols, Samuel W. 7, 155
Nicolay, John 83
Nolan, John (Detective Sergeant) 144
Norreys, Lord, Hon. Montague Charles Francis Bertie 131, 136
Northcott, Benjamin F. 63

Old Bailey 143–46, *149*
Olney, Lt. Col. John 49, 51–57, 60–61
Ord, Maj. Gen. Edward Otto Creasap 114
Ould, Col. Robert 87
Owen, Robert 9

Paducah, Kentucky 57
Palestine Circuit 16
Palmer, John M. 54–55, 101–2, 104
Paris, Illinois 34–35
Patent 120
Pentonville Prison 150, *151*
Perpetual Scholarship Plan 30–31
Perryville, Battle of 64–66
Persimmon Regiment 64
Petersburg Circuit 17
Pinkerton Detective Agency 80
Pittsburg Landing 57, 59–60
plaque honoring Jaquess 152, *163*, 164
Posey County, Indiana 9–13
Poseyville, Indiana 12
Preachers Regiment 63–64, 71
Presson, Maj. William A. 63, 66, 68–70

Quincy, Illinois 36–48
Quincy English and German Seminary 39–40, *41*, 42–48

Rankin, Amberry 17
Rankin, Henry B. 17
Rankin, James 8, 10
Rapp, George 10–11
Raymond, Henry J. 88
"Rebel Terms of Peace, 1864" 89
Reconstruction 95–100, 114–17
Rosecrans, Gen. William S. 70, 72, 81–82, 84, 86
Rosengarten, Dr. Hermann (Alias Dr. Miller) 104–5, 107

Sciple, Mary 13–14
Scott, Thomas A. 54
Seventy-Third Illinois Volunteer Infantry 63–78
Seymour, Gen. Horatio 93
Shawneetown 49, 54, 57
Shawneetown Circuit 16
Sheridan, Gen. Philip H. 69–70, 76
Sherman, William Tecumseh 92
Shiloh 58
Siebert, Wilbur H. 22
Sixth Illinois Cavalry 49–62
Soldiers Home 89
Stanton, Sec. of War Edwin M. 62, 94
Stones River, Battle of 69–70

Thomas, Gen. George H. 71, 86
Thomas, Howell 134–138, 141–146, 148, 150
Thomas, Judge William 55, 77–78, 132
Thompson, Jacob 91–92
Trotter, Rev. W.D.R. 34
Trumbull, Sen. Lyman 68
Tunica, Mississippi 113–114, 117–18, 120
Turner, Gilbert Cook 14
Turner, Jonathan Baldwin 22
Twain, Mark (Samuel Clemens) 122–23

Underground Railroad 22–23, 38–39
Usher, James 133–34

Wall, George 11
Watson, Rev. Edward L. 154, 156–57
Watters, Mary 29
Weed, Thurlow 79–80
Wesley, John 9
Wheeler, W.W. 98
Whipple, Rev. George 93
Wilde, Oscar 150–51
Williams, Lester 97
Williams, Louisa C. 100–1, 103–6, 108–9
Wilmans, 1, 31–33
Wood, John 37

Yates, Richard (governor of Illinois; Senator) 28, 37, 49–51, 53–55, 58–62, 67–68, 77, 102

www.ingramcontent.com/pod-product-compliance
Ingram Content Group UK Ltd.
Pitfield, Milton Keynes, MK11 3LW, UK
UKHW042008140426
5217IPUK00015B/1044